Faith and Violence

.. That neither the low democracy of a nightmare nor
An army's primitive tidiness may deceive me
About our predicament.
W. H. Auden

(*Collected Poetry of W. H. Auden,*
Random House, p. 129)

Faith and Violence

Christian Teaching and Christian Practice

Thomas Merton

UNIVERSITY OF NOTRE DAME PRESS

Second Printing 1972
Third Printing 1976
Fouth Printing 1981
Fifth Printing 1984
Sixth Printing 1994

Library of Congress Card Catalog Number: 68-20438
Manufactured in the United States of America

To Phil Berrigan and Jim Forest

Acknowledgments

Grateful acknowledgement is herewith made to the following for permission to reprint the material listed below.

Commonweal, "The Unbelief of Believers" and "Honest to God";
Continuum, "Peace and Protest" and "The Meaning of Malcolm X";
Fellowship, "Blessed Are the Meek";
Herder and Herder, "Non-Violence and the Christian Conscience" and "Prison Meditations of Father Delp";
Katallagete, "Events and Pseudo-Events," "The Hot Summer of Sixty-Seven" and "Godless Christianity?";
The Mountain Path, "Contemplative Life in the Modern World";
New Blackfriars, "Is Man a Gorilla with a Gun?" and "Race and Religion in the United States";
Peace News, "An Enemy of the State" and "Pacifism and Resistance in Simone Weil";
Pendle Hill Pamphlets, "A Note on *The Psychological Causes of War* by Eric Fromm";
Theoria to Theory, "The Death of God and the End of History"; and Simon and Schuster, Inc., "Taking Sides on Vietnam," from *Authors Take Sides on Vietnam,* © 1967 by Simon and Schuster, Inc., New York.

Contents

CONTENTS

By Way of Preface

THE HASSIDIC RABBI, BAAL-SHEM-TOV, ONCE TOLD THE following story. Two men were traveling through a forest. One was drunk, the other was sober. As they went, they were attacked by robbers, beaten, robbed of all they had, even their clothing. When they emerged, people asked them if they got through the wood without trouble. The drunken man said: "Everything was fine; nothing went wrong; we had no trouble at all!"

They said: "How does it happen that you are naked and covered with blood?"

He did not have an answer.

The sober man said: "Do not believe him: he is drunk. It was a disaster. Robbers beat us without mercy and took everything we had. Be warned by what happened to us, and look out for yourselves."

For some "faithful"—and for unbelievers too—"faith" seems to be a kind of drunkenness, an anesthetic, that keeps you from realizing and believing that anything can ever go wrong. Such faith can be immersed in a world of violence and make no objection: the violence is perfectly all right. It is quite normal—unless of course it happens to be exercised by Negroes. Then it must be put down instantly by superior force. The drunkenness of this kind of faith—whether in a religious message or merely in a political ideology—enables us to go through life without seeing that our own violence is a disaster and that the overwhelming force by which we seek to assert ourselves and our own self-interest may well be our ruin.

Is faith a narcotic dream in a world of heavily-armed robbers, or is it an awakening?

Is faith a convenient nightmare in which we are attacked and obliged to destroy our attackers?

What if we awaken to discover that *we* are the robbers, and our destruction comes from the root of hate in ourselves?

ABBEY OF GETHSEMANI
Advent 1967

Part One

Toward a Theology of Resistance

THEOLOGY TODAY NEEDS TO FOCUS CAREFULLY UPON THE crucial problem of violence. The commandment "Thou shalt not kill" is more than a mere matter of academic or sentimental interest in an age when man not only is more frustrated, more crowded, more subject to psychotic and hostile delusion than ever, but also has at his disposition an arsenal of weapons that make global suicide an easy possibility. But the so-called "nuclear umbrella" has not simplified matters in the least: it may (at least temporarily) have caused the nuclear powers to reconsider their impulses to reduce one another to radioactive dust. But meanwhile "conventional" wars go on with unabated cruelty, and already more bombs have been exploded on Vietnam than were dropped in the whole of World War II. The population of the affluent world is nourished on a steady diet of brutal mythology and hallucination, kept at a constant pitch of high tension by a life that is intrinsically violent in that it forces a large part of the population to submit to an existence which is humanly intolerable. Hence murder, mugging, rape, crime, corruption. But it must be remembered that the crime that breaks out of the ghetto is only the fruit of a greater and more pervasive violence: the injustice which forces people to live in the ghetto in the first place. The problem of violence, then, is not the problem of a few rioters and rebels, but the problem of a whole social structure which is outwardly ordered and respectable, and inwardly ridden by psychopathic obsessions and delusions.

It is perfectly true that violence must at times be re-

3

strained by force: but a convenient mythology which simply legalizes the use of force by big criminals against little criminals—whose small-scale criminality is largely *caused* by the large-scale injustice under which they live—only perpetuates the disorder.

Pope John XXIII in *Pacem in Terris* quoted, with approval, a famous saying of St. Augustine: "What are kingdoms without justice but large bands of robbers?" The problem of violence today must be traced to its root: not the small-time murderers but the massively organized bands of murderers whose operations are global.

This book is concerned with the defense of the dignity and rights of man against the encroachments and brutality of massive power structures which threaten either to enslave him or to destroy him, while exploiting him in their conflicts with one another.

The Catholic moral theology of war has, especially since the Renaissance, concerned itself chiefly with casuistical discussion of how far the monarch or the sovereign state can justly make use of force. The historic context of this discussion was the struggle for a European balance of power, waged for absolute monarchs by small professional armies. In a new historical context we find not only a new struggle on a global scale between mammoth nuclear powers provided with arsenals capable of wiping out the human race, but also the emergence of scores of small nations in an undeveloped world that was until recently colonial. In this Third World we find not huge armed establishments but petty dictatorships (representing a rich minority) armed by the great powers, opposed by small, volunteer guerilla bands fighting for "the poor." The Great Powers tend to intervene in these struggles, not so much by the threat and use of nuclear weapons (with which however they continue to threaten one another) but with armies of draftees and

4

with new experimental weapons which are sometimes incredibly savage and cruel and which are used mostly against helpless non-combatants. Although many Churchmen, moved apparently by force of habit, continue to issue mechanical blessings upon these draftees and upon the versatile applications of science to the art of killing, it is evident that this use of force does not become moral just because the government and the mass media have declared the cause to be patriotic. The cliche "My country right or wrong" does not provide a satisfactory theological answer to the moral problems raised by the intervention of American power in all parts of the Third World. And in fact the Second Vatican Council, following the encyclical of John XXIII, *Pacem in Terris,* has had some pertinent things to say about war in the nuclear era. (See below, Chapter V).

To assert that conflict resolution is one of the crucial areas of theological investigation in our time is not to issue an a priori demand for a theology of pure pacifism. To declare that *all* use of force in any way whatever is by the very fact immoral is to plunge into confusion and unreality from the very start, because, as John XXIII admitted, "unfortunately the law of fear still reigns among peoples" and there are situations in which the only way to protect human life and rights effectively is by forcible resistance against unjust encroachment. Murder is not to be passively permitted, but resisted and prevented—and all the more so when it becomes mass-murder. The problem arises not when theology admits that force can be necessary, but when it does so in a way that implicitly favors the claims of the powerful and self-seeking establishment against the common good of mankind or against the rights of the oppressed.

The real moral issue of violence in the twentieth century is obscured by archaic and mythical presuppositions. We tend to judge violence in terms of the individual, the messy,

5

the physically disturbing, the personally frightening. The violence we want to see restrained is the violence of the hood waiting for us in the subway or the elevator. That is reasonable, but it tends to influence us too much. It makes us think that the problem of violence is limited to this very small scale, and it makes us unable to appreciate the far greater problem of the more abstract, more global, more organized presence of violence on a massive and corporate pattern. Violence today is *white-collar violence, the systematically organized bureaucratic and technological destruction of man.*

The theology of violence must not lose sight of the real problem which is not the individual with a revolver but *death and even genocide as big business.* But this big business of death is all the more innocent and effective because it involves a long chain of individuals, each of whom can feel himself absolved from responsibility, and each of whom can perhaps salve his conscience by contributing with a more *meticulous efficiency* to his part in the massive operation.

We know, for instance, that Adolf Eichmann and others like him felt no guilt for their share in the extermination of the Jews. This feeling of justification was due partly to their absolute obedience to higher authority and partly to the care and efficiency which went into the details of their work. This was done almost entirely on paper. Since they dealt with numbers, not with people, and since their job was one of abstract bureaucratic organization, apparently they could easily forget the reality of what they were doing. The same is true to an even greater extent in modern warfare in which the real moral problems are not to be located in rare instances of hand-to-hand combat, but in the remote planning and organization of technological destruction. The real crimes of modern war are committed not at the front (if

6

any) but in war offices and ministries of defense in which no one ever has to see any blood unless his secretary gets a nosebleed. Modern technological mass murder is not directly visible, like individual murder. It is abstract, corporate, businesslike, cool, free of guilt-feelings and therefore a thousand times more deadly and effective than the eruption of violence out of individual hate. It is this polite, massively organized white-collar murder machine that threatens the world with destruction, not the violence of a few desperate teen-agers in a slum. But our antiquated theology myopically focused on *individual* violence alone fails to see this. It shudders at the phantasm of muggings and killings where a mess is made on our own doorstep, but blesses and canonizes the antiseptic violence of corporately organized murder because it is respectable, efficient, clean, and above all profitable.

In another place I have contrasted, in some detail, the mentality of John XXIII on this point with the mentality of Macchiavelli (see *Seeds of Destruction*, Part III). Macchiavelli said: "There are two methods of fighting, one by law and the other by force. The first method is that of men, the second of beasts; but as the first method is often insufficient, one must have recourse to the second." I submit that a theology which merely seeks to justify the "method of beasts" and to help it disguise itself as law—since it is after all a kind of "prolongation of law"—is not adequate for the problems of a time of violence.

On the other hand we also have to recognize that when oppressive power is thoroughly well-established, it does not always need to resort openly to the "method of beasts" because its laws are already powerful—perhaps also bestial—enough. In other words, when a system can, without resort to overt force, *compel* people to live in conditions of abjection, helplessness, wretchedness that keeps them on the level of beasts rather than of men, it is plainly violent. To make men live on a subhuman level against their will, to constrain them in such a way that they have no hope of escaping their condition, is an unjust exercise of force. Those who in some way or other concur in the oppression—and perhaps profit by it—are exercising violence even though they may be preaching pacifism. And their supposedly peaceful laws, which maintain this spurious kind of order, are in fact instruments of violence and oppression. If the oppressed try to resist by force—which is their right—theology has no business preaching non-violence to them. Mere blind destruction is, of course, futile and immoral: but who are we to condemn a desperation we have helped to cause!

However, as John XXIII pointed out, the "law of fear" is not the only law under which men can live, nor is it really the normal mark of the human condition. To live under the law of fear and to deal with one another by "the methods of beasts" will hardly help world events "to follow a course in keeping with man's destiny and dignity." In order for us to realize this, we must remember that "one of the profound requirements of (our) nature is this: . . . it is not fear that should reign but love—a love that tends to express itself in mutual collaboration."

"Love" is unfortunately a much misused word. It trips easily off the Christian tongue—so easily that one gets the impression it means others ought to love us for standing on their necks.

A theology of love cannot afford to be sentimental. It cannot afford to preach edifying generalities about charity, while identifying "peace" with mere established power and legalized violence against the oppressed. A theology of love cannot be allowed merely to serve the interests of the rich and powerful, justifying their wars, their violence and their bombs, while exhorting the poor and underprivileged

8

to practice patience, meekness, longsuffering and to solve their problems, if at all, non-violently.

The theology of love must seek to deal realistically with the evil and injustice in the world, and not merely to compromise with them. Such a theology will have to take note of the ambiguous realities of politics, without embracing the specious myth of a "realism" that merely justifies force in the service of established power. Theology does not exist merely to appease the already too untroubled conscience of the powerful and the established. A theology of love may also conceivably turn out to be a theology of revolution. In any case, it is a theology of *resistance*, a refusal of the evil that reduces a brother to homicidal desperation.

On the other hand, Christian faith and purity of intention —the simplicity of the dove—are no guarantee of political acumen, and theological insight is no substitute for the wisdom of the serpent which is seldom acquired in Sunday school. Should the theologian or the priest be too anxious to acquire that particular kind of wisdom? Should he be too ambitious for the achievements of a successful political operator? Should he be more careful to separate authentic Christian witness from effectiveness in political maneuvering? Or is the real place of the priest the place which Fr. Camilo Torres took, with the Colombian guerillas?

This book cannot hope to answer such questions. But it can at least provide a few materials for a theology, not of pacifism and non-violence in the sense of *non-resistance,* but for a theology of resistance which is at the same time *Christian* resistance and which therefore emphasizes reason and humane communication rather than force, but which also admits the possibility of force in a limit-situation when everything else fails.

Such a theology could not claim to be Christian if it did not retain at least some faith in the meaning of the Cross and of the redemptive death of Jesus who, instead of using force against his accusers, took all the evil upon himself and overcame that evil by his suffering. This is a basic Christian pattern, but a realistic theology will, I believe, give a new practical emphasis to it. Instead of preaching the Cross *for others* and advising them to suffer patiently the violence which we sweetly impose on them, with the aid of armies and police, we might conceivably recognize the right of the less fortunate to use force, and study more seriously the practice of non-violence and humane methods on our own part when, as it happens, we possess the most stupendous arsenal of power the world has ever known.

General MacArthur was no doubt sincerely edified when the conquered Japanese wrote into their Constitution a clause saying they would never again arm and go to war. He warmly congratulated them for their wisdom. But he never gave the slightest hint of thinking the United States ought to follow their example. On the contrary, he maintained to the end that for *us* there could be no other axiom than that "there is no substitute for victory." Others have come after him with even more forceful convictions. They would probably be glad to see all Asian nations disarm on the spot: but failing that we can always bomb them back to the stone age. And there is no reason to believe that the United States may not eventually try to do so.

The title of this book is *Faith and Violence*. This might imply several interesting possibilities. The book might, for instance, study the violence of believers—and this, as history shows, has sometimes been considerable. The disciples of the Prince of Peace have sometimes managed to prove themselves extremely bloodthirsty, particularly among themselves. They have rather consistently held, in practice, that the way to prove the sincerity of faith was not so much non-violence as the generous use of lethal weapons. It is a curious fact that in this present century there have been two world wars of unparalleled savagery in which Christians, on both sides, were exhorted to go out and kill each other if not in the name of Christ and faith, at least in the name of "Christian duty." One of the strange facts about this was that, in the second World War, German Christians were exhorted by their pastors to die for a government that was not only non-Christian but anti-Christian and which had evident intentions of getting rid of the Church. An official theology which urged Christians, as a matter of Christian duty, to fight for such a government, surely calls for examination. And we shall see that few questioned it. Few question it still. One man did, and we shall devote a few pages to his unusual case. Possibly he was what the Catholic Church might conceivably call a "saint." If so, it was because he dared to refuse military service under the Fuehrer whom his bishop told him he was obliged to obey.

In the case of Franz Jägerstätter we have a faith that stood up against an unjust but established power and refused to practice violence in the service of that power. On the other side, we have Simone Weil who was a French pacifist before World War II and who later joined the French resistance against the Nazis. Simone Weil was not a Christian in the official sense of the word, but no matter: her motives and reservations were Christian, and the limits which she set to force when she decided to resist were also Christian.

Father Delp, Franz Jägerstätter and Simone Weil all resisted the same evil, the same violent, destructive and anti-human political force of Nazism and they all resisted it for the same motives. Their resistance took somewhat different forms. But one can see in them three possible examples of Christian resistance. In each case the resistance was more or less non-violent. It might conceivably have involved

11

a use of force (for instance by those Christians who plotted against Hitler's life—as Father Delp was accused of doing). The point to be emphasized however is not only that these Christians were non-violent but that they *resisted*. They refused to submit to a force which they recognized as anti-human and utterly destructive. They refused to accept this evil and to palliate it under the guise of "legitimate authority." In doing so they proved themselves better theologians than the professionals and the pontiffs who supported that power and made others obey it, thus cooperating in the evil.

The first section of this book studies various aspects of non-violent resistance to the evil of war as waged by the "large bands of robbers." Its approach assumes that non-violent resistance can be an effective means of conflict resolution, perhaps more effective than the use of force. At no point in these pages will the reader find the author trying to prove that evil should not be resisted. The reason for emphasizing non-violent resistance is this: he who resists force with force in order to seize power may become contaminated by the evil which he is resisting and, when he gains power, may be just as ruthless and unjust a tyrant as the one he has dethroned. A non-violent victory, while far more difficult to achieve, stands a better chance of curing the illness instead of contracting it.

There is an essential difference here, for non-violence seeks to "win" not by destroying or even by humiliating the adversary, but by *convincing him* that there is a higher and more certain common good than can be attained by bombs and blood. Non-violence, ideally speaking, does not try to overcome the adversary by winning over him, but to turn him from an adversary into a collaborator by winning him over. Unfortunately, non-violent resistance as practiced by those who do not understand it and have not been trained

12

in it, is often only a weak and veiled form of psychological aggression.

The second part of the book, devoted to Vietnam, takes into account the fact that the use of force in Vietnam is curing and settling nothing. With incredible expense and complication, and with appalling consequences to the people we claim to be helping, we are inexorably destroying the country we want to "save." Part three considers the racial conflict in the United States, where non-violence was first adopted as the best method and later discredited as ineffective, in favor of an appeal to force. The last section considers the rather ambiguous "death of God" which has curiously coincided with these other events and may perhaps cast some light on them.

At any rate, faith itself is in crisis along with the society which was once officially Christian, officially supported by God and his representatives, and which is now seeking to consolidate itself by an ever more insistent appeal to violence and brute power.

In brief: without attempting a systematic treatment of that theology of love which, in crisis situations, may become a theology of resistance, we will examine principles and cases all of which help us to see the unacceptable ambiguities of a theology of "might makes right" masquerading as a Christian theology of love.

Blessed Are the Meek

IT WOULD BE A SERIOUS MISTAKE TO REGARD CHRISTIAN NON-violence simply as a novel tactic which is at once efficacious and even edifying, and which enables the sensitive man to participate in the struggles of the world without being dirtied with blood. Non-violence is not simply a way of proving one's point and getting what one wants without being involved in behavior that one considers ugly and evil. Nor is it, for that matter, a means which anyone can legitimately make use of according to his fancy for any purpose whatever. To practice non-violence for a purely selfish or arbitrary end would in fact discredit and distort the truth of non-violent resistance. To use non-violence merely in order to gain political advantage at the expense of the opponent's violent mistakes would also be an abuse of this tactic.

Non-violence is perhaps the most exacting of all forms of struggle, not only because it demands first of all that one be ready to suffer evil and even face the threat of death without violent retaliation, but because it excludes mere transient self-interest, even political, from its considerations. In a very real sense, he who practices non-violent resistance must commit himself not to the defense of his own interests or even those of a particular group: he must commit himself to the defense of objective truth and right and above all of *man*. His aim is then not simply to "prevail" or to prove that he is right and the adversary wrong, or to make the adversary give in and yield what is demanded of him.

Nor should the non-violent resister be content to prove *to himself* that *he* is virtuous and right, that *his* hands and

14

heart are pure even though the adversary's may be evil and
defiled. Still less should he seek for himself the psychological gratification of upsetting the adversary's conscience and
perhaps driving him to an act of bad faith and refusal of the
truth. We know that our unconscious motives may, at times,
make our non-violence a form of moral aggression and even
a subtle provocation designed (without our awareness) to
bring out the evil we hope to find in the adversary, and thus
to justify ourselves in our own eyes and in the eyes of
"decent people." Wherever there is a high moral ideal there
is an attendant risk of pharisaism and non-violence is no
exception. The basis of pharisaism is division: on one hand
this morally or socially privileged self and the elite to which
it belongs. On the other, the "others," the wicked, the unen-
lightened, whoever they may be, communists, capitalists, co-
lonialists, traitors, international Jewry, racists, and so forth.

Christian non-violence is not built on a presupposed division, but on the basic unity of man. It is not out for the conversion of the wicked to the ideas of the good, but for the
healing and reconciliation of man with himself, man the
person and man the human family.

The non-violent resister is not fighting simply for "his"
truth or for "his" pure conscience, or for the right that is on
"his side." On the contrary, both his strength and his weakness come from the fact that he is fighting for *the* truth,
common to him and to the adversary, *the* right which is
objective and universal. He is fighting for *everybody*.

For this very reason, as Gandhi saw, the fully consistent
practice of non-violence demands a solid metaphysical and
religious basis both in being and in God. This comes before
subjective good intentions and sincerity. For the Hindu this
metaphysical basis was provided by the Vedantist doctrine
of the Atman, the true transcendent Self which alone is
absolutely real, and before which the empirical self of the

15

individual must be effaced in the faithful practice of *dharma*.
For the Christian, the basis of non-violence is the Gospel
message of salvation for *all men* and of the Kingdom of God
to which *all* are summoned. The disciple of Christ, he who
has heard the good news, the announcement of the Lord's
coming and of His victory, and is aware of the definitive
establishment of the Kingdom, proves his faith by the gift
of his whole self to the Lord in order that *all* may enter the
Kingdom. This Christian discipleship entails a certain way
of acting, a *politeia,* a *conversatio,* which is proper to the
Kingdom.

The great historical event, the coming of the Kingdom,
is made clear and is "realized" in proportion as Christians
themselves live the life of the Kingdom in the circumstances
of their own place and time. The saving grace of God in the
Lord Jesus is proclaimed to man existentially in the love,
the openness, the simplicity, the humility and the self-
sacrifice of Christians. By their example of a truly Christian
understanding of the world, expressed in a living and active
application of the Christian faith to the human problems of
their own time, Christians manifest the love of Christ for
men (Jn 13:35, 17:21), and by that fact make him visibly
present in the world. The religious basis of Christian non-
violence is then faith in Christ the Redeemer and obedience
to his demand to love and manifest himself in us by a certain
manner of acting in the world and in relation to other men.
This obedience enables us to live as true citizens of the
Kingdom, in which the divine mercy, the grace, favor and
redeeming love of God are active in our lives. Then the Holy
Spirit will indeed "rest upon us" and act in us, not for our
own good alone but for God and his Kingdom. And if the
Spirit dwells in us and works in us, our lives will be a continuous and progressive conversion and transformation in
which we also, in some measure, help to transform others

16

and allow ourselves to be transformed by and with others, in Christ.

The chief place in which this new mode of life is set forth in detail is the Sermon on the Mount. At the very beginning of this great inaugural discourse, the Lord numbers the beatitudes, which are the theological foundation of Christian non-violence: Blessed are the poor in spirit . . . blessed are the meek (Matt 5:3–4).

This does not mean "blessed are they who are endowed with a tranquil natural temperament, who are not easily moved to anger, who are always quiet and obedient, who do not naturally resist!" Still less does it mean "blessed are they who passively submit without protest to unjust oppression." On the contrary, we know that the "poor in spirit" are those of whom the prophets spoke, those who in the last days will be the "humble of the earth," that is to say the oppressed who have no human weapons to rely on and who nevertheless resist evil. They are true to the commandments of Yahweh, and who hear the voice that tells them: "Seek justice, seek humility, perhaps you will find shelter on the day of the Lord's wrath" (Soph 2:3). In other words they seek justice in the power of truth and of God, not by the power of man. Note that Christian meekness, which is essential to true non-violence, has this eschatological quality about it. It refrains from self-assertion and from violent aggression because it sees all things in the light of the great judgment. Hence it does not struggle and fight merely for this or that ephemeral gain. It struggles for the truth and the right which alone will stand in that day when all is to be tried by fire (I Cor 3:10–15).

Furthermore, Christian non-violence and meekness imply a particular understanding of the power of human poverty and powerlessness when they are united with the invisible strength of Christ. The beatitudes indeed convey a pro-

17

found existential understanding of the dynamic of the Kingdom of God—a dynamic made clear in the parables of the
mustard seed and of the yeast. This is a dynamism of patient
and secret growth, in belief that out of the smallest, weakest
and most insignificant seed the greatest tree will come. This
is not merely a matter of blind and arbitrary faith. The early
history of the Church, the record of the apostles and martyrs
remains to testify to this inherent and mysterious dynamism
of the ecclesial "event" in the world of history and time.
Christian non-violence is rooted in this consciousness and
this faith.

This aspect of Christian non-violence is extremely important and it gives us the key to a proper understanding of
the meekness which accepts being "without strength"
(*gewaltlos*) not out of masochism, quietism, defeatism or
false passivity, but trusting in the strength of the Lord of
truth. Indeed, we repeat, Christian non-violence is nothing
if not first of all a formal profession of faith in the Gospel
message that the Kingdom has been established and that the
Lord of truth is indeed risen and reigning over his Kingdom, defending the deepest values of those who dwell in it.

Faith of course tells us that we live in a time of eschatological struggle, facing a fierce combat which marshalls
all the forces of evil and darkness against the still invisible
truth, yet this combat is already decided by the victory of
Christ over death and over sin. The Christian can renounce
the protection of violence and risk being humble, therefore
vulnerable, not because he trusts in the supposed efficacy
of a gentle and persuasive tactic that will disarm hatred and
tame cruelty, but because he believes that the hidden power
of the Gospel is demanding to be manifested in and through
his own poor person. Hence in perfect obedience to the
Gospel, he effaces himself and his own interests and even
risks his life in order to testify not simply to "the truth" in

18

a sweeping, idealistic and purely platonic sense, but to the truth that is incarnate in a concrete human situation, involving living persons whose rights are denied or whose lives are threatened.

Here it must be remarked that a holy zeal for the cause of humanity in the abstract may sometimes be mere lovelessness and indifference for concrete and living human beings. When we appeal to the highest and most noble ideals, we are more easily tempted to hate and condemn those who, so we believe, are perversely standing in the way of their realization.

Christian non-violence does not encourage or excuse hatred of a special class, nation or social group. It is not merely *anti*-this or that. In other words, the Evangelical realism which is demanded of the Christian should make it impossible for him to generalize about "the wicked" against whom he takes up moral arms in a struggle for righteousness. He will not let himself be persuaded that the adversary is totally wicked and can therefore never be reasonable or well-intentioned, and hence need never be listened to. This attitude, which defeats the very purpose of non-violence—openness, communication, dialogue—often accounts for the fact that some acts of civil disobedience merely antagonize the adversary without making him willing to communicate in any way whatever, except with bullets or missiles. Thomas à Becket, in Eliot's play *Murder in the Cathedral,* debated with himself, fearing that he might be seeking Martyrdom merely in order to demonstrate his own righteousness and the King's injustice: "This is the greatest treason, to do the right thing for the wrong reason."

Instead of trying to use the adversary as leverage for one's own effort to realize one's ends however ideal, non-violence seeks only to enter into a dialogue with him in order to attain, together with him, the common good of

19

man. Non-violence must be realistic and concrete. Like ordinary political action, it is no more than the "art of the possible." But precisely the advantage of non-violence is that is lays claim to a *more Christian and more humane notion of what is possible.* Where the powerful believe that only power is efficacious, the non-violent resister is persuaded of the superior efficacy of love, openness, peaceful negotiation and above all of truth. For power can guarantee the interests of *some men* but it can never foster the good of *man.* Power always protects the good of some at the expense of all the others. Only love can attain and preserve the good of all. Any claim to build the security of *all* on force is a manifest imposture.

Now all these principles are fine and they accord with our Christian faith. But once we view the principles in the light of current *facts,* a practical difficulty confronts us. If the "Gospel is preached to the poor," if the Christian message is essentially a message of hope and redemption for the poor, the oppressed, the underprivileged and those who have no power humanly speaking, how are we to reconcile ourselves to the fact that Christians belong for the most part to the rich and powerful nations of the earth? Seventeen percent of the world's population control eighty percent of the world's wealth, and most of these seventeen percent are supposedly Christian. Admittedly those Christians who are interested in non-violence are not ordinarily the wealthy ones. Nevertheless, like it on not, they share in the power and privilege of the most wealthy and mighty society the world has ever known. Even with the best subjective intentions in the world, how can they avoid a certain ambiguity in preaching non-violence? Is this not a mystification?

We must remember Marx's accusation that, "The social principles of Christianity encourage dullness, lack of self-respect, submissiveness, self-abasement, in short all the characteristics of the proletariat." We must frankly face the possibility that the non-violence of the European or American preaching Christian meekness may conceivably be adulterated by bourgeois feelings and by an unconscious desire to preserve the status quo against violent upheaval.

On the other hand, Marx's view of Christianity is obviously tendentious and distorted. A real understanding of Christian non-violence (backed up by the evidence of history in the Apostolic Age) shows not only that it is a *power*, but that it remains perhaps the only really effective way of transforming man and human society. After nearly fifty years of communist revolution, we find little evidence that the world is improved by violence. Let us however seriously consider at least the *conditions* for relative honesty in the practice of Christian non-violence:

1. Non-violence must be aimed above all at the transformation of the present state of the world, and it must therefore be free from all occult, unconscious connivance with an unjust and established abuse of power. This poses enormous problems—for if non-violence is too political it becomes drawn into the power struggle and identified with one side or another in that struggle, while if it is totally a-political it runs the risk of being ineffective or at best merely symbolic.

2. The non-violent resistance of the Christian who belongs to one of the powerful nations and who is himself in some sense a privileged member of world society will have to be clearly not *for himself* but *for others*, that is for the poor and underprivileged. (Obviously in the case of Negroes in the United States, though they may be citizens of a privileged nation their case is different. They are clearly entitled to wage a non-violent struggle for their rights, but even for them this struggle should be primarily for *truth itself*—this being the source of their power.)

3. In the case of non-violent struggle for peace—the threat

21

of nuclear war abolishes all privileges. Under the bomb there is not much distinction between rich and poor. In fact the richest nations are usually the most threatened. Non-violence must simply avoid the ambiguity of an unclear and *confusing protest* that hardens the warmakers in their self-righteous blindness. This means in fact that *in this case above all non-violence must avoid a facile and fanatical self-righteousness,* and refrain from being satisfied with dramatic self-justifying gestures.

4. Perhaps the most insidious temptation to be avoided is one which is characteristic of the power structure itself— this fetishism of immediate visible results. Modern society understands "possibilities" and "results" in terms of a super-ficial and quantitative idea of efficacy. One of the missions of Christian non-violence is to restore a different standard of practical judgment in social conflicts. This means that the Christian humility of non-violent action must establish itself in the minds and memories of modern man not only as *conceivable* and possible, but as a *desirable alternative* to what he now considers the only realistic possibility, namely political manipulation backed by force. Here the human dignity of non-violence must manifest itself clearly in terms of a freedom and a nobility which are able to resist political manipulation and brute force and show them up as arbitrary, barbarous and irrational. This will not be easy. The temptation to get publicity and quick results by spec-tacular tricks or by forms of protest that are merely odd and provocative but whose human meaning is not clear may defeat this purpose.

The realism of non-violence must be made evident by humility and self-restraint which clearly show frankness and open-mindedness and invite the adversary to serious and reasonable discussion.

It is here that genuine humility is of the greatest importance. Such humility, united with true Christian courage (because it is based on trust in God and not in one's own ingenuity and tenacity), is itself a way of communicating the message that one is interested only in truth and in the genuine rights of others. Conversely, our authentic interest in the common good above all will help us to be humble, and to distrust our own hidden drive to self-assertion.

5. Christian non-violence, therefore, is convinced that the manner in which the conflict for truth is waged will itself manifest or obscure the truth. To fight for truth by dishonest, violent, inhuman, or unreasonable means would simply betray the truth one is trying to vindicate. The absolute refusal of evil or suspect means is a necessary element in the witness of non-violence.

As Pope Paul said before the United Nations Assembly: "Men cannot be brothers if they are not humble. No matter how justified it may appear, pride provokes tensions and struggles for prestige, domination, colonialism and egoism. In a word *pride shatters brotherhood.*" He went on to say that attempts to establish peace on the basis of violence were in fact a manifestation of human pride. "If you wish to be brothers, let the weapons fall from your hands. You cannot love with offensive weapons in your hands."

6. A test of our sincerity in the practice of non-violence is this: are we willing to *learn something from the adversary?* If a *new truth* is made known to us by him or through him, will we admit it? Are we willing to admit that he is not totally inhuman, wrong, unreasonable, cruel? This is important. If he sees that we are completely incapable of listening to him with an open mind, our non-violence will have nothing to say to him except that we distrust him and seek to outwit him. Our readiness to see some good in him and to agree with some of his ideas (though tactically this might look like a weakness on our part) actually gives us power,

23

the power of sincerity and of truth. On the other hand, if we are obviously unwilling to accept any truth that we have not first discovered and declared ourselves, we show by that very fact that we are interested not in the truth so much as in "being right." Since the adversary is presumably interested in being right also, and in proving himself right by what he considers the superior argument of force, we end up where we started. Non-violence has great power, provided that it really witnesses to truth and not just to self-righteousness.

The dread of being open to the ideas of others generally comes from our hidden insecurity about our own convictions. We fear that we may be "convicted"—or perverted—by a pernicious doctrine. On the other hand, if we are mature and objective in our open-mindedness, we may find that in viewing things from a basically different perspective—that of our adversary—we discover our own truth in a new light and are able to understand our own ideal more realistically.

Our willingness to take *an alternative approach* to a problem will perhaps relax the obsessive fixation of the adversary on his view, which he believes is the only reasonable possibility and which he is determined to impose on everyone else by coercion.

It is the refusal of alternatives—a compulsive state of mind which one might call the "ultimatum complex"—which makes wars in order to force the unconditional acceptance of one oversimplified interpretation of reality. The mission of Christian humility in social life is not merely to edify, but *to keep minds open to many alternatives.* The rigidity of a certain type of Christian thought has seriously impaired this capacity, which non-violence must recover.

Needless to say, Christian humility must not be confused with a mere desire to win approval and to find reassurance by conciliating others superficially.

24

7. Christian hope and Christian humility are inseparable. The quality of non-violence is decided largely by the purity of the Christian hope behind it. In its insistence on certain human values, the second Vatican Council, following *Pacem in Terris,* displayed a basically optimistic trust *in man himself.* Not that there is not wickedness in the world, but today trust in God cannot be completely divorced from a certain trust in man. The Christian knows that there are radically sound possibilities in every man, and he believes that love and grace always have power to bring out those possiblities at the most unexpected moments. Therefore if he has hopes that God will grant peace to the world it is because he also trusts that man, God's creature, is not basically evil: that there is in man a potentiality for peace and order which can be realized provided the right conditions are there. The Christian will do his part in creating these conditions by preferring love and trust to hate and suspiciousness. Obviously, once again, this "hope in man" must not be naive. But experience itself has shown, in the last few years, how much an attitude of simplicity and openness can do to break down barriers of suspicion that had divided men for centuries.

It is therefore very important to understand that Christian humility implies not only a certain wise reserve in regard to one's own judgments—a good sense which sees that we are not always necessarily infallible in our ideas— but it also cherishes positive and trustful expectations of others. A supposed "humility" which is simply depressed about itself and about the world is usually a false humility. This negative, self-pitying "humility" may cling desperately to dark and apocalyptic expectations, and refuse to let go of them. It is secretly convinced that only tragedy and evil can possibly come from our present world situation. This secret conviction cannot be kept hidden. It will manifest

25

itself in our attitudes, in our social action and in our protest. It will show that in fact we despair of reasonable dialogue with anyone. It will show that we expect only the worst. Our action therefore seeks only to block or frustrate the adversary in some way. A protest that from the start declares itself to be in despair is hardly likely to have positive or constructive results. At best it provides an outlet for the personal frustrations of the one protesting. It enables him to articulate his despair in public. This is not the function of Christian non-violence. This pseudo-prophetic desperation has nothing to do with the beatitudes, even the third. No blessedness has been promised to those who are merely sorry for themselves.

In resume, the meekness and humility which Christ extolled in the Sermon on the Mount and which are the basis of true Christian non-violence, are inseparable from an eschatological Christian hope which is completely open to the presence of God in the world and therefore to the presence of our brother who is always seen, no matter who he may be, in the perspectives of the Kingdom. Despair is not permitted to the meek, the humble, the afflicted, the ones famished for justice, the merciful, the clean of heart and the peacemakers. All the beatitudes "hope against hope," "bear everything, believe everything, hope for everything, endure everything" (I Cor 13:7). The beatitudes are simply aspects of love. They refuse to despair of the world and abandon it to a supposedly evil fate which it has brought upon itself. Instead, like Christ himself, the Christian takes upon his own shoulders the yoke of the Savior, meek and humble of heart. This yoke is the burden of the world's sin with all its confusions and all its problems. These sins, confusions and problems are our very own. We do not disown them.

Christian non-violence derives its hope from the promise

of Christ: "Fear not, little flock, for the Father has prepared for you a Kingdom" (Lk 12:32).

The hope of the Christian must be, like the hope of a child, pure and full of trust. The child is totally available in the present because he has relatively little to remember, his experience of evil is as yet brief, and his anticipation of the future does not extend very far. The Christian, in his humility and faith, must be as totally available to his brother, to his world, in the present, as the child is. But he cannot see the world with childlike innocence and simplicity unless his memory is cleared of past evils by forgiveness, and his anticipation of the future is hopefully free of craft and calculation. For this reason, the humility of Christian non-violence is at once patient and uncalculating. The chief difference between non-violence and violence is that the latter depends entirely on its own calculations. The former depends entirely on God and on his Word.

At the same time the violent or coercive approach to the solution of human problems considers man in general, in the abstract, and according to various notions about the laws that govern his nature. In other words, it is concerned with man as subject to necessity, and it seeks out the points at which his nature is consistently vulnerable in order to coerce him physically or psychologically. Non-violence on the other hand is based on that respect for the human person without which there is no deep and genuine Christianity. It is concerned with an appeal to the liberty and intelligence of the person insofar as he is able to transcend nature and natural necessity. Instead of forcing a decision upon him from the outside, it invites him to arrive freely at a decision of his own, in dialogue and cooperation, and in the presence of that truth which Christian non-violence brings into full view by its sacrificial witness. The key to non-violence is the willingness of the non-violent resister to suffer a certain amount of accidental evil in order to bring about a change of mind in the oppressor and awaken him to personal openness and to dialogue. A non-violent protest that merely seeks to gain publicity and to show up the oppressor for what he is, without opening his eyes to new values, can be said to be in large part a failure. At the same time, a non-violence which does not rise to the level of the personal, and remains confined to the consideration of nature and natural necessity, may perhaps make a deal but it cannot really make sense.

The distinction suggested here, between two types of thought—one oriented to nature and necessity, the other to person and freedom—calls for further study at another time. It seems to be helpful. The "nature oriented" mind treats other human beings as objects to be manipulated in order to control the course of events and make the future conform to certain rather rigidly determined expectations. "Person-oriented" thinking does not lay down these draconian demands, does not seek so much to *control* as to *respond,* and to *awaken response.* It is not set on determining anyone or anything, and does not insistently demand that persons and events correspond to our own abstract ideal. All it seeks is the openness of free exchange in which reason and love have freedom of action. In such a situation the future will take care of itself. This is the truly Christian outlook. Needless to say that many otherwise serious and sincere Christians are unfortunately dominated by this "nature-thinking" which is basically legalistic and technical. They never rise to the level of authentic interpersonal relationships outside their own intimate circle. For them, even today, the idea of building peace on a foundation of war and coercion is not incongruous—it seems perfectly reasonable!

It is understandable that the Second Vatican Council,

28

which placed such strong emphasis on the dignity of the human person and the freedom of the individual conscience, should also have strongly approved, "those who renounce the use of violence in the vindication of their rights and who resort to methods of defense which are otherwise available to weaker parties too." (Constitution on the Church in the Modern World, n. 78) In such a confrontation between conflicting parties, on the level of personality, intelligence and freedom, instead of with massive weapons or with trickery and deceit, a fully human solution becomes possible. Conflict will never be abolished but a new way of solving it can become habitual. Man can then act according to the dignity of that adulthood which he is now said to have reached—and which yet remains, perhaps, to be conclusively demonstrated. One of the ways in which it can, without doubt, be proved is precisely this: man's ability to settle conflicts by reason and arbitration instead of by slaughter and destruction.

Non-Violence and the
Christian Conscience

SHORTLY AFTER THE ASSASSINATION OF PRESIDENT JOHN F. Kennedy, one of the most widely read American news magazines had this to say about the suspected assassin who had, himself, just been shot down. *"Oswald was a lone wolf whose background showed that he was inclined to non-violence up to a point where his mind apparently snapped."*

This little gem of double-think deserves our attention. Pages of exegesis would barely suffice to untangle the explicit and implicit mythology which it contains.

What especially recommends it to us here is its curious mythological conception of non-violence, a conception which is in fact diametrically opposed to reality and which, nevertheless, seems to be rather widely accepted in America. The most curious thing about this myth and its acceptance is that non-violence which is the one political philosophy today which appeals directly to the Gospel, should be regarded as unchristian, while reliance on force and cooperation with massive programs of violence is sometimes seen as an obvious and elementary Christian duty.

The French Dominican P.-R. Régamey confronts these ambiguities in his theological study of non-violence. We can prepare ourselves for his conclusions by meditating on the magazine writer's curious insistence on what he thought was Oswald's non-violence. After all, murder is hardly a non-violent act, and Oswald's past record showed him to be "inclined," if anything, to support a philosophy of violent revolution. How could the writer simply take it for granted that this statement, a pure self-contradiction as it stands,

30

would be accepted by American readers without question and without comment as a perfect truism?

Bearing in mind the fact that this statement is typical of popular thinking on non-violence, let us examine its more obvious implications.

1. To begin with, this was an article which took it for granted, a few hours after Oswald's death and before any serious investigation was possible, that Oswald's guilt was so obvious as to require no further proof. All the writer thought he needed was an "explanation" which would give his readers the satisfaction of knowing all about what had happened, once for all. It is understood that the purpose of such magazines is to provide the reader with omniscience and endow him with the capacity to judge everything finally and forever, without the need to resort to any further effort, once he has mastered the concatenations of cliches which pass for news in those lively columns.

2. The explanation, delivered with lordly and absolute finality, amounts to this: Oswald was a non-conformist. A non-conformist is capable of anything. Because Oswald the non-conformist was capable of anything, he killed the President. In order to drive home the point that Oswald was capable of anything, the writer deemed it sufficient to state that the man was "inclined to non-violence." What more could you want? Non-violence is so irrational and so dangerous that anyone "inclined" to it would obviously be capable of any atrocity.

3. Non-violence is here impressionistically represented as a kind of addiction, to which one may be "inclined," as for example to alcoholism or drugs. It is enough to suggest that he was inclined. To be inclined is to be predetermined. The reader's imagination fills in the details for itself. Before the mind's eye rises the fateful image of one who is led in a hypnotic trance to perpetrate mysterious evils. He is in

31

reality a drug addict looking for a fix. A drug addict will do anything in order to get a fix. A man "inclined to non-violence" is in no way different from a drug addict. He will do anything, because he is "inclined." Such is the logic of suggestion.

4. It is taken for granted that addiction to non-violence follows the same (mythical) pattern of all other addictions. One's mind eventually "snaps." Hence, though people who believe in non-violence and practice it may not yet have reached the point where, with briskly snapping minds, they have shot a president or two, they are already virtually insane. This, in fact, brings us back to the basic principle on which the whole thing rests. Not to conform to the standards of reasonable and right thinking men (in this case the readers of the magazine in question) is to be insane, capable of anything.

Here a great deal can be implied because it is all given and understood in the basic, vague, general presupposition of *all* the thinking in the magazine. Everything in such a magazine, and in the mass-media generally, assumes in the reader a particular mode of self-understanding which would be too complex to analyze here. Suffice it to say that this mode of self-understanding is a myth rather than a philosophy, a global secular faith which is assumed without question to be the only right view of life and of political and social actuality. It is a positivist, pragmatic, fundamentally a-moral view of things, completely confident of its own logic, its own superiority (proved by power and affluence), its own mission to judge and direct the rest of the world, and to do so by the cheerful assertion of unlimited power. If necessary this world view appeals to a few semi-Christian slogans, as if to point out, in a modest, offhand way, that the possession of this superiority, this power and this manifest destiny is a warrant of divine and messianic vocation.

Any other way of self-understanding is dismissed as heretical. Non-violence is based on radically different principles which bring it into head-on collision with this mode of self-understanding. It is therefore heretical and in fact insane.

Conclusion: If a crime is committed, and if a person suspected of an inclination to non-violence was in a position where it was physically possible for him to commit the act, then he must have committed it. No further proof needed. You have your man. Or, as a practical corollary: if a crime has been committed, and if one wants to make sure that a suspect is convicted, one can help the cause along by discovering that at one time or other he showed an "inclination to non-violence."

Now in fact, there is nothing to indicate that Oswald was ever seriously interested in non-violence. On the contrary, the same argument, in the same breath, would insist that he was also a Communist. Communists, as the same source repeatedly asserts, are intent upon the *violent* overthrow of peaceful and democratic society. Pushing the logic to its conclusion, in order to discover the nature of non-violence according to this source, we come up with the answer: non-violence is violence. *Quod erat demonstrandum.*

*   *   *

What is the purpose of our semantic meditation? Simply this. It shows how average Americans, not excluding average American Catholics, tend to understand the exotic and disturbing phenomenon of non-violence. Their understanding is no understanding at all. They have heard a great deal about it. They have their minds filled with confused and confusing images associated with it. They have never been seriously and accurately informed of its true nature, and it ferments in their minds as one of the more inscrutable myths of a world in crisis.

33

Those who have read a little on the subject may perhaps associate the origins of non-violence with Tolstoy, Thoreau, the Quakers. All this is, to a Catholic, religiously odd. As for those who have never heard of Tolstoy, Thoreau and the Quakers, they know non-violence as something invented by Negroes (Gandhi was, of course, a "Negro"). They include it in the category of underworld activities which whites get into when they associate too intimately with Negroes. From there on, the shape the myth takes depends on your own regional outlook. If you are from the North, non-violence rates as something odd and irrational if not actually sinister, like smoking marihuana. If you are from the South, it is classed in the same sociological hell as all the other suspect activities in which Negroes and whites intermingle socially (exception made, of course, for lynching which is perfectly respectable, and in no way tainted with non-violence).

Here we come to the heart of the myth. While non-violence is regarded as somehow sinister, vicious and evil, violence has manifold acceptable forms in which it is not only tolerated but approved by American society. Let us turn now from Oswald, who was obviously not non-violent, to some who obviously were: for example the Civil Rights workers murdered in Mississippi in the summer of 1964. Quite apart from the question of who murdered them, it is obvious that in the society where they met their death there was a fairly unanimous acceptance of their murder and of the inhuman brutality and cruelty with which one of them in particular was destroyed. If. in the practice of non-violent civil disobedience, civil rights workers should violate some trifling ordinance placed on the books to obstruct and harass a section of the population which is deprived of its rights, they are regarded with horror, treated as the most sinister and maniacal emissaries of hell. If on the other hand someone should proceed to commit murder or any other violent or unjust act, in defense of the prevailing myths, this may be on occasion publicly deplored in suitable terms, but in fact it is accepted as normal, sane, healthy, reasonable and indeed as fully consonant not only with democratic but even Christian ideals. Hence, whatever may be said about the supposed murderers of the civil rights workers (the supposition is known to everybody), no one has ever suggested that they were inclined to non-violence or that their minds snapped. As for the civil rights workers themselves, not only were they inclined to non-violence, but they had succumbed, they had gone all the way, they were poisoning the pure air of the South by its open practice.

* * *

We can now say it seriously, without irony and without exaggeration: *there exists in the American mind today an image of non-violence which is largely negative and completely inadequate.*

Non-violence is represented at best as an unhealthy kind of idealism, which implicitly becomes subversion and treason by virtue of its effects. At worst, it is purely and simply a tool of Communist deceit, another gambit in the game of violent revolution.

This myth is systematically kept in existence by the mass media because, as was said above, non-violence is based on principles which call into question the popular self-understanding of the society in which we live. Even though in fact the number of people who are interested enough in non-violence to dedicate their lives to it is infinitesimally small, they are regarded as a serious and mysterious potential threat to the entire nation insofar as they bear witness to a radically different way of looking at life.

Now we know that from the first this has been the mode

of action of God's word and of the Gospel in the world: it calls into question the routine self-understanding of man and of his society. It fractures the idols, it unmasks dead works, and it opens the way to new life. All history is full of examples to teach us that this mode of action is unacceptable. Those who decide in favor of the routines which are profitable and pleasant to themselves can always manage to do so in the name of truth and of God, and their appeal to truth and God can often be convincingly backed by social authority. But we also know that this tenacity in clinging to routine notions of good and evil always leads to the ossification of living moral organisms. It is by their resistance to the challenge of an unpalatable new truth that these organisms make themselves incapable of living self-renewal.

The real question that is raised by non-violent action is not at all whether the democratic ideal ought to be replaced by something else: it is on the contrary an accusation of those who, while mouthing democratic slogans, have in fact clearly betrayed the democratic ideal and emptied it of meaning. This explains the virulence of the counter-attack against the kind of thinking which non-violence supposes.

Non-violence does not attack the ideals on which democratic society is built, still less the ideals of Christianity. It claims on the contrary to be a genuine fulfillment and implementation of those ideals. And in so claiming, it rejects the counter claim of that popular self-understanding which is in fact a myth and a betrayal of democracy and of Christianity.

The real question which non-violent action poses is this: whether it may in fact be necessary to practice non-violent methods if democracy is to be kept alive and preserved against the sclerosis which is gradually hardening it into a new form of Totalism.

If, instead of fabricating for ourselves a mythical and

inadequate self-understanding made up of the postures and antics of TV westerns, we return to a deeper awareness of our professed ideals, we may find that non-violence is very relevant to them. After all, the basic principle of non-violence is respect for the personal conscience of the opponent. Non-violent action is a way of insisting on one's just rights without violating the rights of anyone else. In many instances, non-violence offers the only possible way in which this can be effected. The whole strength of non-violence depends on this absolute respect for the rights even of an otherwise unjust oppressor: his legal rights and his moral rights as a person. If non-violence is allied with civil disobedience, and it certainly is, this disobedience is however strictly limited. It is confined to *disobeying an unjust law,* for only this disobedience can be carried out without violation of rights.

Where an unjust law is disobeyed, authentic non-violent resistance nevertheless requires implicit acceptance of the penalty which is imposed for violation of the law. The purpose of this disobedience and the prompt acceptance of punishment for it is, according to Gandhian principles, to make abundantly clear the injustice of the law, in such a way that even the unjust oppressor will come to admit the fact, and will himself be willing to change the situation.

In this way non-violence claims to work not only for the good of the one who is unjustly oppressed, but also for the good of the oppressor. Ideally speaking, non-violent action is supposed to be conducted in such a way that both sides come to see the injustice as a disadvantage and a dishonor to both, and they then agree to work together to remedy things. In this way non-violence aims not at disruption and disintegration of society, but at a more real and living collaboration, based on truth and love.

So much for the ideal.

It must certainly be admitted that not all those who claim to be practicing non-violence have kept themselves strictly within the limits so prescribed. On the contrary, many have in fact a very imperfect understanding of these principles and have made their non-violence simply another form of violence. But on the other hand those who have taken non-violence seriously enough to dedicate their lives to it, have undergone the necessary training, and have carried out their tasks with the required discipline, have not only achieved great success but have demonstrated the truth of their principles. In spite of all attempts at misrepresentation and denigration, these achievements have been evident and impressive. The witness of genuine non-violence has been incontestable.

Nevertheless, in spite of this, the whole concept of non-violence remains, as far as most Americans are concerned, on the level of pure myth.

We badly need a clear, sound, fundamental treatment of the principles of Non-Violent Action. In particular, Christians need a theological exposition of these principles. Father Régamey is not only a theologian, he has also been active in the French Gandhian non-violent movement and therefore knows his subject both theologically and existentially. His treatment is particularly valuable, not only as clarification but as witness. Above all, at a time when so many American Catholics have come to the point where they seem to think that to question the justice of the use of force is to betray the nation and to deny the faith, we need this perfectly sound, reasonable and exact argument in favor of Christian non-violence.

The chief value of such an exposition is that it clearly shows the difference between *non-violence* and *non-resistance*. Not only does non-violence resist evil but, if it is properly practiced, it often resists evil more effectively than

38

violence ever could. Indeed, the chief argument in favor of non-violent resistance is that it is, per se and ideally, *the only really effective resistance to injustice and evil.*

This does not mean that in practice the solution to grave international and civil problems can be had merely by good will and pious gestures of appeasement. The non-violent ideal does not contain in itself all the answers to all our questions. These will have to be met and worked out amid the risks and anguish of day to day politics. But they can never be worked out if non-violence is never taken seriously.

Whoever reads Father Régamey's study carefully and objectively should put it down, if not convinced that non-violent resistance is the Christian way par excellence to resist evil, at least persuaded that it is a form of positive resistance which deserves respectful consideration. In any event, the reader may rest assured that if, on putting down the book, he feels himself "inclined to non-violence," he does not have to fear that his mind will presently snap and that he will go berserk. At least one thing should be clear, after one has studied these pages. Far from being a fanatical manifestation of misguided idealism, non-violence demands a lucid reason, a profound religious faith and, above all, an uncompromising and courageous spirit of self-sacrifice.

Peace and Protest

"WAR NEVER AGAIN!" CRIED POPE PAUL ADDRESSING THE UNITED Nations in October, 1965, and many who solemnly assented to his plea as reasonable and right, assented with equal solemnity a few weeks later when a retired Air Force General suggested that the way to bring peace to Southeast Asia was to "bomb North Vietnam back into the stone age." It was in this atmosphere that Cardinal Spellman, addressing troops in Vietnam, deplored the protest against the war articulated at home and summed up his view with, "My country right or wrong!" All of which goes to show that when war is actually being waged, emotional cliches come easier than creative thinking.

The Vatican Council took note of the fact that even without nuclear weapons, or the horrendous chemical and bacteriological methods of extermination which are being held in reserve, modern war can easily reach a level of "savagery far surpassing that of the past." Even "conventional" modern war is in fact no longer the war that used to be waged in the past between armed forces. Systematic terrorism involves the whole population of a beleaguered area. This is now a normal feature of war. All war is now total wherever it is waged.

Frankly denouncing as criminal all acts of war which deliberately conflict with natural law, the council said that blind obedience could not excuse those who carried them out. "Such actions must be vehemently condemned as horrendous crimes. The courage of those who fearlessly and openly resist those who issue such commands merits supreme commendation." (Constitution on the Church in the Modern World, n. 79)

In the language of most American Catholics today this rates as an incitement to treason.

The council intended by these and other statements to drive home one point: We must take an entirely new attitude in evaluating war today. (n. 80)

Current familiar attitudes no longer provide us with the right perspective from which to judge acts of war. Therefore to judge according to our old, habitual ways of thought means to judge wrongly. Consequently the entire human race has a most serious obligation to face the inadequacy of these familiar attitudes and to do something about getting re-educated. Each one of us has to unlearn an ingrained tendency to violence and to destructive thinking. Each of us has to get rid of a systematic moral myopia which excuses acts of barbarism when justified by appeals to patriotism, freedom and so on. But every time we renounce reason and patience in order to solve a conflict by violence we are side-stepping this great obligation and putting it off. Appeal to nationalistic or other ideological cliches only serves to obscure this issue and to justify unreason. How long can we continue to do this? Our time is limited, and we are not taking advantage of our opportunities. In fact, even with a certain semblance of goodwill, we are just not able to.

The human race today is like an alcoholic who knows that drink will destroy him and yet always he has "good reasons" why he must continue drinking. Such is man in his fatal addiction to war. He is not capable of seeing a realistic alternative to massive violence. He does not really want peace, in the sense that he is not capable of making an efficacious decision in favor of peace rather than war in any situation where he feels himself seriously threatened. All his theoretical approval for peace applies only to remote and unreal

41

situations, which do not affect him or his interests.

If this task of building a peaceful world is the most important task of our time, it is also the most difficult. It will, in fact, require far more discipline, more sacrifice, more planning, more thought, more cooperation and more heroism than war ever demanded.

If it were possible for the political leaders of the world to agree to "abolish war" and then organize an international police force to restrain every impulse to belligerency, the problem would be simple. Actually, of course no political system at present seriously contemplates abolishing war. All still assume that the only way to peace is to abolish the enemy—or reduce him to helplessness. And this is in fact what the average citizen still believes. The mere problem of getting people to think otherwise is in fact an awesome challenge to human courage and intelligence. Can we meet this challenge? Do we have the moral strength and the faith that are required to make so drastic a change in a short time?

Sometimes the prospect seems almost hopeless, for man is more addicted to violent fantasies and obsessions now than he ever has been before, and we are today spending more for war alone than we spent for everything, war included, thirty years ago.

We also live in a double crisis of faith and reason in which man is haunted by uncertainties and is reduced to confusion by the total insecurity of all moral standards. The Church can serenely point to natural law but what does the average G.I. in Vietnam know about natural law? True, it is "inscribed in his nature" but the training he receives to prepare him for active service and perhaps also the life he has previously led in civilian society have made a palimpsest of the inscription!

In such a situation, protest and discussion are vitally necessary, and there has been no lack of protest against the war in Vietnam. It is to the honor of America that so many citizens have raised so many of the right questions about such a war.

The big question, however, is the validity of the protest as communication. Is the current protest making any real headway in re-educating us, in giving us a new attitude towards war? Or is it simply an outlet for the indignation, the frustration and the anxiety of those who see that the war is irrational, but fear they can do nothing to stop it? The important thing about protest is not so much the short-range possibility of changing the direction of policies, but the longer range aim of helping everyone gain an entirely new attitude towards war. Far from doing this, much current protest simply reinforces the old positions by driving the adversary back into the familiar and secure mythology of force. Hence the strong "patriotic" reaction against protests in the United States. How can one protest against war without implicitly and indirectly contributing to the war-mentality?

I do not advocate the burning of draft cards; I can understand the arguments of those who have burned their cards. I just do not know if their position is comprehensible to a lot of frightened and confused people: in any case I certainly believe that we must admit patriotic dissent and argument at a time like this. Such dissent must be responsible. It must give a clear and reasonable account of itself to the nation, and it must help sincere and concerned minds to accept alternatives to war without surrendering the genuine interests of our own national community.

There is however considerable danger of ambiguity in protests that seek mainly to capture the attention of the press, to gain publicity for a cause, and that are more concerned with their impact upon the public than with the meaning of that impact. Such dissent tends to be at once

43

dramatic and superficial. It may cause a slight commotion, but in a week everything is forgotten—some new shock has occurred in some other area. What is needed is a constructive, consistent and clear dissent that recalls people to their senses, makes them think deeply, plants in them a seed of change, and awakens in them the profound need for truth, reason and peace which is implanted in man's nature. Such dissent implies belief in openness of mind and in the possibility of mature exchange of ideas. When protest becomes desperate and seemingly extreme, then perhaps one reason for this is that the ones protesting have given up hope of a fair hearing, and therefore seek only to shock or to horrify. On the other hand, perhaps the public is too eager to be shocked and horrified and to refuse a fair hearing. The reaction of shock always seems to dispense from serious thought.

There is no question of the evident ambiguities of the communist peace-line, particularly that of China, for which "peace" seems to consist in an all-out world uprising of small nations against "neo-colonialist imperialism" (i.e., the United States). It is obviously to the interest of such a line to draw to itself the American peace protest which has nothing to do essentially with communism. To argue that because it can be used in favor of communism and is therefore communist by implication is to resort to the logic which governed Stalin's purges in the thirties and forties. As a matter of fact, nothing is more "useful" to world-communism than the kind of war effort we are now engaged in.

The great problem is to maintain clarity, objectivity and openness even in resisting manifest error.

We have a duty to live up to our heritage of open-mindedness. We must always be tolerant and fair and never simply revile others for their opinions. The way to silence error is by truth, not by various subtle forms of aggression. But we will always prefer violence to truth if our imaginations are at every moment over-stimulated by frenzied and dangerous fantasies.

Therefore one of the most important tasks of the moment is to recognize the great problem of the mental climate in which we live. Our minds are filled with images which call for violent and erratic reactions. We can hardly recover our senses long enough to think calmly and make reasoned commitments. We are swept by alternate fears and hopes which have no relation to deep moral truth. A protest which merely compounds these fears and hopes with a new store of violent images can hardly help us become men of peace.

Is it perhaps this insatiable hunger for visible and quick returns that has driven the majority of Americans to accept the war in Vietnam as reasonable? Are we so psychologically constituted and determined that we find real comfort in a daily score of bombed bridges and burned villages, forgetting that the price of our psychological security is the burned flesh of women and children who have no guilt and no escape from the fury of our weapons?

Or perhaps our scientific and technological mentality makes us war-minded. We believe that any end can be achieved from the moment one possesses the right instruments, the right machines, the right technique. The problem of war turns into a problem of engineering. We forget that we are dealing with human beings instead of rocks, oil, steel, water, or coal. Hence the signal failure of the bulldozer mentality in Vietnam. Yet apparently the only answer of the Pentagon is to get a bigger bulldozer. The answer is neither scientific nor humane.

One thing that gives such a drastic character to the protest against war is the realization which the peace people have of this unjust suffering inflicted on the innocent largely as a result of our curious inner psychological needs, fo-

45

mented by the climate of our technological culture.

In order to resist this appeal to mercy, those who want and "need" the violence in Vietnam disregard the sufferings of "the enemy" and concentrate on the very real and desperate hardships of our own G.I.'s in Vietnam.

Yet there remains a difference.

The sufferings of our own men are avoidable. There are alternatives. It is even possible that these alternatives would be more effective and would restore the honor of our country in the eyes of those nations that feel threatened by us and therefore hate us.

All protest against war and all witness for peace should in some way or other strive to overcome the desperation and hopelessness which lead man now, in fact, to regard all his existing peace-making machinery as futile beyond redemption. It is this practical despair of effective peace-making that drives man more and more to embrace the conclusion that only war is effective and that because violence seems to pay off, we must finally resort to it.

The great value of Pope Paul's visit to the United Nations was precisely this: it was a positive and constructive witness which, together with a clear and firm protest against war and injustice, re-awakened a definite hope in peaceful alternatives to war. It was a most serious and highly credible reminder that instruments for peaceful conflict solution are at hand. These instruments are abused and discredited, but if men want to make serious and effective use of them, they are still free to do so.

The Prison Meditations
of Father Delp

1

THOSE WHO ARE USED TO THE NORMAL RUN OF SPIRITUAL books and meditations will have to adjust themselves to a new and perhaps disturbing outlook if they read the *Prison Meditations* of the Jesuit Alfred Delp (New York, 1963). Written literally by a man in chains, condemned to be executed as a traitor to Nazi Germany in time of war, these pages are completely free from the myopic platitudes and the insensitive complacencies of routine piety. Set in the familiar framework of seasonal meditations on the Church year, these are new and often shocking insights into realities which we sometimes discuss academically but which are here experienced in their naked, uncompromising truth. These are the thoughts of a man who, caught in a well-laid trap of political lies, clung desperately to a truth that was revealed to him in solitude, helplessness, emptiness and desperation. Face to face with inescapable physical death, he reached out in desperation for the truth without which his spirit could not breathe and survive. The truth was granted him, and we share it in his surreptitious writings, awed by the realization that it was given him not for himself alone, but for us, who need it just as desperately, perhaps more desperately, than he did.

One of the most sobering aspects of Father Delp's meditations is the conviction they impart that we may one day be in the same desperate situation as the writer. Though we may perhaps still seem to be living in a world where, in spite of wars and rumors of wars, business goes on as usual, and Christianity is what it has always been, Father Delp reminds us that somewhere in the last fifty years we have crossed a mysterious limit set by Providence and have entered a new era. We have, in some sense, passed a point of no return, and it is both useless and tragic to continue to live as if we were still in the nineteenth century. Whatever we may think of the new era, whether we imagine it is the millennium, the noosphere, as the beginning of the end, there has been a violent disruption of society and a radical overthrow of that western Christian culture which goes back to Charlemagne and St. Augustine.

In this new era the social structures into which Christianity had fitted so comfortably and naturally have all but collapsed. The thought patterns which began to assert themselves in the Renaissance, and which assumed control at the French Revolution, have now so deeply affected modern man that even where he preserves certain traditional beliefs, they tend to be emptied of their vital inner reality, and to mask instead the common pseudo-spirituality or the outright nihilism of mass-man. The meditations of Father Delp were written not only in the face of his own death, but in the terrifying presence of this specter of a faceless being that was once the image of God, and toward which the Church nevertheless retains an unchanging responsibility.

The first pages were written in Advent of 1944, when the armies of the Reich launched their last, hopeless offensive in the Ardennes. Defeat was already certain. The Nazis alone refused to see it. Hitler was still receiving lucky answers from the stars. Father Delp had long since refused to accept the collective delusion. In 1943 at the request of Count Von Moltke and with the permission of his religious superiors, he had joined in the secret discussions of the "Kreisau Circle," an anti-Nazi group that was planning a new social order to be built on Christian lines after the war. That was all. But since it implied a complete repudiation of the compulsive myths and preposterous fictions of Nazism, it constituted high treason. Since it implied that Germany might not win, it was "defeatism"—a crime worthy of death.

The trial itself was a show, staged by a specialist in such matters. It was handled with ruthless expertise and melodramatic arrogance before an obedient jury and docile public of SS men and Gestapo agents. The scenario did not provide for a serious defense of the prisoners. Such efforts as they made to protest their innocence were turned against them and only made matters worse. Count Von Moltke and Father Delp were singled out as the chief villains, and in Delp's case the prosecution smeared not only the prisoner but the Jesuit Order and the Catholic Church as well. Moltke came under special censure because he had had the temerity to consult bishops and theologians with sinister "re-Christianizing intentions." The prosecution also tried to incriminate Moltke and Delp in the attempted assassination of Hitler the previous July, but this was obviously out of the question and the charge was dropped. This was plainly a religious trial. The crime was heresy against Nazism. As Father Delp summed it up in his last letter: "The actual reason for my condemnation was that I happened to be and chose to remain a Jesuit."

Nearly twenty years have passed since Father Delp was executed in the Plotzensee prison on February 2, 1945. During these twenty years the world has been supposedly "at peace." But in actual fact, the same chaotic, inexhaustible struggle of armed nations has continued in a different form. A new weaponry, unknown to Father Delp, now guarantees that the next total war will be one of titanic destructiveness, when a single nuclear weapon contains more explosive force than all the bombs in World War II put

49

together. In the atmosphere of violent tension that now pre-
vails, there is no less cynicism, no less desperation, no less
confusion than Father Delp saw around him. Totalitarian
fanaticisms have not disappeared from the face of the earth:
on the contrary, armed with nuclear weapons, they threaten
to possess it entirely. Fascism has not vanished: the state
socialism of the Communist countries can justly be rated
as a variety of fascism. In the democratic countries of the
west, armed to the teeth in defense of freedom, fascism is
not unknown. Fanatical right wing para-military organizations are growing in America. In France, a secret terrorist
organization has attempted to gain power by intimidation,
violence, torture, blackmail, murder. The principles of this
organization were explicitly fascist principles. Curiously
enough, Nazism, returning to life in Germany, recognized
its affinities with the French Terrorists and proclaimed its
solidarity with them. Yet among the French crypto-fascists
were many who appeal paradoxically to Christian principles,
in justification of their ends!

What in fact is the position of Christians? It is ambiguous
and confused. Though the Holy See and more recently the
Vatican Council repeatedly affirmed the traditional classical
ethic of social and international justice, and though these
pronouncements are greeted with a certain amount of
respectful interest, it is increasingly clear that their actual
influence is often negligible. Christians themselves are confused and passive, looking this way and that for indications
of what to do or think next. The dominating factor in the
political life of the average Christian today is fear of Communism. But, as Father Delp shows, the domination of fear
completely distorts the true perspectives of Christianity and
it may well happen that those whose religious activity
reduces itself in the long run to a mere negation, will find
that their faith has lost all content.

In effect, the temptation to negativism and irrationality, the urge to succumb to pure pragmatism and the massive use of power, is almost overwhelming in our day. Two huge blocs, each armed with a quasi-absolute, irresistible offensive force capable of totally annihilating the other, stand face to face. Each one insists that it is armed in defense of a better world and for the salvation of mankind. But each tends more and more explicitly to assert that this end cannot be achieved until the enemy is wiped out.

A book like the Delp meditations forces us to stand back and re-examine these oversimplified claims. We are compelled to recall that in the Germany of Father Delp's time Christians were confronted with more or less the same kind of temptation. First there must be a war. After that a new and better world. This was nothing new. It was by now a familiar pattern, not only in Germany but in Russia, England, France, America and Japan.

Was there another choice? Is there another choice today? The western tradition of liberalism has always hoped to attain a more equable world order by peaceful collaboration among nations. This is also the doctrine of the Church. Father Delp and Count Von Moltke hoped to build a new Germany on Christian principles. Pope John XXIII in his encyclicals *Mater et Magistra* and *Pacem in Terris* clarified and exposed these principles. The Vatican Council promulgated its Constitution on the Church and the World. If there remains a choice confronting man today, it is the crucial one between global destruction or global order. Those who imagine that in the nuclear age it may be possible to clear the way for a new order with nuclear weapons are even more deluded than the people who followed Hitler, and their error will be a thousand times more tragic, above all if they commit it in the hope of defending their religion.

Father Delp had no hesitation in evaluating the choice

of those who, in the name of religion, followed the Nazi government in its policy of conquest first and a new world later. He said: "The most pious prayer can become a blasphemy if he who offers it tolerates or helps to further conditions which are fatal to mankind, which render him unacceptable to God, or weaken his spiritual, moral or religious sense."

2

What did Father Delp mean by "conditions fatal to mankind"?

His prison meditations are a penetrating diagnosis of a devastated, gutted, faithless society in which man is rapidly losing his humanity because he has become practically incapable of belief. Man's only hope, in this wilderness which he has become, is to respond to his inner need for truth, with a struggle to recover his spiritual freedom. But this he is unable to do unless he first recovers his ability to hear the voice that cries to him in the wilderness: in other words, he must become aware of his devastated and desperate condition before it is too late. There is no question of the supreme urgency of this revival. For Father Delp it seems clear that the time is running out.

In these pages we meet a stern, recurrent foreboding that the "voice in the wilderness" is growing fainter and fainter, and that it will soon no longer be heard at all. The world may then sink into godless despair.

Yet the "wilderness" of man's spirit is not yet totally hostile to all spiritual life. On the contrary, its silence is still a healing silence. He who tries to evade solitude and confrontation with the unknown God may eventually be destroyed in the meaningless chaotic atomized solitariness of mass society. But meanwhile it is still possible to face one's inner solitude and to recover mysterious sources of hope and strength. This is still possible. But fewer and fewer men are aware of the possibility. On the contrary: "Our lives today have become godless to the point of complete vacuity."

This is not a cliche of pulpit rhetoric. It is not a comforting slogan to remind the believer that he is "right" and that the unbeliever is "wrong." It is a far more radical assertion, which questions even the faith of the faithful and the piety of the pious. Far from being comforting, this is an alarming declamation of almost Nietszchean scandalousness. "Of all messages this is the most difficult to accept—*we find it hard to believe that the man of active faith no longer exists.*" An extreme statement, but he follows it with another: "Modern man is not even capable of knowing God." In order to understand these harsh assertions by Father Delp we must remember they were written by a man in prison, surrounded by Nazi guards. When he speaks of "modern man," he is in fact speaking of the Nazis or of their accomplices and counterparts. Fortunately not all modern men are Nazis. And even in reference to Nazis, when stated thus bluntly and out of context, these statements are still too extreme to be true. They are not meant to be taken absolutely, for if they were simply true, there would be no hope left for anyone, and Father Delp's message is in fact a message of hope. He believes that "the task in the education of present and future generations is to *restore man to a state of fitness for God.*" The Church's mission in the world today is a desperate one of helping create conditions in which man can return to himself, recover something of his lost humanity, as a necessary preparation for his ultimate return to God. But as he now is, alienated, void, internally dead, modern man has in effect no capacity for God.

Father Delp is not saying that human nature is vitiated in its essence, that we have been abandoned by God or become radically incapable of grace. But the dishonesty and injustice of our world are such, Father Delp believes, that we are blind to spiritual things even when we think we are seeing them: and indeed perhaps most blind when we are convinced that we see. "Today's bondage," he says, speaking of Germany in 1944, "is the sign of our untruth and deception."

The predicament of man, from which comes his faithlessness, is basically a matter of alienation expressed in arrogance or in fear. These two are only the two sides of one coin—attachment to material things for their own sake, love of wealth and power. Alienation results in the arrogance of those who have power or in the passive servility of the functionary who, unable to have wealth and power himself, gladly participates in a power structure which employs him as a utensil. Modern man has surrendered himself to be used more and more as an instrument, as a means, and in consequence his spiritual creativity has dried up at its source. No longer alive with passionate convictions, but centered on his own empty and alienated self, man becomes destructive, negative, violent. He loses all insight, all compassion, and his instinctual life is cruelly perverse. Or else his soul, shocked into insensitivity by suffering and alienation, remains simply numb, inert and hopeless. In such varying conditions, man continues in "blind conflict with reality" and hence his life is a repeated perpetration of a basic untruth. Either he still hopes in matter and in the power he acquires by its manipulation, and then his heart is one to which "God Himself cannot find access, it is so hedged around with insurance." Or else, in abject self-contempt, alienated man "believes more in his own unworthiness than in the creative power of God."

Both these conditions are characteristic of materialist man, but they also appear in a pseudo-Christian guise. This is particularly true of the negative, lacrymose and "resigned" Christianity of those who manage to blend the cult of the status quo with a habit of verbalizing on suffering and submission. For such as these, indifference to real evil has become a virtue, and preoccupation with petty or imaginary problems of piety substitutes for the creative unrest of the truly spiritual man. A few phrases about the Cross and a few formal practices of piety concord, in such religion, with a profound apathy, a bloodless lassitude, and perhaps an almost total incapacity to love. It is the indifference of a man who, having surrendered his humanity, imagines that he is therefore pleasing to God. Unfortunately Father Delp suggests that such a one is already faithless, already prepared for any one of the modern pseudo-religions, the worship of the Class, Race or State.

What can be done to save such resigned and negative Christians from becoming crypto-fascists? Certainly no amount of "baroque glamorizing" of the mysteries of faith, no dramatic banalities, no false glitter of new apologetic techniques. Seen from the silence of Father Delp's prison cell, the much publicized movements dedicated to so many worthy ends, take on a pitiable air of insignificance. Too often, he says, these efforts represent a failure to meet the genuine needs of man. Sometimes they do not imply even an elementary awareness of man's real desperation. Instead of being aimed at those whom the Church most needs to seek, these movements seem to him in many cases to concern themselves with the hunger of pious souls for their own satisfaction: they produce an illusion of holiness and a gratifying sense that one is "accomplishing something."

Instead of the difficult exploratory and diagnostic work of seeking modern man in his spiritual wilderness with all its baffling problems, these movements are scarcely aware of anything new in the world—except new means of communication. For them, *our problems are still the same ones* the Church has been confronting and solving for two thousand years. It is assumed that we know what is wrong, and that all we lack is zeal and opportunity to fix it: then everything will be all right. It is not a question of truth or insight but of power and will, we imagine: all we need is the capacity to do what we already know. Hence we concentrate on ways and means of gaining influence so that we can obtain a hearing for our familiar answers and solutions. But in actual fact we are, with everybody else, in a new world, unexplored. It is as though we were already on the moon or on Saturn. The walking is not the same as it was on earth.

Too much religious action today, says Father Delp, concentrates on the relatively minor problems of the religious minded minority and ignores the great issues which compromise the very survival of the human race. Man has gradually had the life of the spirit and the capacity for God crushed out of him by an inhuman way of life of which he is both the "product and the slave." Instead of striving to change these conditions, and to build an order in which man can gradually return to himself, regain his natural and supernatural health, and find room to grow and respond to God, we are rather busying ourselves with relatively insignificant details of ritual, organization, ecclesiastical bureaucracy, the niceties of law and ascetical psychology. Those who teach religion and preach the truths of faith to an unbelieving world are perhaps more concerned with proving themselves right than with really discovering and satisfying the spiritual hunger of those to whom they speak. Again, we are too ready to assume that we know better than the unbeliever what ails him. We take it for granted that the only answer he needs is contained in formulas so familiar to us that we utter them without thinking. We do not realize that he is listening not for words but for the evidence of thought and love behind the words. Yet if he is not instantly converted by our sermons we console ourselves with the thought that this is due to his fundamental perversity.

Father Delp says: "None of the contemporary religious movements take for their starting point the position of mankind as human beings . . . they do not help man in the depths of his need but merely skim the surface. . . . They concentrate on the difficulties of the religious minded man who still has religious leanings. They do not succeed in coordinating the forms of religion with a state of existence that no longer accepts its values." Before we can interest non-Christians in the problems of cult and of conduct that seem important and absorbing to us, we must first try to find out what they need, and perhaps also we might devote a little more thought to the question whether it is not possible that, in a dialogue with them *they* might have something to give *us*. Indeed, if we do not approach the dialogue as a genuine dialogue, if it is simply a benign monologue in which they listen to us in abashed and grateful awe, we cannot give them the one thing they most need: the love which is our own deepest need also. "Man" says Father Delp, "must be educated to resume his proper status of manhood, and religion must be taught intensively by truly religious teachers. The profession has fallen into disrepute and it will have to be re-established." What is needed, he says, is not simply goodwill and piety, but "truly religious men *ready to cooperate in all efforts for the betterment of mankind and human order.*"

However these efforts must not be a matter of an interested and manipulative religious politics. The world has become disillusioned with religious politics devoid of genuine human and spiritual concern, interested only in preparing the way for peremptory doctrinal and moral demands.

57

Father Delp makes it clear that we are in no position to make such demands on modern man. The following paragraph is one of the most sobering and perhaps shocking in the book, but it contains profound truths for those who know how to listen:

> A church that makes demands in the name of a peremptory God no longer carries weight in a world of changing values. The new generation is separated from the clear conclusions of traditional theology by a great mountain of boredom and disillusion thrown up by past experience. We have destroyed man's confidence in us by the way we live. We cannot expect two thousand years of history to be an unmixed blessing and recommendation. History can be a handicap too. But recently a man turning to the Church for enlightenment has all too often found only a tired man to receive him—a man who then had the dishonesty to hide his fatigue under pious words and fervent gestures. At some future date the honest historian will have some bitter things to say about the contribution of the Churches to the creation of the mass mind, of collectivism, dictatorships and so on.

More than this, Father Delp realizes the profound responsibility of the Christian to his persecutors themselves "lest those who are our executioners today may at some future time be our accusers for the suppression of truth."

In such statements as these, Father Delp makes no attempts to gloss over what he believes to be the truth, and he speaks with all the authority of a confessor of the faith who knows that he must not waste words. He himself adds, in all frankness: "Whoever has fulfilled his duty of obedience has a right to cast a critical eye over the realities of the Church and where the Church fails the shortcomings should not be glossed over." It is impossible to dismiss these criticisms as the words of an embittered rebel, disloyal to the Church. Father Delp *died* for the Church. The words of one who has been obedient unto death cannot be dismissed or gainsaid. These meditations "in face of death" have a sustained, formidable seriousness unequalled in any spiritual book of our time. This imposes upon us the duty to listen to what he has said with something of the same seriousness, the same humility and the same courage.

Nevertheless it must be recognized that since 1945 other voices have joined themselves to Father Delp's and have reiterated the same criticisms. Perhaps they have done so in milder or more general terms, but there is a widespread recognition of the fact that the Church is seriously out of contact with modern man and can in some sense be said to have failed in her duty to him. This awareness, though stated in general terms, can be discerned in statements of certain bishops, even of the Pope himself. Certainly the convocation of the Second Vatican Council was intended, in the mind of John XXIII, to meet precisely the situation which Father Delp described with an almost brutal forthrightness.

Archbishop Hurley of Durban has recommended a radical reform in seminary education to enable priests to meet the new needs that confront the Church. Though stated with less urgency than the strictures of Father Delp, these recommendations of the South African Archbishop reflect something of the same sense of crisis.

> Unless the change of methods is systematically pursued, a first-class crisis will result, for there is no better way of promoting a crisis than by allowing a situation to drift into change without adjusting the approach of those most directly involved in the situation. Priests engaged in the pastoral ministry are the persons most directly involved in the Church's day-to-day life and activity. There is therefore no more urgent task confronting us than a reconsideration of the methods by which our priests are trained for their ministry. If we fail to face up to it the developing crisis may strain to a breaking point the relations between a laity in desperate need of a new approach and to some extent lead to expect it, and a clergy incapable of supplying the need.

(Pastoral Emphasis in Seminary Studies, Maynooth, 1962)

3

The diagnosis of our modern sickness has been given to us by Father Delp in the most serious unambiguous terms. What of the prognosis?

First of all, he asks us to face the situation squarely, but warns that it is not enough to take a perverse pleasure in contemplating our own ruin. "Pious horror at the state of the world will not help us in any way." An apocalyptic mood of general disgust and contempt for the hopes of our struggling fellow-Christians would only further aggravate the negativism and despair which he has so lucidly pointed out to us. Yet at the same time there can be no question that we must start from where we are: we must begin with the fact that in the midst of a twisted and shattered humanity we too are leading an "existence that has become a reproach." Yet here he lays open to us the paradox on which our salvation depends: the truth that even in our blindness and apparent incapacity for God, God is still with us, and that an encounter with Him is still possible. Indeed, it is our only hope.

Impatience, willfulness, self-assertion and arrogance will not help us. There is no use in Promethean self-dramatization. Things have gone too far for that. The encounter with God is not something we can produce at will. It is not something we can conjure up by some magic effort of psychological and spiritual force. Indeed, these are the temptations of the secular false prophets: the masters of autonomy, for whom "untrammeled subjectivity is the ultimate secret of being," the artists of Faustian self-assertion whose efforts "have silenced the messengers of God" and reduced the world to a spiritual waste land.

The Advent discovery which Father Delp made, pacing up and down his cell in chains, was that in the very midst

60

of his desolation the messengers of God were present. This discovery was in no way due to his own spiritual efforts, his own will to believe, his own purity of heart. The "blessed messages" were pure gifts from God, which could never have been anticipated, never foreseen, never planned by a human consciousness. Unaccountably, while he saw with a terrible and naked clarity the horror of his world gutted by bombs, he saw at the same time the meaning and the possibilities of man's condition. In the darkness of defeat and degradation, the seeds of light were being sown.

> What use are all the lessons learned through our suffering and misery if no bridge can be thrown from one side to the other shore? What is the point of our revulsion from error and fear if it brings no enlightenment and does not penetrate the darkness and dispel it? What use is it shuddering at the world's coldness which all the time grows more intense, if we cannot discover the grace to conjure up better conditions?

In his Advent meditations, with all the simplicity of traditional Christian faith, and in images that are seldom remarkable for any special originality, Father Delp proceeds to describe the ruin of Germany and of the Western world as an "advent" in which the messengers of God are preparing for the future. But this golden future is not a foregone conclusion. It is not a certainty. It is an object of hope. But it is contingent upon the spiritual alertness of man. And man, as Father Delp has already repeated so often, is utterly confused.

Man must begin by recognizing and accepting his desolation, in all its bitterness.

"Unless a man has been shocked to his depths at himself and the things he is capable of, as well as the failings of humanity as a whole, he cannot understand the full import of Advent."

61

The tragedy of the concentration camps, of Eichmann and of countless others like him is not only that such crimes were possible, but that the men involved could do what they did *without being in the least shocked and surprised at themselves.* Eichmann to the very last considered himself an obedient and God-fearing man! It was this dehumanized bureaucratic conscientiousness that especially appalled Father Delp: the absurd and monumental deception that practices the greatest evil with ritual solemnity as if it were somehow noble, intelligent and important. The inhuman complacency that is *totally incapable* of seeing in itself either sin, or falsity, or absurdity, or even the slightest impropriety.

Two things then are necessary to man. Everything depends on these.

First he must accept without reserve the truth "that life . . . by itself has neither purpose nor fulfillment. It is both powerless and futile within its own range of existence and also as a consequence of sin. To this must be added the rider that life demands both purpose and fulfillment."

"Secondly it must be recognized that it is God's alliance with man, his being on our side, ranging himself with us, that corrects this state of meaningless futility. *It is necessary to be conscious of God's decision to enlarge the boundaries of His own supreme existence by condescending to share ours, for the overcoming of sin.*"

In other words, Father Delp is reiterating the basic truth of Christian faith and Christian experience, St. Paul's realization of the paradox of man's helplessness and God's grace, not as somehow opposed, fighting for primacy in man's life, but as a single existential unity: Sinful man redeemed in Christ.

Acceptance does not guarantee a sudden illumination which dispels all darkness forever. On the contrary it means seeing life as a long journey in the wilderness, but a journey with an invisible Companion, toward a secure and promised fulfillment not for the individual believer alone but for the community of man to whom salvation has been promised in Jesus Christ. But as soon as these familiar words are uttered, we imagine that it is now once again a question of lulling ourselves to sleep in devout psychological peace. "Everything will be all right. Reality is not so terrible as it seems."

On the contrary, Father Delp will have us turn back to the real contemporary world in all its shocking and inhuman destructiveness. We have no other option. This is the prime necessity. The urgent need for courage to face the truth of untruth, the cataclysmic presence of an apocalyptic lie that is at work not only in this or that nation, this or that class, and party, this or that race, but in all of us, everywhere. "These are not matters that can be postponed to suit our convenience. They call for immediate action because untruth is both dangerous and destructive. It has already rent out souls, destroyed our people, laid waste our land and our cities; it has already caused our generation to bleed to death."

Yet at the same time, truth is hidden in the very heart of untruth. "Our fate, no matter how much it may be entwined with the inescapable logic of circumstance, is still nothing more than the way to God, the way the Lord has chosen for the ultimate consummation of His purpose."

The light and truth which are hidden in the suffocating cloud of evil are not to be found only in a stoical and isolated individual here and there who has surmounted the horror of his fate. They must appear somehow in a renewal of our entire social order. "Moments of grace both historical and personal are inevitably linked with an awakening and restoration of genuine order and truth." This is most important. It situates the profound and mystical intuitions of Father Delp in a securely objective frame of reference. His vision has meaning not for himself alone but for our society, our Church and for the human race.

In other words, Father Delp prescribes not only accept- ance of our "fate" but much more, acceptance of a divinely appointed task in history. It is, note clearly, not simply the decision to accept one's personal salvation from the hands of God, in suffering and tribulation, but the decision to become *totally engaged in the historical task of the Mystical Body of Christ* for the redemption of man and his world.

It is then not only a question of accepting suffering, but much more, of accepting *happiness.* This in its turn implies much more than a stoical willingness to put up with the blows of fortune, even though they may be conceived as "sent by God." It means a total and complete *openness to God.* Such openness is impossible without a full reorienta- tion of man's existence according to exact and objective order which God has place in His creation and to which the Church bears infallible witness.

If we surrender completely to God, considered not only as an inscrutable and mysterious Guest within ourselves, but as the Creator and Ruler of the world, the Lord of His- tory and the Conqueror of evil and of death, then we can recover the meaning of existence, we rediscover our sense of direction. "We regain faith in our own dignity, our mis- sion and our purpose in life precisely to the extent that we grasp the idea of our own life flowing forth within us from the mystery of God."

Perfect openness, total receptivity, born of complete self- surrender, bring us into uninhibited contact with God. In finding him we find our true selves. We return to the true order He has willed for us.

Such texts show that Father Delp was at the same time profoundly mystical and wide open to the broadest ideals of Christian humanism. It was by the gift of mystical intui-

64

tion that he not only found himself in God but also situated himself perfectly in God's order and man's society, even though paradoxically his place was to be a condemned man in the prison of an unjust and absurd government. Yet it was here that, as this book so eloquently proves to us, he fulfilled all that God asked of him. It was here that he could write, without exaggeration, "To restore divine order and to proclaim God's presence—these have been my vocation."

Father Delp's exact obedience to God, his perfect acceptance of God's order in the midst of disorder, was what gave him a sublime authority in denouncing the cowardice of Christians, who seek refuge from reality in trifling concerns, petty sectarian opinions, futile ritualism or religious technicalities which they alone can understand. Christians must not be afraid to be people and to enter into a genuine dialogue with other men, precisely perhaps with those men they most fear or stand most ready to condemn.

"The genuine dialogue no longer exists," says Father Delp, "because there are no genuine partners to engage in it. People are frightened. They are scared to stride out firmly and honestly to the boundaries of their potential powers because they are afraid of what they will find at the borderline."

In his impassioned plea for Christian liberty and personal dignity, Father Delp stands out as an advocate of true Christian humanism. This is exactly the opposite of the Promethean pseudo-humanism of anti-Christian culture since the Renaissance.

The supposed "creativity" claimed by the untrammeled subjectivism of men who seek complete autonomy defeats itself, because man centered on himself inevitably becomes destructive.

The humanism of Father Delp, which is also the humanism of the Church, recognizes that man has to be rescued precisely from this spurious autonomy which can only ruin him. He must be liberated from fixation upon his own subjective needs and compulsions and recognize that he cannot fully become himself until he knows his need for the world and his duty of serving it.

In bare outline, man's service of the world consists not in brandishing weapons to destroy other men and hostile societies, but in creating an order based on God's plan for His creation, beginning with minimum standard for a truly human existence for all men. Living space, law and order, nourishment for *all*, are basic needs without which there can be no peace and no stability on earth. "No faith, no education, no government, no science, no art, no wisdom will help mankind if the unfailing certainty of the minimum is lacking."

There is also an ethical minimum: honesty in every field, self-respect and mutual respect for all men, human solidarity among all races and nations. There must finally be a "minimum of transcendence"; in other words the cultural and spiritual needs of man must be met. In the words of Pope John XXIII, in *Mater et Magistra:* "Today the Church is confronted with *the immense task of giving a human and Christian note to modern civilization:* a note that is almost asked by that civilization itself for its further development *and even for its continued existence.*" It is no easy task to meet these minimal standards. At the present moment the fury and compassion of the Cold War seem to be the chief obstacle to our progress. Yet we too are in the same "advent" as Father Delp, and its laws are the same for us. If we pay attention, rouse ourselves from our despairing sleep, open our hearts without reserve to the God who speaks to us in the very wilderness where we now are, we can begin the work He asks of us: the work of restoring order to society, and bringing peace to the world, so that eventually man may begin to be healed of his mortal sickness, and that one day a sane society may emerge from our present confusion.

Is this impossible? When Father Delp died, he surrendered his life into the hands of God with the full conviction that it was not only possible, but that the work would one day be done.

But he also believed that the only hope for the world was this return to order and the emergence of the "new man," who knows that "adoration of God is the road that leads man to himself."

Unless man is made new, in the new order for which Father Delp laid down his life, there is no hope for our society, there is no hope for the human race. For man, in his present condition, has been reduced to helpless confusion in which he grimly tries to straighten himself out with technological instruments. Each apparent solution only serves to aggravate his problems.

Such then is the deeply disturbing yet hopeful message of these pages. It is the message not of a politician, but of a mystic. Yet this mystic recognized his inescapable responsibility to be involved in politics. And because he followed messengers of God into the midst of a fanatical and absurd political crisis, he was put to death for his pains.

What remains now is to understand this final most important lesson. The place of the mystic and the prophet in the twentieth century is not totally outside of society, not utterly remote from the world. Spirituality, religion, mysticism are not an unequivocal rejection of the human race in order to seek one's own individual salvation without concern for the rest of men. Nor is true worship a matter of standing aside and praying for the world, without any concept of its problems and its desperation.

The mystic and the spiritual man who in our day remain indifferent to the problems of their fellow men, who are not fully capable of facing those problems, will find themselves inevitably involved in the same ruin. They will suffer the same deceptions, be implicated in the same crimes. They will go down to ruin with the same blindness and the same insensitivity to the presence of evil. They will be deaf to the voice crying in the wilderness, for they will have listened to some other, more comforting voice, of their own making. This is the penalty of evasion and complacency.

Even contemplative and cloistered religious, perhaps especially these, need to be attuned to the deepest problems of the contemporary world. This does not mean that they must leave their solitude and engage in the struggle and confusion in which they can only be less useful than they would be in their cloister. They must preserve their unique perspective, which solitude alone can give them, and from their vantage point they must understand the world's anguish and share it in their own way, which may, in fact, be very like the experience of Father Delp.

No one has a more solemn obligation to understand the true nature of man's predicament than he who is called to a life of special holiness and dedication. The priest, the religious, the lay-leader must, whether he likes it or not, fulfill in the world the role of a prophet. If he does not face the anguish of being a true prophet, he must enjoy the carrion comfort of acceptance in the society of the deluded by becoming a false prophet and participating in their delusions.

An Enemy of the State

ON AUGUST 9, 1943, THE AUSTRIAN PEASANT FRANZ JÄGER-stätter was beheaded by the German military authorities as an "enemy of the state" because he had repeatedly refused to take the military oath and serve in what he declared to be an "unjust war." His story has a very special importance at a time when the Catholic Church, in the Second Vatican Council, is confronting the moral problem of nuclear weaponry. This Austrian peasant was not only simultaneously a Catholic and a conscientious objector, but he was a fervent Catholic, so fervent that some who knew him believe him to have been a saint. His lucid and uncompromising refusal to fight for Germany in the Second World War was the direct outcome of his religious conversion. It was the political implementation of his desire to be a perfect Christian.

Franz Jägerstätter surrendered his life rather than take the lives of others in what he believed to be an "unjust war." He clung to this belief in the face of every possible objection not only on the part of the army and the state, but also from his fellow Catholics, the Catholic clergy and of course his own family. He had to meet practically every "Christian" argument that is advanced in favor of war. He was treated as a rebel, disobedient to lawful authority, a traitor to his country. He was accused of being selfish, self-willed, not considering his family, neglecting his duty to his children.

His Austrian Catholic friends understood that he was unwilling to fight for Hitler's Germany, but yet they argued

69

that the war was justified because they hoped it would lead to the destruction of Bolshevism and therefore to the preservation of "European Christianity." He was therefore refusing to defend his faith. He was also told that he was not sufficiently informed to judge whether or not the war was just. That he had an obligation to submit to the "higher wisdom" of the state. The government and the Fuehrer know best. Thousands of Catholics, including many priests, were serving in the armies, and therefore he should not try to be "more Catholic than the Church."

He was even reminded that the bishops had not protested against this war, and in fact not only his pastor but even his bishop tried to persuade him to give up his resistance because it was "futile." One priest represented to him that he would have innumerable opportunities to practice Christian virtue and exercise an "apostolate of good example" in the armed forces. All these are very familiar arguments frequently met with in our present situation, and they are still assumed to be so conclusive that few Catholics dare to risk the disapproval they would incur by conscientious objection and dissent.

Jäggerstätter's fellow villagers thought his refusal was evidence of fanaticism due to his religious conversion at the time of his marriage in 1936, followed by an "excess of Bible reading." His conscientious objection is still not fully understood in his native village, though on the local war memorial his name has been added to those of the villagers who were killed in action.

The peasant refused to give in to any of these arguments, and replied to them with all simplicity:

"I cannot and may not take an oath in favor of a government that is fighting an unjust war. . . . I cannot turn the responsibility for my actions over to the Führer. . . . Does

70

anyone really think that this massive blood-letting can save European Christianity or bring it to a new flowering? . . . Is it not more Christian to offer oneself as a victim right away rather than first have to murder others who certainly have a right to live and want to live—just to prolong one's own life a little while?"

When reminded that most Catholics had gone to war for Hitler without any such qualms of conscience, he replied that they obviously "had not received the grace" to see things as they were. When told that the bishops themselves expressed no such objections he repeated that "they had not received the grace" either.

Jägerstätter's refusal to fight for Hitler was not based on a personal repugnance to fighting in any form. As a matter of fact Jägerstätter was, by temperament, something of a fighter. In his wilder youthful days he had participated rather prominently in the inter-village gang wars. He had also undergone preliminary military training without protest, though his experience at that time had convinced him that army life presented a danger to morals.

Shortly after Hitler took over Austria in 1938, Jägerstätter had a dream in which he saw a splendid and shining express train coming round a mountain, and thousands of people running to get aboard. "No one could prevent them from getting on the train." While he was looking at this he heard a voice saying: "This train is going to hell." When he woke up he spontaneously associated the "train" with Nazism. His objection to military service was, then, the fruit of a particular religious interpretation of contemporary political events. His refusal to fight was not only a private matter of conscience: it also expressed a deep intuition concerning the historical predicament of the Catholic Church in the twentieth century. This intuition was articulated in several

71

long and very impressive meditations or "commentaries"
in which he says:

> "The situation in which we Christians of Germany find our-
> selves today is much more bewildering than that faced by
> the Christians of the early centuries at the time of their
> bloodiest persecution. . . . We are not dealing with a small
> matter, but the great (apocalyptic) life and death struggle
> has already begun. Yet in the midst of it there are many
> who still go on living their lives as though nothing had
> changed. . . . That we Catholics must make ourselves tools
> of the worst and most dangerous anti-Christian power that
> has ever existed is something that I cannot and never will
> believe. . . . Many actually believe quite simply that things
> have to be the way they are. If this should happen to mean
> that they are obliged to commit injustice, then they believe
> that others are responsible. . . . I am convinced that it is
> still best that I speak the truth even though it costs me my
> life. For you will not find it written in any of the command-
> ments of God or of the Church that a man is obliged under
> pain of sin to take an oath committing him to obey what-
> ever might be commanded him by his secular ruler. We
> need no rifles or pistols for our battle, but instead spiritual
> weapons—and the foremost of these is prayer."

The witness of this Austrian peasant is in striking contrast
to the career of another man who lived and worked for a
time in the nearby city of Linz: Adolf Eichmann.

The American sociologist, Gordon Zahn, who is also a
Catholic and a pacifist, has written an absorbing, objective, fully documented life of Jäggerstätter,* in which he
studies with great care not only the motives and actions of
the man himself, but the reactions and recollections of
scores of people who knew him, from his family and neigh-
bors to fellow prisoners and prison chaplains. One of the
most striking things about the story is that repeated attempts
were made to save the peasant-objector's life not only by

* *In Solitary Witness* (New York: Holt, Rinehart & Winston, 1964).

his friends, by priests, by his attorney but even by his military judges (he was not in the hands of the SS).

Jägerstätter could have escaped execution if he had accepted non-combatant service in the medical corps, but he felt that even this would be a compromise, because his objection was not only to killing other men but to the act of saving his own life by an implicit admission that the Nazis were a legitimate regime carrying on a just war. A few minutes before his execution Jägerstätter still calmly refused to sign a document that would have saved him. The chaplain who was present, and who had tried like everyone else to persuade the prisoner to save himself, declared that Jägerstätter "lived as a saint and died as a hero."

It is important to observe that though the Catholic villagers of his native St. Radcgund still tend to regard Jägerstätter as an extremist and a fanatic, or even as slightly touched in the head, the priests who knew him and others who have studied him have begun to admit the seriousness and supernatural impact of his heroic self-sacrifice. There are some who do not hesitate to compare his decision with that of Thomas More.

One of the prison chaplains who knew him said: "Not for an instant did I ever entertain the notion that Jägerstätter was "fanatic" or even possibly mentally deranged. He did not give the slightest impression of being so." And a French cellmate said of him that he was "one of the heroes of our time, a fighter to the death for faith, peace and justice."

Finally, it is interesting to read the very reserved judgment of the bishop who, when consulted by Jägerstätter about this moral problem, urged him to renounce his "scruples" and let himself be inducted into the army.

"I am aware of the 'consistency' of his conclusions and respect them—especially in their intention. At that time I could see that the man thirsted after martyrdom and for

73

the expiation of sin, and I told him that he was permitted to choose that path only if he knew he had been called to it through some special revelation originating from above and not in himself. He agreed with this. For this reason Jagerstatter represents a completely exceptional case, one more to be marveled at than copied."

The story of the Austrian peasant as told by Gordon Zahn is plainly that of a martyr, and of a Christian who followed a path of virtue with a dedication that cannot be fully accounted for by human motivation alone. In other words, it would seem that already in this biography one might find plausible evidence of what the Catholic Church regards as sanctity. But the Bishop of Linz, in hinting at the possibility of a special calling that might have made Jägerstätter an "exceptional case," does not mean even implicitly to approve the thesis that the man was a saint, still less a model to be imitated. In other words the bishop, while admitting the remote possibility of Catholic heroism in a conscientious objector, is not admitting that such heroism should be regarded as either normal or imitable.

The Second Vatican Council in its Constitution on the Church in the Modern World (n. 79) recognized, at least implicitly, the right of a Catholic to refuse on grounds of conscience to bear arms. It did not propose conscientious objection as a sweeping obligation. Nevertheless it clearly declared that no one could escape the obligation to *refuse obedience* to criminal orders issued by the state or the military command. The example of genocide was given. In view of the fact that total war tends more and more in fact to be genocidal, the Council's declaration obviously bears above all on war.

The Bishop of Linz, however, did not propose conscientious objection as a rational and Christian option. For him, the true heroes remain "those exemplary young Catholic

74

men, seminarians, priests and heads of families who fought and died in heroic fulfillment of duty and in the firm conviction that they were fulfilling the will of God at their post. . . ."

It is still quite possible that even today after the Council and in an era of new war technology and new threats of global destruction, when the most urgent single problem facing modern man is the proliferation of atomic and nuclear weaponry, many Catholic bishops will continue to agree with this one. It is true, they admit that there is such a thing as an erroneous conscience which is to be followed provided it is "invincible." "All respect is due to the innocently erroneous conscience," says the Bishop of Linz, "it will have its reward from God."

Of whom is he speaking? Of the Catholic young men, the priests and the seminarians who died in Hitler's armies "in the firm conviction that they were fulfilling the will of God"? No. These, he says, were men (and the word is underlined) acting in the light of "a clear and correct conscience." Jägerstätter was "in error" but also "in good faith."

Certainly the bishop is entitled to his opinion: but the question of whose conscience was erroneous and whose was correct remains one that will ultimately be settled by God, not man. Meanwhile there is another question: the responsibility of those who help men to form their conscience—or fail to do so. And here, too, the possibility of firm convictions that are "innocently erroneous" gives food for some rather apocalyptic thought.

The real question raised by the Jägerstätter story is not merely that of the individual Catholic's right to conscientious objection (admitted in practice even by those who completely disagreed with Jägerstätter) but the question of the Church's own mission of protest and prophecy in the gravest spiritual crisis man has ever known.

75

Pacifism and Resistance in Simone Weil

LIKE BERNANOS AND CAMUS, SIMONE WEIL IS ONE OF THOSE brilliant and independent French thinkers who were able to articulate the deepest concerns of Europe in the first half of this century. More controversial, perhaps more of a genius than the others, certainly harder to situate, she has been called all kinds of names, both good and bad and often contradictory: gnostic and Catholic, Jew and Albigensian, medievalist and modernist, platonist and anarchist, rebel and saint, rationalist and mystic. De Gaulle said he thought she was out of her mind. The doctor in the sanatorium at Ashford, Kent, where she died on August 24, 1943, said, "she had a curious religious outlook and (probably) no religion at all."

Whatever is said about her, she will perhaps always be treated as "an enigma," which is simply to say that she is somewhat more difficult to categorize than most people, since in her passion for integrity she absolutely refused to take up any position she had not first thought out in the light of what she believed to be a personal vocation to "absolute intellectual honesty." When she began to examine any accepted position, she easily detected its weaknesses and inconsistencies.

None of the books of Simone Weil (seventeen in French, eight in English) were written as books. They are all collections of notes, essays, articles, journals and letters. Though she has conquered a certain number of fans by the force of her personality, most readers remember her as the author of some fragment or other that they have found in some way both impressive and disconcerting. One cannot help admiring her lucid genius, and yet one can very easily disagree with her most fundamental and characteristic ideas. But this is usually because one does not see her thought as a whole.

The new biography by Jacques Cabaud* not only tells of her active and tormented life, but studies in detail a large number of writings (of which a complete bibliography is given), together with the testimony of those who knew her. Cabaud has fortunately avoided treating Simone Weil either as a problem or as a saint. He accepts her as she evidently was. Such a book is obviously indispensable, for without a comprehensive and detached study it would be impossible for us to see her in perspective. In fact, no one who reads this book carefully and dispassionately can treat Simone Weil merely as an enigma or a phenomenon, still less as deluded or irrelevant: few writers have more significant thought than she on the history of our time and a better understanding of our calamities.

On the other hand, probably not even Mr. Cabaud would claim that this book says the last word on Simone Weil or that it fully explains, for instance, the "Christian mysticism" that prompted her to remain deliberately outside the Church and refuse baptism even on the point of death because she felt that her natural element was with "the immense and unfortunate multitude of unbelievers." This "unbeliever," we note, was one who had been "seized" by Christ in a mystical experience the marks of which are to all appearances quite authentic, though the Catholic theologian has trouble keeping them clearly in a familiar and traditional focus. (Obviously, one of her charisms was that of living

* *Simone Weil, a Fellowship in Love* (New York: Channel Press, 1964).

and dying as a sign of contradiction for Catholics, and one feels that the climate of Catholic thought in France at the time of Vatican II has been to some extent affected by at least a vague awareness of her experiences at Solesmes and Marseilles.)

Though her spirit was at times explicitly intended to be that of the mediaeval Cathars and though her description of her mystical life is strongly Gnostic and intellectual, she has had things to say of her experience of sufferings of Christ which are not only deeply Christian but also speak directly to the anguish and perplexity of modern man. This intuition of the nature and meaning of suffering provides, in Simone Weil, the core of a metaphysic, not to say a theology, of non-violence. And a metaphysic of non-violence is something that the peace movement needs.

Looking back at Simone Weil's participation in the peace movement of the thirties, Cabaud speaks rather sweepingly of a collapse of pacifism in her thought and political action. It is quite true that the pacifism of the thirties was as naive as it was popular, and that for many people at that time pacifism amounted to nothing more than the disposition to ignore unpleasant realities and to compromise with the threat of force, as did Chamberlain at Munich. It is also true that Simone Weil herself underestimated the ruthlessness of Hitler at the time of the Munich crisis, though her principles did not allow her to agree with the Munich pact.

Cabaud quotes a statement of Simone Weil accusing herself of a "criminal error committed before 1939 with regard to pacifist groups and their actions." She had come to regard her earlier tolerance of a passive and inert pacifism as a kind of cooperation with "their disposition towards treason"—a treason she said she had not seen because she had been disabled by illness.

This reflects her disgust with Vichy and with former pacifists who now submitted to Hitler without protest. But we cannot interpret this statement to mean that after Munich and then after the fall of France, Simone Weil abandoned all her former principles in order to take up an essentially new position in regard to war and peace. This would mean equating her "pacifism" with the quietism of the uncomprehending and inactive. It would also mean failure to understand that she became deeply committed to non-violent resistance. Before Munich her emphasis was, however, on non-violence; after the fall of France it was on resistance, including resistance by force where non-violence was ineffective.

It is unfortunate that Cabaud's book does not sufficiently avoid the cliched identification of pacifism with quietist passivity and non-resistance. Simone Weil's love of peace was never sentimental and never quietistic; and though her judgment sometimes erred in assessing concrete situations, it was seldom unrealistic. An important article she wrote in 1937 remains one of the classic treatments of the problem of war and peace in our time. Its original title was "Let us not start the Trojan War all over again." It appears in her *Selected Essays* as "The Power of Words." Cabaud analyzes it in his book (pp. 155–160), concluding that it marks a dividing line in her life. It belongs in fact to the same crucial period as her first mystical experiences.

But there is nothing mystical about this essay. It develops a theme familiar to Montaigne and Charron: the most terrible thing about war is that, if it is examined closely, it is discovered to have no rationally definable objective. The supposed objectives of war are actually myths and fictions which are all the more capable of enlisting the full force of devotion to duty and hatred of the enemy when they are completely empty of content. Let us briefly resume this article, since it contains the substance of Simone Weil's ideas on

79

peace and is (apart from some of her topical examples) just as relevant to our own time as it was to the late thirties.

The article begins with a statement which is passed over by Cabaud but which is important for us. Simone Weil remarks that while our technology has given us weapons of immense destructive power, the weapons do not go off by themselves (we hope). Hence, it is a primordial mistake to think and act as if the weapons were what constituted our danger, rather than the people who are disposed to fire them. But more precisely still: the danger lies not so much in this or that group or class, but in the climate of thought in which all participate (not excluding pacifists). This is what Simone Weil set herself to understand. The theme of the article is, then, that war must be regarded as a problem to be solved by rational analysis and action, not as a fatality to which we must submit with bravery or desperation. We see immediately that she is anything but passively resigned to the evil of war. She says clearly that the acceptance of war as an unavoidable fatality is the root of the power politician's ruthless and obsessive commitment to violence.

This, she believed, was the "key to our history."

If, in fact, conflicting statesmen face one another only with clearly defined objectives that were fully rational, there would be a certain measure and limit which would permit of discussion and negotiation. But where the objectives are actually nothing more than capital letter slogans without intelligible content, there is no common measure, therefore no possibility of communication, therefore, again, no possibility of avoiding war except by ambiguous compromises or by agreements that are not intended to be kept. Such agreements do not really avoid war. And of course they solve no problems.

The typology of the Trojan war, "known to every educated man," illustrates this. The only one, Greek or Trojan,

80

who had any interest in Helen was Paris. No one, Greek or Trojan, was fighting for Helen, but for the "real issue" which Helen symbolized. Unfortunately, there was no real issue at all for her to symbolize. Both armies, in this war, which is the type of all wars, were fighting in a moral void, motivated by symbols without content, which in the case of the Homeric, heroes took the form of gods and myths. Simone Weil considered that this was relatively fortunate for them, since their myths were thus kept within a well-defined area. For us, on the other hand (since we imagine that we have no myths at all), myth actually is without limitation and can easily penetrate the whole realm of political, social and ethical thought.

Instead of going to war because the gods have been arguing among themselves, we go because of "secret plots" and sinister combinations, because of political slogans elevated to the dignity of metaphysical absolutes: "our political universe is peopled with myths and monsters—we know nothing there but absolutes." We shed blood for high sounding words spelled out in capital letters. We seek to impart content to them by destroying other men who believe in enemy-words, also in capital letters.

But how can men really be brought to kill each other for what is objectively void? The nothingness of national, class or racial myth must receive an apparent substance, not from intelligible content but from the will to destroy and be destroyed. (We may observe here that the substance of idolatry is the willingness to give reality to metaphysical nothingness by sacrificing to it. The more totally one destroys present realities and alienates oneself to an object which is really void, the more total is the idolatry, i.e., the commitment to the falsehood that the non-entity is an objective absolute. Note here that in this context the God of the mystics is not "an object" and cannot be described properly

81

as "an entity" among other entities. Hence, one of the marks of authentic mysticism is that God as experienced by the mystic can in no way be the object of an idolatrous cult.)

The will to kill and be killed grows out of sacrifices and acts of destruction already performed. As soon as the war has begun, the first dead are there to demand further sacrifice from their companions since they have demonstrated by their example that the objective of the war is such that no price is too high to pay for its attainment. This is the "sledge hammer argument," the argument of Minerva in Homer: "You must fight on, for if you now make peace with the enemy, you will offend the dead."

These are cogent intuitions, but so far they do not add anything, beyond their own vivacity, to the ideas that prevailed in the thirties. In effect, everyone who remembered the First World War was capable of meditating on the futility of war in 1938. Everyone was still able to take sarcastic advantage of slogans about "making the world safe for democracy." But merely to say that war, in its very nature, was totally absurd and totally meaningless was to run the risk of missing the real point. Mere words without content do not suffice, of themselves, to start a war. Behind the empty symbols and the objectiveless motivation of force, there is a real force, the grimmest of all the social realities of our time: collective power, which Simone Weil, in her more Catharist mood, regarded as the "great beast." "How will the soul be saved," she asked her philosophy students in the Lycee, "after the great beast has acquired an opinion about everything?"

The void underlying the symbols and the myths of nationalism, of capitalism, communism, fascism, racism, totalism is in fact filled entirely by the presence of the beast—the urge to collective power. We might say, developing her image, that the void thus becomes an insatiable demand for power: it sucks all life and all being into itself. Power is then generated by the plunge of real and human values into nothingness, allowing themselves to be destroyed in order that the collectivity may attain to a theoretical and hopeless ideal of perfect and unassailable supremacy: "What is called national security is a chimerical state of things in which one would keep for oneself alone the power to make war while all other countries would be unable to do so. . . . War is therefore made in order to keep or to increase the means of making war. All international politics revolve in this vicious circle." But she adds, "why must one be able to make war? This no one knows any more than the Trojans knew why they had to keep Helen."

Nevertheless, when Germany overran France she herself found a reason for joining the resistance: the affirmation of human liberty against the abuse of power. "All over the world there are human beings serving as means to the power of others without having consented to it." This was a basic evil that had to be resisted. The revision of Simone Weil's opinion on pacifism and non-violence after Munich does not therefore resolve itself, as Cabaud seems to indicate, with a practical repudiation of both. Munich led her to clarify the distinction between ineffective and effective non-violence. The former is what Gandhi called the non-violence of the weak, and it merely submits to evil without resistance. Effective non-violence ("the non-violence of the strong") is that which opposes evil with serious and positive resistance, in order to overcome it with good.

Simone Weil would apparently have added that if this non-violence had no hope of success, then evil could be resisted by force. But she hoped for a state of affairs in which human conflict could be resolved non-violently rather than by force. However, her notion of non-violent resistance was never fully developed. If she had survived (she would be fifty-six now) she might possibly have written some exciting things on the subject.

Once this is understood, we can also understand Simone Weil's revulsion at the collapse of that superficial and popular pacifism of Munich, which, since it was passive and also without clear objective, was only another moment in the objectiveless dialectic of brute power. And we can also understand the passion with which she sought to join the French resistance. But she did not change her principles. She did not commit herself to violent action, but she did seek to expose herself to the greatest danger and sacrifice, non-violently. Though her desire to form a "front line nursing corps" (regarded by de Gaulle as lunacy) was never fulfilled, she nevertheless worked—indeed overworked—until the time of her death, trying to clarify the principles on which a new France could be built. She never gave up the hope that one might "substitute more and more in the world effective non-violence for violence."

Part Two

Vietnam-An Overwhelming Atrocity

"No country may unjustly oppress others or unduly meddle in their affairs."

(*Pacem in Terris*, n. 120)

"As men in their private enterprises cannot pursue their own interests to the detriment of others, so too states cannot lawfully seek that development of their own resources which brings harm to other states and unjustly oppresses them."

(*Pacem in Terris*, n. 92)

IN 1967 SEVERAL YOUNG MEMBERS OF THE INTERNATIONAL Volunteer Service in Vietnam resigned and returned to America, in protest against the way the war was, in their opinion, needlessly and hopelessly ravaging the country.

The International Volunteer Service is a non-profit organization meant to help American Youth to contribute to international goodwill by person-to-person contacts and service programs in other countries. Ambassador Lodge had called it "one of the success stories of American assistance," and obviously the men serving in Vietnam were in very close touch with the people, knew the language, and were perhaps better able to judge the state of affairs than most other Americans. As they said, they "dealt with people, not statistics," and they were in a position to know that the story of the Vietnam war is a very different one when it is learned from women and children whose flesh has been

87

burned by napalm than it is when those same women and children appear in statistics as "enemy" casualties.*

At this point, in case the reader is not fully aware of what napalm is, we might quote from a report of four American physicians on "Medical Problems of South Vietnam":

> "Napalm is a highly sticky inflammable jelly which clings to anything it touches and burns with such heat that all oxygen in the area is exhausted within moments. Death is either by roasting or suffocation. Napalm wounds are often fatal (estimates are 90%). Those who survive face a living death. The victims are frequently children."

---

* Though this very unpleasant truth is admitted rather grudgingly, it is inescapable, and the American press has recognized that there have been many casualties among Vietnamese non-combatants, including large numbers of children. *Time* takes note of the Committee of Responsibility which was organized in 1966 to do something about these children "less a medical project than an exorcism of guilt" (in *Time*'s words). It is of course a medical project. The COR, with the aid of voluntary and governmental agencies in Vietnam and the U.S., and with funds raised by Americans who are aware of the tragic problem, have flown badly burned children from Vietnam to the U.S. for hospital care and plastic surgery. The plight of civilian war victims in Vietnam is outlined in a pamphlet which shows some gruesome pictures of children disfigured by this burning jelly, and reminds us that in South Vietnam: "Hospitals are overcrowded to the extent that beds often sleep two or three. Supplies and equipment are usually absent; sanitation and ventilation are primitive and frequently nonexistent. There is approximately one doctor and nine nurses to care for every 100,000 people. . . ." This pamphlet may be obtained from the COR, 60 Madison Ave., Suite 1209, New York, New York 10010. Needless to say, only a very small number of victims can be flown to America. But this and other organizations which have tried to meet a fantastically desperate human need naturally have serious claims on the American conscience. To help them is not a moral luxury but a plain duty.

Another American physician (Dr. R. E. Perry, *Redbook*, January, 1967) wrote:

> "I have been an orthopedic surgeon for a good number of years with rather a wide range of medical experience. But nothing could have prepared me for my encounters with Vietnamese women and children burned by napalm. It was shocking and sickening even for a physician to see and smell the blackened and burned flesh."

By their resignation and by the statement they issued in an open letter to President Johnson, these men attempted to get through to the American public with a true idea of what the war really means to the Vietnamese—our allies, the ones we are supposedly "saving" from Communism. The attitude and feelings of the Vietnamese *people* (as distinct from the government) are too little known in the United States. They have been systematically ignored.

Pictures of GI's bestowing candy bars upon half-naked "native" children are supposed to give us all the information we need in this regard. These are happy people who love our boys because we are saving them from the Reds and teaching them "democracy." It is of course important, psychologically and politically, for the public to believe this because otherwise the war itself would be questioned, and as a matter of fact it *is* questioned. Never was there a war in American history that was so much questioned! The official claim that such questioning is "betrayal" is a transparently gross and authoritarian attack on democratic liberty.

According to these Americans in the International Volunteer Service, men who cannot be considered leftists, still less as traitors, the American policy of victory at any price is simply destroying Vietnam. It is quite possible that the United States may eventually "win," but the price may be so high that there will be few left around to enjoy the fruits of victory and democracy in a country which we will, of course, obligingly reconstruct according to ideas of our own.

The people of South Vietnam have already had some experience of this kind of resettlement and reconstruction. Having seen their own homes burned or bulldozed out of existence, their fields and crops blasted with defoliants and herbicides, their livelihood and culture destroyed, they have been forcibly transplanted into places where they cannot live as they would like or as they know how, and forced into a society where, to adapt and be "at home" one has to be a hustler, a prostitute, or some kind of operator who knows how to get where the dollars are.

The people we are "liberating" in Vietnam are caught between two different kinds of terrorism and the future presents them with nothing but a more and more bleak and hopeless prospect of unnatural and alienated existence. From their point of view, it doesn't matter much who wins. Either way it is going to be awful: but at least if the war can stop before everything is destroyed, and if they can somehow manage their own destiny, they will settle for that.

This, however, does not fit in with our ideas. We intend to go on bombing, burning, killing, bulldozing and moving people around while the numbers of plague victims begin to mount sharply and while the "civilization" we have brought becomes more and more rotten. The people of South Vietnam believe that we are supporting a government of wealthy parasites they do not and cannot trust. They believe that the 1967 election was rigged, and they know that the two newspapers which protested about it were immediately silenced and closed down by the "democratic" government which we are supporting at such cost.

To put it plainly, according to the men who resigned from the International Volunteer Service the people of South Vietnam are hardly grateful for "democracy" on such terms, and while they are quite willing to accept our dollars when they have a chance, they do not respect us or trust us. In point of fact, they have begun to hate us.

Far from weakening communism in Asia by our war policy, we are only strengthening it. The Vietnamese are no lovers of China, but by the ruthlessness of our war for "total victory" we are driving them into the arms of the Red Chinese. "The war as it is now being waged" say the Volunteers, "is self-defeating." They support their contentions by quoting people they have known in Vietnam.

A youth leader: "When the Americans learn to respect the true aspirations in Vietnam, true nationalism will come to power. Only true nationalists can bring peace to the South, talk to the North and bring reunification."

While a Catholic Bishop in the United States was soothing President Johnson with the assurance the war in Vietnam is "a sad and heavy obligation imposed by the mandate of love," a Buddhist nun said in Vietnam: "You Americans come to help the Vietnamese people, but have brought only death and destruction. Most of us Vietnamese hate from the bottom of our hearts the Americans who have brought the suffering of this war. . . ." After which she burned herself to death. That, too, was a drastic act of violence. Whether or not we may agree with it, we must admit that it lends a certain air of seriousness to her denunciation! Unfortunately, such seriousness does not seem to get through to those Americans who most need to hear and understand it.

Meanwhile Billy Graham declared that the war in Vietnam was a "spiritual war between good and evil." A plausible statement, certainly, but not in the way in which he meant it. At the same time a Saigon Catholic Youth Leader gave another view of the picture: "We are caught in a struggle between two power blocs. . . . Many people told me you cannot trust Americans, but I never accepted it.

91

Now I am beginning to believe it. You come to help my people, but they will hate you for it."

The tragic thing about Vietnam is that, after all, the "realism" of our program there is so unrealistic, so rooted in myth, so completely out of touch with the needs of the people whom we know only as statistics and to whom we never manage to listen, except where they fit in with our own psychopathic delusions. Our external violence in Vietnam is rooted in an inner violence which simply ignores the human reality of those we claim to be helping. The result of this at home has been an ever mounting desperation on the part of those who see the uselessness and inhumanity of the war, together with an increasing stubbornness and truculence on the part of those who insist they want to win, regardless of what victory may mean.

What will the situation be when this book appears in print? Will the 1968 Presidential election force the issue one way or another? Will the candidates *have to* make sense out of this in spite of everything? We are getting to the point where American "victory" in Vietnam is becoming a word without any possible human meaning. What matters is the ability and willingness to arrive at some kind of workable solution that will save the identity of the nation that still wants to survive in spite of us, in spite of communism, in spite of the international balance of power. This cannot be arrived at unless the United States is willing to de-escalate, stop bombing the North, stop destroying crops, and recognize the NLF as among those with whom we have to deal if we want to make peace. Obviously a perfect solution is impossible but some solution can be realized and lives can be saved.

It is still possible to learn something from Vietnam: and above all we should recognize that the United States has received from no one the mission to police every country in the world or to decide for them how they are to live. No single nation has the right to try to run the world according to its own ideas. One thing is certain, the Vietnam war is a tragic error and, in the words of the resigned volunteers, "an overwhelming atrocity."

How do we explain such atrocities? Obviously, they are well-meant and the Americans who support the war are, for the most part, convinced that it is an inescapable moral necessity. Why? For one thing, as the more sophisticated reader is well aware, the picture of the war given by the mass media and the official version of what is happening are both extremely one-sided and oversimplified, to say the least. Some claim that the public has been deliberately misinformed. In any case, Americans do not seem to realize what effect the war is really having. The hatred of America which it is causing everywhere (analogous to the hatred of Russia after the violent suppression of the Hungarian revolt in 1956) is not just the result of Red propaganda. On the contrary, the Communists could never do such a fine job of blackening us as we are doing all by ourselves.

There is another, deeper source of delusion in the popular mythology of our time. One example of this popular mythology is examined in the first chapter of this section. It is the myth that all biological species in their struggle for survival must follow a law of aggression in which the stronger earns the right to exist by violently exterminating all his competitors. This pseudo-scientific myth is simply another version of the cliche that "might makes right" and of course it was explicitly used and developed by the ideologists of Nazism. This canonization of violence by pseudo-science has come to be so much taken for granted, that when Konrad Lorenz, in his carefully thought out study *On Aggression* sought to qualify it in very important ways, his book has simply been lumped with others, like Mr. Ardrey's,

93

as one more rationalization of the aggression theory. Thus in the *New York Times Book Review* (Christmas issue, 1967) the paperback edition of *On Aggression* is summarized with approval in this one line: "Like all other animals man is instinctively aggressive." True, of course, up to a point. But this contains the same implicit false conclusion ("therefore he *has to* beat up and destroy members of his own kind") and explicitly ignores the real point of Lorenz's book. The point is that man is the *only* species, besides the rat, who wantonly and cruelly turns on his own kind in *unprovoked* and murderous hostility. Man is the only one who deliberately seeks to *destroy* his own kind (as opposed to merely resisting encroachment).

To quote a prominent Dutch psychoanalyst who, among other things, has studied the mentality of Nazi war criminals:

> What we usually called hatred or hostility is different from normal self-assertive aggression. The former are hyper-charged fantasy products, mixed with reactions to frustrations. They form an aura of intense anticipation of revenge and greater discharge in the future. . . . This finds its most paradoxical action in the hatred of those who want to break out into history. They destroy because they want to be remembered. NO OTHER ANIMAL AVAILS HIMSELF OF PLANS FOR MOBILIZATION AND FUTURE ATTACK. However, man gets caught in his own trap, and what he once dreamed up in a fatal hour often takes possession of him so that he is finally compelled to act it out.*

Now this develops the point made by Lorenz in *On Aggression*. Lorenz *distinguishes* the destructive hostility of men and of rats from the natural self-assertive aggression common to all species, and indicates that far from pointing

---

* I am grateful to my friend Dr. Joost A. M. Meerloo for permission to quote from his unpublished manuscript of the English version of *Homo Militans*.

to the "survival of the fittest" this drive toward intraspecific aggression may perhaps lead to the self-destruction of the human race. That is the thesis developed in detail by Dr. Meerloo. Mr. Ardrey's book, like so much other popular mythology on the subject, serves to contribute to those "hypercharged fantasies" by which modern man at once excuses and foments his inner hostilities until he is compelled to discharge them, as we are now doing, with immense cost for innocent and harmless people on the other side of the globe.**

It is because of these obsessions and fantasies that we continue to draft our young men into the army when in fact a professional army of enlisted men would suffice, along with our fabulous nuclear arsenal, to meet any conceivable need for national defense. The Vietnam war has called the legality and justice of the draft law into question, and rightly. Our young men feel that they are simply being imposed upon and that their lives are being stupidly sacrificed, not to defend the country but to act out the manias of politicians and manufacturers who think they have a mission to police the world and run the affairs of smaller countries in the interests of American business. The draft law ought to be abolished. That would somewhat lessen the temptation to get involved in any more "overwhelming atrocities" like the one in Vietnam.

** I have examined elsewhere the psychological connection between the Indian wars of extermination in the last century, and the Vietnam war. See: "Ishi: A Meditation," in the *Catholic Worker*, March 1967.

Is Man a Gorilla with
a Gun?

"EXTRAPOLATION," SAY THE DICTIONARIES, "IS THE METHOD of finding by calculation, based on the known terms of a series, other terms, whether preceding or following." The method is proper to mathematics and works efficiently when dealing with number and quantity. When it is transferred to the realm of quality and of organic life, more still to that of history and of culture, it tends to lose its precisely exact scientific quality and becomes a venture in creativity, or even a work of fantasy. Imagination now takes the place of calculation. There can be no doubt that the scientist who seeks to learn the origin of man from a fossilized remnant of a skull that might have belonged to man or to a baboon must be blessed with a creative imagination as well as with a scientifically exact intelligence. I suppose that when Robert Ardrey, a playwright rather than a professional scientist, subtitles his book* "A personal investigation into the animal origins and nature of man" he is serving notice that he intends to extrapolate with unrestrained imaginative abandon. At any rate, this is what he does!

There is of course a good basis of scientific evidence in *African Genesis.* The most recent discoveries of palaeontology made in Africa, especially the most notable, those of Dr. L. S. B. Leakey at Olduvai in Tanganyika, give very convincing indications that the origin of man was in Africa not in Asia. The Olduvai gorge is a deep canyon, fantastically rich in fossils and in primitive tools, which has pre-

* *African Genesis* (New York: Athenium, 1961).

96

served a seemingly completely and continuous record of the million year period in which man appeared. And here it must be clearly said that the conclusions of this very tendentious book differ radically from those of Dr. Leakey, who is certainly the most credible authority on the subject. Dr. Leakey says that the tools at Olduvai were the work of man in his earliest known form (*Zinjanthropus*). Mr. Ardrey's thesis is that the tools are the work not of man but of an ape. Indeed of an inferior ape, a vegetarian and pacifist ape, who was not even to be the "ancestor of man." The real ancestor of man in Ardrey's thesis was an ape who made not tools but weapons—and was a killer.

So while admitting that L. S. B. Leakey is a "great scientist," Mr. Ardrey says that on this point he has gone wrong, misled by sentimentality and romanticism. The term "romantic fallacy" occurs everywhere in the book, and is used to discredit any and every theory of man's origin which does not admit that he is a descendant, in the direct line, from a "killer ape." And therefore it must be said that the reader who picks up this book looking for precise and coherent information about the important new discoveries in Africa is himself the victim of an illusion. What information there is concerns mainly the discoveries and hypotheses of certain South Africans whom Mr. Ardrey greatly admires, and even this information is buried in autobiographical reminisence, picaresque anecdote and pages of philosophical improvization.

On the basis of the remote possibility that there were, in Africa, perhaps a million years ago, tool-and-weapon using hominids, or pre-human apes, Mr. Ardrey delivers a very aggressive homily in atheistic evolutionism. He attacks not only the traditional Christian world-view but also, much more radically, the world-views of Marx, Freud, Darwin and practically everyone else you can think of. One theory of man after another is tossed out the window with glorious enthusiasm as "romantic fallacy"—and all because some ape seems to have picked up the leg bone of an antelope and used it to crack the skull of one of his fellows. This is all the author needs in order to reconstruct entirely all social philosophy, all history, all anthropology, all psychology, all economics. For Mr. Ardrey, this one monumental act of violence explains everything.

Homo sapiens is therefore, he declares, the direct "legitimate" descendent of a transitional, carnivorous, erect-walking, right-handed and weapon-using anthropoid. Because this ape was no ordinary mild-mannered vegetarian, no "generalized fruit-eating ape," but a ruthless "killer ape," man emerged. Man is, according to Ardrey, the child not only of the ape but of the weapon. It was "the weapon that fathered man." Not only that, but Mr. Ardrey even goes so far as to hint that, instead of man developing weapons for himself, he was in some way developed by biology to be a user of weapons. "Whether man is in fact a biological invention to suit the purposes of the weapon must be a matter of future debate." Whatever that debate may be, to suppose that instead of weapons being developed for man, man was developed for weapons is carrying alienation pretty far! But it is quite characteristic of Mr. Ardrey's world-view and of its South African sources. The consequence follows immediately. Man is by his very nature an inventor and user of weapons and a defender of territory. The essence of human nature is therefore not so much rationality as trigger-happiness, or at least club-happiness and "territoriality." Even sex is set aside as a secondary, relatively meaningless urge compared with man's essential drive to beat up anything and anyone that threatens to invade his "territory." Yes, "territory" is very important here, crucially important. Man is not really interested in woman, in love, in the warmth of satisfied libido (as Freud may have thought). Man is not so deeply engaged in making a living that his very existence is shaped and dominated by the system of production (according to Marxist ideas). Man is an ape that goes berserk when he thinks he is running out of *Lebensraum*, and I must admit that Mr. Ardrey's description of two rival teams of howling monkeys trying to jam each others' broadcasts is very suggestive of modern political life.

The chief contention of Robert Ardrey's high-powered social message is that any philosophy, religious or otherwise, which takes an optimistic view of man, regards him as basically rational and progressive, and postulates that he can better himself by using his intelligence to improve his social system, is basically a "romantic illusion." It is absurd, says Mr. Ardrey, to hope that man can settle his differences over "territory" by means of arbitration rather than by bombs. "Man is a predator whose natural instinct is to kill with a weapon." It is fortunate that some members of the human race are still capable of thinking otherwise (for instance Pope John XXIII in his encyclical *Pacem in Terris*).

Quite apart from religious faith and Christian hope, it seems to me that Mr. Ardrey's thesis negates any real hope there may be for man in evolutionism. After all, the theory of natural selection postulates that a species is able to survive by progressive adaptation to new and more difficult conditions. We armed gorillas have now reached a rather crucial point in our evolutionary development in which "killing with a weapon" is about the least effective way of settling our problems and guaranteeing our survival. It would seem that if we cannot get beyond the stage where we seem to have been a million years ago, in other words, if we cannot adapt to a new situation and settle our problems by reason instead of with clubs, we are soon going to

be as extinct as any dinosaur. The amusing thing about all
that is that we are a species that has been given the choice
of survival or non-survival. We have very large skulls and,
presuming there is still a proportionate content inside them,
it is up to us to make use of it for something besides in-
venting ways to blow ourselves up. This is so obvious that
even Mr. Ardrey, after ignoring and skirting it for over
three hundred pages, finally has to face it in his last chapter ("Cain's Children") with conclusions that we shall
presently see.

The author of *African Genesis* is totally and slavishly
committed to a philosophy of ironbound determinism which
is dominated by one inexorable obsession: the "killer ape"
armed with the leg-bone of an antelope. Because man
"descended in a direct line" from an ape with a weapon,
then he is predetermined to be a killer, he is before all else
a killer, and it is folly to even consider him being anything
else, at least until his "lucky genes" have had a few hundred
thousand more years. Mr. Ardrey confesses himself to be
firmly convinced of "man's pristine depravity." Thus he is
commited to a world-view in which aggression, barbarism,
murder, and every form of violence are bound to prevail.

Yet the whole picture is not all of unrelieved darkness—
otherwise the book would hardly have been a best seller in
America. What about freedom? Man is predetermined to be
a killer, but fortunately (says Mr. Ardrey) his killing habits
are the basis of his freedom—freedom from vegetarianism,
freedom to leave the jungle and roam around the world living on high-calorie foods and having a wonderful time.
Man is a gorilla with a gun—and a credit card! "Freedom
was the first gift of the predatory way," and doubtless, as
man exists for the weapon, so does freedom! In any case, he
says, the progress of the weapon is mankind's "most signifi-

cant cultural endowment!" and to many American readers
this has evidently seemed quite reasonable.

However, the idea that man is capable of destroying all
life with his weapons is dismissed by Mr. Ardrey as "neo-
romantic." It presumes too much of man's capacities.
"While a giant effort on the part of man could conceivably
bring extinction to all land vertebrates, it is impossible to
believe that a world of insects would not survive." Though
a nuclear disaster is, according to him, very likely, it cannot
be more than a "partial disaster" as a result of which "over-
population will cease to be a problem in India" and instead
there will be plague and anarchy everywhere. A depleted
population of radiated mutants may end up being devoured
by rats, says our author cheerfully, but even then evolution
will doubtless come out on top. This is not explained, since
it is an article of faith.

Nevertheless, he has another "optimistic" alternative
which is a surprising variant of the new "red or dead" realism. Man has indeed reached his peak, he has developed
the absolute weapon—but now he must learn to live without
it. At this point we begin to wonder if Mr. Ardrey is suddenly going to say something useful. What he says is this:
if man has to live without war, he is heading for a decline.
Society and culture will disintegrate without armed conflict
to keep them going. Moral order "sheltered throughout all
history by the judgment of arms" will collapse. But perhaps
evolution will finally develop out of our race a new breed
that really has and uses reason! This may take another million years. However, Mr. Ardrey would not have us be
romantics, putting our trust in conscience to preserve sanity
and life, for conscience is "irrational," is in league with our
illusions, entirely subjective and "provincial." It is consequently a-moral. It operates with symbols and emotions,

101

not with ideas and principles. It is animal, not rational. In fact, he regards conscience as "an anti-rational power." It has created a "chamber of dull horrors" called civilization, and neither conscience nor civilization can save us. Our only hope is the presence of Cain, our unpredictable ancestor living in our "wild genes." Cain will take care of everything, whether it be firing the weapon or avoiding a general disaster because he prefers to fight in the back streets with a switchblade knife. It is old daddy Cain who alone knows the answers and makes the choices. "We are children of Cain and were it not so, then for humanity there would be small hope."

I am prompted to reflect that this is where you end up when you lose your grasp on the real import of the higher religions. No man can really exist completely without a religion and a philosophy. If he gets rid of good ones, he will unconsciously exchange them for bad ones. If he is impatient of "myth" in higher religion then he will end up fabricating a myth of his own, and organizing his own crude fantasies into another homemade "system" which pleases him better—with consequences that are only too well known.

Now Mr. Ardrey's exploits in myth-making are not hard to observe. They are evident on every page of his book. To take just one example: on page twenty-one, he wants to give a brief description of Lake Victoria, as the spot near which man came into existence. There are innumerable ways in which one could describe Lake Victoria. Out of a hundred possible qualifiers Mr. Ardrey, characteristically, selects the following: "A hundred miles to the east spreads sprawling and enormous the cynically smiling face of Lake Victoria, poisonous with disease, crawling with crocodiles, the probable focus of our earliest human experience." I submit that people who read books like this need a little elementary training in semantics, in the interests of their basic mental

102

and spiritual hygiene. Such a sentence (and there are hundreds like it in the book) has one function above all others: it attempts to predispose the reader a suitable feeling of disillusionment, an awareness of the general dominion of evil and violence as the basic law of all existence. Once one "feels" this, one will resist the "romantic fallacy," and will experience less compunction in reaching for a gun or firing an ICBM.

This kind of thinking is all too common in the twentieth century. Theories which substituted genes for intelligence and conscience abounded in the Europe of Mussolini, of Hitler, of Goebbels. The Second World War was the direct consequence of mental conditioning by pseudo-scientific myth. The Nazi dogma of race, blood and land developed an ideology of war and conquest out of just this kind of emotionally loaded anthropology. Everyone is aware that Hitler's racism was, in part, simply a crudely misunderstood mish-mash of popular evolutionism. Hitler's attempts to help the processes of natural selection with his gas chamber are mentioned in this book with no particular expression of romantic disapproval.

Once when the quiet and distinguished Spanish philosopher Miguel de Unamuno was lecturing at Salamanca in the early thirties, a one-armed Falangist general leaped up and expressed his impatience with all forms of humanism by shouting "Viva la Muerte!" The heroes of *African Genesis* are the killer gorilla and daddy Cain. The "God" (if we can call it that) which has watched over the gorilla's fortune and destiny is no other than Death. Mr. Ardrey is cool toward all other gods, particularly to the ones that favor non-violence and compassion. About Death he waxes lyrical. "Death is the evaluator . . . Death chooses . . . Death disposes. . . . We should all be lost in a wilderness of chance had not Death through a billion choosings erected the values

103

of the world I know." If this last sentence had a meaning (and I am not able to find much meaning in it myself) it would be that Death is a kind of free and personal Absolute and Mr. Ardrey turns out to be no atheist after all.

Nothing can better dispose us for a third world war than the conviction that we are doomed to fight anyway, that our enemies are all well-armed gorillas too, and the only smart thing to do is to let them have it before they ambush us. In the chaotic atmosphere of a nation torn by race riots, deafened by the stridency of hate groups and of fanatics, it is understandable that readers may derive a kind of perverse comfort from this mythology—made to order for the "radical right." They will do so all the more readily because there is an unquestionably important basis of scientific data mixed in with the theatrical rhetoric and sermonizing of *African Genesis*.

Romanticism has more forms than one. The sentimentally optimistic kind that served the purposes of nineteenth-century laissez faire and the liberal myth of perpetual easy progress has obviously had its day. But it has yielded to the tough and callous romanticism of the street gang or of the fascist storm troop—a romanticism no less fallacious and deceptive for the fact that it also on occasion covers itself with a veneer of "realism" and pseudo-science. This second kind of romantic fallacy is that which we find developed and indeed monstrously over-developed in *African Genesis*. It is all the more regrettable because it is rooted in an intuition—one which in our day has become completely inescapable—of the desperateness of the human situation.

This is the greatest and most urgent truth of our time: we live in the presence of the meaningless and absurdity to which we have been inexorably reduced by our own more or less dishonest attempts to convince ourselves that we were progressing toward a definite and even a noble goal.

104

The pessimism of the existentialists may indeed be dour and frustrated, but it has at least a certain stoic dignity about it. But this fraudulent attempt to organize the negativity and desperation of modern man around a stupidly melodramatic killer image, assembled from the less responsible surmises of popular anthropology, can do nothing whatever to help modern man in his quest for identity and for meaning. It is one thing to admit our violence and face it humbly and realistically: quite another to turn that "acceptance" into the shouting and posturing of racist self-congratulation. I do not know if this book is being read in Europe where—surely—people have had enough opportunities to grow tired of the formula. But it is still all too acceptable in America.

Nhat Hanh Is My Brother

THIS IS NOT A POLITICAL STATEMENT. IT HAS NO ULTERIOR motive, it seeks to provoke no immediate reaction "for" or "against" this or that side in the Vietnam war. It is on the contrary a human and personal statement and an anguished plea for Thich Nhat Hanh who is my brother. He is more my brother than many who are nearer to me by race and nationality, because he and I see things exactly the same way. He and I deplore the war that is ravaging his country. We deplore it for exactly the same reasons: human reasons, reasons of sanity, justice and love. We deplore the needless destruction, the fantastic and callous ravaging of human life, the rape of the culture and spirit of an exhausted people. It is surely evident that this carnage serves no purpose that can be discerned and indeed contradicts the very purpose of the mighty nation that has constituted itself the "defender" of the people it is destroying.

Certainly this statement cannot help being a plea for peace. But it is also a plea for my Brother Nhat Hanh. He represents the least "political" of all the movements in Vietnam. He is not directly associated with the Buddhists who are trying to use political manipulation in order to save their country. He is by no means a Communist. The Vietcong is deeply hostile to him. He refuses to be identified with the established government which hates and distrusts him. He represents the young, the defenseless, the new ranks of youth who find themselves with every hand turned against them except those of the peasants and the poor, with whom they are working. Nhat Hanh speaks truly

for the people of Vietnam, if there can be said to be a
"people" still left in Vietnam.

Nhat Hanh has left his country and has come to us in
order to present a picture which is not given us in our newspapers and magazines. He has been well received—and
that speaks well for those who have received him. His visit
to the United States has shown that we are a people who
still desire the truth when we can find it, and still decide in
favor of man against the political machine when we get
a fair chance to do so. But when Nhat Hanh goes home,
what will happen to him? He is not in favor with the government which has suppressed his writings. The Vietcong
will view with disfavor his American contacts. To have
pleaded for an end to the fighting will make him a traitor
in the eyes of those who stand to gain personally as long
as the war goes on, as long as their countrymen are being
killed, as long as they can do business with our military.
Nhat Hanh may be returning to imprisonment, torture, even
death. We cannot let him go back to Saigon to be destroyed
while we sit here, cherishing the warm humanitarian glow
of good intentions and worthy sentiments about the ongoing
war. We who have met and heard Nhat Hanh, or who have
read about him, must also raise our voices to demand that
his life and freedom be respected when he returns to his
country. Furthermore, we demand this not in terms of any
conceivable political advantage, but purely in the name of
those values of freedom and humanity in favor of which
our armed forces declare they are fighting the Vietnam war.
Nhat Hanh is a free man who has acted as a free man in
favor of his brothers and moved by the spiritual dynamic of
a tradition of religious compassion. He has come among us
as many others have, from time to time, bearing witness to
the spirit of Zen. More than any other he has shown us that
Zen is not an esoteric and world denying cult of inner illumi-

nation, but that it has its rare and unique sense of responsibility in the modern world. Wherever he goes he will walk in the strength of his spirit and in the solitude of the Zen monk who sees beyond life and earth. It is for our own honor as much as for his safety that we must raise our voices to demand that his life and personal integrity be fully respected when he returns to his smashed and gutted country, there to continue his work with the students and peasants, hoping for the day when reconstruction can begin.

I have said Nhat Hanh is my brother, and it is true. We are both monks, and we have lived the monastic life about the same number of years. We are both poets, both existentialists. I have far more in common with Nhat Hanh than I have with many Americans, and I do not hesitate to say it. It is vitally important that such bonds be admitted. They are the bonds of a new solidarity and a new brotherhood which is beginning to be evident on all the five continents and which cuts across all political, religious and cultural lines to unite young men and women in every country in something that is more concrete than an ideal and more alive than a program. This unity of the young is the only hope of the world. In its name I appeal for Nhat Hanh. Do what you can for him. If I mean something to you, then let me put it this way; do for Nhat Hanh whatever you would do for me if I were in his position. In many ways I wish I were.

Taking Sides on Vietnam

I MIGHT PREFACE THESE REMARKS BY SAYING THAT I AM NO longer a very enthusiastic side-taker. For instance in the U.S. presidential election of 1964 along with the majority of voters I took the side of Lyndon Johnson against Barry Goldwater, and my reason for doing so was that I did not want Goldwater's belligerent policy in Vietnam. However, though Johnson won the election, Goldwater's policy in Vietnam was what we got. The taking of sides, politically, may not always be a useful or significant exercise. But it may nevertheless remain morally necessary.

In my opinion the exorbitant U.S. war effort in Vietnam can not be explained or justified by the reasons that are officially given ("to prevent South Vietnam from being overrun by Communism from the North"). The game of escalation continues to be more and more aggressive. Why is the U.S. anxious to maintain such huge military bases in South East Asia? Are these necessary for the "defense" of South Vietnam?

No matter what side we may have taken in 1937, World War II was prepared in Spain by the great Belligerents. It was their training field and the proving ground for their new weapons. Who suffered most cruelly? The innocent, the defenseless, the unarmed. Who gained by it? Not Spain. The same can be said of Vietnam today.

Therefore when I take a side in this question, it is not the side of the United States and it is not the side of Communism. Peking, Washington, Saigon and Hanoi want the war to go on. I am on the side of the people who are being burned, cut to pieces, tortured, held as hostages, gassed, ruined, destroyed. They are the victims of both sides. To take sides with massive power is to take sides against the innocent. The side I take is then the side of the people who are sick of war and want peace in order to rebuild their country.

Once this has been said, it must be admitted that the American policy of escalation is what makes peace and order impossible in Vietnam. As long as bombings continue in North Vietnam, as long as rumors of an invasion of North Vietnam continue to grow, it is useless to expect an end to the horrors and inhumanities of the war. Resistance and counter-escalation are the obvious result. U.S. aggression must stop. The problems of South Vietnam must be settled by arbitration, and by the free unhampered action of the people of Vietnam themselves, not by force or by military might. The initiative can only come from the U.S. and must begin with de-escalation and a cessation of bombings in North Vietnam.

Can President Johnson understand this? Perhaps not. But in that case the responsibility for World War Three may be found resting on his shoulders and on those of the U.S. military-industrial complex which is the chief beneficiary of this callous and inhuman conflict.

I, therefore, join with those who deplore it.

A Note on the Psychological Causes of War by Eric Fromm

THE CHRISTIAN CONCEPT OF MAN, A CONCEPT WHICH IS HELD in common by all the religions which can be called "higher" or "mystical," is one which sees man as a spiritual, or self-transcending being. That is to say that man, unlike other animals, does not find his fulfillment or self-realization merely on the level of his own nature. Even the most satisfactory exercise of those biological functions which preserve and propagate the life of the species is not enough to fulfill man's inner capacities, even when this exercise is also psychologically mature and rewarding. As long as man acts *only* as a member of the human species, within his limits as an individual subservient to the inescapable finalities of his common "nature," he is still subject to the deepest and most radical form of spiritual alienation. He is not fully "free" because he is not able to transcend his specific individuality and function on the level of a spiritual *person* with all the perfection and autonomy implied by that concept.

In other words, it seems to me that we must remember the need to explore the full spiritual depths of such concepts as "life" and "love of life," "freedom" and so on. This will necessarily imply at the same time a deepening and in some way an apparent complicating of the notion of man's alienation. I fully accept Fromm's analysis of alienation as it is hinted at here and developed more fully in his other books. But I think the concept needs a great deal of further exploration, beyond the limits of sociology and psychology, even of depth psychology.

I think it has too often been forgotten that there are two

111

aspects of that vast, mysterious area of our being which we call the unconscious. There is the psychosomatic area which is so to speak rooted in man's biological substratum, but there is an infinitely more spiritual and metaphysical substratum in man's being, which the Rhenish mystics called the "ground" or "base" of the soul, and which the Zen Masters continually point to, but which they refuse to describe except by incomprehensible and paradoxical terms like "your original face before you were born." So, to put my point briefly, I would like to suggest the overwhelming and almost totally neglected importance of exploring this spiritual unconscious of man. There is no real love of life unless it is oriented to the discovery of one's true, spiritual self, beyond and above the level of mere empirical individuality, with its superficial enjoyments and fears.

In fact I would like to suggest what would seem to me to be perhaps the most fruitful avenue of approach, at least for one in my own field: namely, the clear recognition of the ambiguities and ambivalences generated by false personalism. I refer to the fateful error of reducing the "person" or "spirit" to the individual and empirical ego, the "self-as-object," the self which we observe as it goes about its biological business, the machine which we regulate and tune up and feed with all kinds of stimulants and sedatives, constantly trying to make it run more and more smoothly, to fit the patterns prescribed by the salesman of pleasure-giving and anxiety-allaying commodities.

A mediaeval writer of great finesse, Guigo the Carthusian, points out the state of idolatry and alienation of a man who is in all things "subject to what he himself destroys"— that is to the pleasures and gratifications which the transient and exterior self takes in evanescent things. One might say that this leads us to the crux of the problem: the hope of finding life and joy in the mere *processes* of natural existence

112

leads to the contradiction which tries to *construct* and *create* in acts which have at least an implicitly destructive character. The self-affirmation that springs from "using up" something or someone else in the favor of one's own pitiable transiency, leads to the outright destruction of others in open despair at our own evanescence.

So Guigo says: "He who loves nothing destructible has no place in himself where he can be wounded by the man of power and he becomes inviolable, since he loves inviolable values as they ought to be loved." One might add that such a one has no need and no incentive to defend himself violently or to destroy. He does not despise or hate evanescent things. He simply hears them as "syllables which God utters at their proper time" and passes on.

When our empirical ego is taken, without further qualification, as the true "person," the true "self," as the being who is the genuine subject of life, freedom, joy and fulfillment, or indeed of religious salvation, then we arrive at the most tragic frustrations and errors, because this implies a radical alienation of our true being. While recognizing the great importance of depth psychology (we cannot get along without it today!) I would like to say—and I am sure all analysts worthy of their salt will agree—that considerable mystification is involved in the complacent and beatific sort of counseling that aims only to remove "guilt feelings" and adjust the empirical self to a society of which Fromm has, here and elsewhere, questioned the basic sanity. We *ought* to feel guilty and we *ought* to experience anguish in the fabulous irresponsibilities and panics we are generating every week of the Cold War. The trouble is rather our moral obtuseness and our spiritual insensibility to fundamental human values.

It would seem that we ought to pay a great deal more attention than we do to the traditional spiritual and con-

113

templative wisdoms which prescribe disciplines (in the deepest sense of "discipleships") to help man transcend his empirical self and find his "true self" in an emptiness that is completely "awake" because completely free of useless reflection. This is a realm of paradox and risk, because there are false and unsatisfactory spiritualities which do not go far enough, which indulge in Platonic oversimplifications, which objectify that which can only be grasped as subject, and even then is lost as soon as it is "grasped." Some spiritualities generate divisive contempts which flower in destructiveness. In other words there is great danger in facile and thoughtless verbalizations of spiritual reality. All true spiritual disciplines recognize the peril of idolatry in the irresponsible fabrication of pseudo-spiritual concepts which serve only to delude man and to subject him once again to a deeper captivity just when he seems on the point of tasting the true bliss and the perfect poverty of liberation. The supreme risk in this quest for liberation resides in the paradox of transcendence itself. For the Transcendent is also at the same time Immanent, and the mystery is that while man's spiritual liberation consists in a self-renunciation and self-recovery "beyond self," it is also at the same time a fantastic awakening to the truth and transcendent value of one's *ordinary self*.

I know that this apparent contradiction is thoroughly outrageous and I have perhaps no real excuse for introducing it in so short a piece of writing, except that even the longest and most complex explanation would not serve to clear it up. All I can say is that for those who are interested, there are documents of all kinds which say that the highest and most "biophilic" expression of man's extraordinary capacities is precisely in this *ecstasis* in which the person is at once totally empty (of separateness and material individuation) and totally full, realizing himself in unity not only with all being(s) but with the very source and finality of Being. It is the paradox of D. T. Suzuki's formula that zero equals infinity, or the *todo y nada* of St. John of the Cross.

Hence I want to say that the highest form of life is this "spiritual life" in which the infinitely "fontal" (source-like) creativity of our being in Being is somehow attained, and becomes in its turn a source of action and creativity in the world around us. The common jargon of religions tends to speak of this sometimes as "contemplation," sometimes as "liberation," sometimes as "salvation," sometimes as "divination." The words are not indifferent, because they do have definite implications, some of which can easily be unfortunate.

Now I think the point is this: where Fromm speaks of *abundance* as against *scarcity*, saying abundance is a possible support for a biophilic orientation, I think there are unresolved ambiguities left lying around, and they have explosive possibilities. I agree by all means that it is necessary to make wise use of all the techniques which man now has at his disposal to eliminate want, misery and injustice from the face of the earth. But our conquest of matter is illusory if it is at the same time only a more radical and more total subjection of ourselves to matter. When we had to strugle *against* a hostile nature, the challenge enabled us to preserve intact a life-giving and central integrity. Now that matter has yielded to us, we have also yielded ourselves to it so that we no longer expect life and joy from our own spiritual "center" but from things which are outside us and alien to us. I think we have to recognize the hollowness (and Fromm himself certainly does) of the kind of material and depersonalized abundance which we presently enjoy in the United States. Not only does this tend to stifle and corrupt the real spiritual depths of man's being, not only does it imprison him in every possible kind of spiritual delusion, but I think the very frustrations and self contradictions of materialistic affluence, coupled with frantic and useless activism, do much to explain the death-wish of our warfare economy and culture.

We live in a society that tries to keep us dazzled with euphoria in a bright cloud of lively and joy-loving slogans. Yet nothing is more empty and more dead, nothing is more insultingly insincere and destructive than the vapid grins on the billboards and the moron beatitude in the magazines which assure us that we are all in bliss right now. I know of course that we are fools, but I do not think any of us are fools enough to believe that we are now in heaven, even though the Russians are breaking their necks in order to become as rich as we are. I think the constant realization that we are exhausting our vital spiritual energy in a waste of shame, the inescapable disgust at the idolatrous vulgarity of our commercial milieu (or the various other apocalyptic whoredoms that abound elsewhere on the face of the earth), is one of the main sources of our universal desperation. Other writers have analyzed this with great finesse, and indeed since the phenomenon is more subtle and more sophisticated in Europe than in America, I can only refer to to those who have done such a good job on it over there. Gabriel Marcel is, I think, a case in point. Better still, perhaps, the less well-known and more explosive Leon Bloy, who saw the whole thing with a devastatingly prophetic clarity some fifty years ago.

I might doubtless be expected to conclude with gestures of congratulation in the direction of popular religion. I am afraid this is impossible. Popular religion has to a great extent betrayed man's inner spirit and turned him over, like Samson, with his hair cut off and his eyes dug out, to turn the mill of a self-frustrating and self-destroying culture. The cliches of popular religion have in many cases become every bit as hollow and as false as those of soap salesmen, and far more dangerously deceptive because one cannot so easily verify the claims made about the product. The sin of religiosity is that it has turned God, peace, happiness, salvation and all that man desires into products to be marketed in a speciously attractive package deal. In this, I think, the fault lies not with the sincerity of preachers and religious writers, but with the worn-out presuppositions with which they are content to operate. The religious mind today is seldom pertinently or prophetically critical. Oh, it is critical all right; but too often of wrong or irrelevant issues. There is still such a thing as straining at gnats and swallowing camels. But I wonder if we have not settled down too comfortably to accept passively the prevarications that the Gospels or the Prophets would have us reject with all the strength of our being. I am afraid the common combination of organizational jollity, moral legalism and nuclear crusading will not pass muster as a serious religion. It certainly has little to do with "spiritual life." Needless to say, this is more generally understood by churchmen than those who resent religious institutions are perhaps likely to realize. There is no question that Pope John XXIII, in his efforts to foster a general spiritual renewal of the Catholic Church by the Second Vatican Council, was aware of where the trouble lay. But even then, I think that the more profoundly and properly *spiritual* issues still lie too deep for common observation and interest, and are certainly far too mysterious to be captured in the concise and technical terminology of an ecumenical council.

Still I would like to conclude on a note of hope. It is precisely because I believe, with Abraham Heschel and a cloud of witnesses before him, that "man is not alone," that I find hope even in this most desperate situation. Man does not have to transcend himself in the sense of pulling himself

117

up by his own bootstraps. He has, rather, to respond to the mysterious grace of a Spirit which is at once infinitely greater than his own and yet which, at the same time, offers itself as the total plenitude of all Gifts, to be in all reality his "own Spirit."

Returning to Guigo the Carthusian: our response to the Spirit of life is itself a living and dynamic progress, a continual attunement to all the "syllables of the great song." Our violence and destructiveness come from the fact that we cling madly to a single syllable, and thus wish the whole song to stop dead while we enjoy what we imagine is final and absolute. But the "most wise singer" is not singing for ourselves alone and we must accept the fact that some of His notes and words are for others and seemingly "against us." We must not react destructively against the notes we do not like. We must learn to respond not to this or that syllable, but to the whole song.

However, the response is not automatic. It demands a great purity of devotion to truth and to life. The delusions of a fat society glutted with the profits begotten by its own death wish hardly dispose us to respond to the *Creator Spiritus,* the *Cantor sapientissimus,* without a fundamental re-orientation of our thought and life. All have the duty to contribute whatever they can to this reorientation. I do not think the word reorientation is strong enough. What is required is a spiritual upheaval such as we seldom see recorded in history. But such things have happened, and let us hope we have not gone so far that they will not happen again.

118

Part Three

From Non-Violence to Black Power

"Violence is as American as cherry pie." (H. Rap Brown)

THE NON-VIOLENT STRUGGLE FOR INTEGRATION WAS WON ON the law books—and was lost in fact. Integration is more myth than real possibility. The result has been that non-violence both as tactic and as mystique has been largely rejected as irrelevant by the American Negro. At the same time, the struggle for racial recognition has taken on an entirely new and more aggressive character.

First of all, Frantz Fanon has become the prophet of Black America, and Malcolm X has become its martyr. Fanon was a black psychoanalyst from the French colony of Martinique. He joined the Algerian conflict and preached a mystique of violence as necessary for the Third World to recover its identity and organize for revolutionary self-liberation. The Black Power movement in America has accepted this doctrine as simpler, and more effective, and more meaningful than Christian non-violence.

It must be admitted that for the majority of black Americans, Christian non-violence remained highly ambiguous. The Negro felt himself imprisoned in the fantasy image of him devised by the white man: an image of subservient, subhuman, passive tutelage and minority. Part of this image was the assumption that the Negro was there to be beaten over the head. Whether he chose to accept his beating with Christian dignity and heroic, self-sacrificial motives was a matter of supreme indifference to white people like Bull Connor.

121

It is true that the Montgomery bus strike and the Birmingham demonstrations did communicate to the whole nation an image of Negro dignity, maturity and integrity—an example of restraint and nobility which should not have been lost on a culture with our professed ideals. It was unfortunately soon forgotten when black people in the North began to ask for open housing. Northern liberals might admire black dignity at a distance, but they still did not want all that nobility right next door: it might affect property values. Nobility is one thing and property values quite another.

Second, the Vietnam war has had a great deal to do with the new trend to Black Power. The Negroes have been more keenly aware than anyone else of the war's ambiguities. They have tended to identify themselves with the Vietnamese—indeed with the Vietcong—and have not paid much heed to the official rhetoric of Washington. They have, on the contrary, seen the Vietnam war as another manifestation of whitey's versatility in beating down colored people. They have naturally concluded that white America is not really interested in non-violence at all.

Rap Brown's statement that "violence is as American as cherry pie" is steeped in the pungent ironies which characterize the new language of racial conflict. (One is tempted to explore possible psychoanalytic insights in the droll image used. Orality, mother love, hate of brother, . . .) Yes, violence is thoroughly American and Rap Brown is saying that it is in fact the real American language. Perhaps so, perhaps not. But in any event, it is the language the Black American has now elected to speak. Oddly enough, he instantly got himself a much better hearing when he did so.

America sat up and began paying a great deal of attention. "Black Power" became an explosive and inexhaustible theme in the white media. It turned out to be a much better money-maker than non-violence (indeed non-violence was found to interest the American public only is so far as it could be seen as an obscure, perverse form of violence—a dishonest and so to speak "inverted" violence—hence the persistent snide allusions attempting to link non-violence with passivity and homosexuality). Black Power was clearly a message that somehow white America *wanted* to hear. Not of course that white America was not scared, it was deliciously afraid. And glad. Because now things were so much simpler. One had perfectly good reasons to call out the cops and the National Guard.

Well, the blacks wanted it that way too. It was also simpler for them. And they turned it into a self-justifying weapon. There is a lot of truth in this arraignment of white America by Rap Brown:

> You sit out there and you pretend violence scares you, but you watch TV every night and you can't turn it on for five minutes without seeing somebody shot to death or karated to death. Violence is part of your culture. There's no doubt about it. You gave us violence and this is the only value that black people can use to their advantage to end oppression. . . . Johnson says every day if Vietnam don't come round, Vietnam will burn down. I say that if America don't come round America should be burned down. *It's the same thing.*

My reason for quoting these lines is not necessarily to approve a program of arson, but to make the point that it is, quite literally, *the same thing* and to congratulate Rap Brown on the firm and acute justice of his ironic insight.

An America that destroys Vietnamese non-combatants with napalm has no right to object when blacks at home burn down their slums. Indeed, if there is a difference, it is that the second case is more justifiable than the first: it is a protest against real injustice.

It is perfectly logical that the America of LBJ should be

at once the America of the Vietnam war and the Detroit riots. It's the same America, the same violence, the same slice of mother's cherry pie.

The people who have been most shocked by the Black Power movement are the white liberals. And of course they are right, because the whole impact of the movement is directed against *them*. It is a rejection of their tender and ambiguous consciences, their taste for compromise, their desire to eat momma's cherry pie and still have it, their semi-conscious proclivity to use the Negro for their own sentimental, self-justifying ends. The black man has definitely seen through and summarily rejected the white liberal. The overtones of racism in the Black Power program are, in their way, an acknowledgement that the Negro feels the white segregationist to be more honest, in his way, than the liberal. Of course this infuriates the liberal, because it is supposed to do just that. And for that reason it is not to be taken too seriously.

The Black Power movement is not just racism in reverse. This racist suggestion is of course a built-in ambiguity which is at once a strength and a weakness of the movement. For two reasons it has to *appear* racist; to help the black man consolidate his sense of identity, and to rebuff the sentimental and meddling integrationism of the white liberal. There is also a third reason: to get the liberals off the black man's back, and to make it quite clear that the Negro wants to run his own liberation movement from now on, without being told what to do by someone who cannot really understand his situation. If the white liberal wants to help, let him do so indirectly. Let him help poor whites, and let him try to show poor whites that they have much the same problems as the blacks, and that they therefore should not mess with the blacks or oppose them.

Stokely Carmichael has aptly summed up the situation in

124

these words: "Black people often question whether or not they are equal to whites because every time they start to do something, white people are around showing them how to do it" (at Berkeley, November 19, 1966). Hence, the Black Power movement means not only that the black people want real and unquestionable political power, but that they want to attain it by their own efforts. It is here that the strategy of Black Power is necessarily most aggressive, most truculent, most anti-white. But there remains a built-in ambiguity because without *some kind* of support from the overwhelmingly large white majority in the United States, Black Power cannot be politically viable at all. This means that whites who support blacks in their struggle for equality in the political and economic fields must be able to adapt to the new situation and understand it correctly. What Black Power asks of them is recognition of the black man's right to fight for his own interests even, if necessary, by revolutionary means. And it also asks a certain acceptance of the new emphasis on black identity—an emphasis which can be called "ethnocentric" rather than "racist"—as a necessary part of the program. As Floyd McKissick defined Black Power (in an admittedly moderate statement) it is " . . . a drive to mobilize the black communities of this country in a monumental effort to remove the basic causes of alienation, frustration, despair, low self-esteem and hopelessness."

But the trouble is that the nature of the revolution is not at all clear, and the future is not guaranteed to conform to the scenario devised by this or that black leader. There is no indication whatever that even the most influential of the new radical leaders have any real control over the course of events in the cities that are always ready to explode into violence.

Obviously, as McKissick points out, Black Power does not

125

and cannot imply the hope of a "black takeover" or of "black supremacy." But it is not crystal clear that McKissick is right in saying that "Black power . . . does not advocate violence and will not start riots." Though the real thrust of the Black Power movement is toward the acquisition of a political power that will ensure real *influence* (which the Negro has never had) and a serious ability to participate in the economic life of the country on equal terms with white people, this perfectly legitimate and just aim gets lost in the anticipation of chaotic and senseless violence aroused both by white fears and by black rhetoric. And in fact the police and military preparations for the summer of 1968 bear witness to a state of polarized conflict in which guns will talk louder than reason.

It is of course to the interests of white society and in particular of the white mass media to confuse and mis-handle the whole Black Power issue. The more it can be treated as an eruption of berserk violence and African blood-lust the better the story will be and the more the white public will be charmed into gooseflesh by it. The frank exploitation of this sensationalist aspect of the race crisis is illustrated by the way *Esquire* got William Worthy to write on Black Power and then, against his will, gave his contribution a highly slanted and misleading publicity compaign (emphasizing "racist" implications). For which Worthy then sued the magazine.

This willful distortion and exploitation make it completely impossible for the average reader to be properly informed about Black Power. He is predisposed to violent and panic reactions, and it can be said that the whole of America is now primed for an explosion of anarchic destructiveness and aimless slaughter. The fault does not lie with Black Power, or not entirely. The Black Power movement has simply elected to act as catalyst, in order that what is deeply

126

hidden in American society may come out into the open. And evidently it will.

The essays that follow cannot pretend to be anything like adequate to the present situation. The first one is by now completely dated: it represents a provisional view of things in 1964. The one on the Summer of 1967 is also provisional, but a few sentences here may serve to retrace the same outlines with firmer and more definite strokes, thanks to better information and to more mature reflection.

The Black Power movement is not really a racist movement, but it is definitely revolutionary. As Rap Brown says, again: "We are not an anti-white movement, we are anti-anybody who is anti-black." It is a frankly violent movement. It is an anti-liberal movement, because it takes as axiomatic the belief that liberals are in favor of the established power institutions and of all liberal ideologies which covertly or otherwise aim at preserving these. Black Power claims it wants to destroy white institutions but in this it is perhaps ambiguous. Doubtless there are many in the Black Power movement who are frankly revolutionary, and passionately desire to destroy the American capitalist system. Others, on the other hand, are already moving toward more sophisticated (or more corrupt?) establishment positions, and are accused of careerism, of professional rhetoric, and of complicity with the government-supported intellectuals. In fact they are accused of *becoming* establishment intellectuals. It is not my place here to say whether or not this is true, but it is obviously a familiar development. It is altogether possible that the American establishment will be smart enough to neutralize Black Power by simply sucking the leaders into the government or academic machine, as was done before with the older and less radical Negro organizations. The question then is: how long before Rap Brown becomes another Uncle Tom?

127

The Black Power movement is explicitly identified with and involved in the world revolutionary ferment in the Third World. "We are members of the Third World." "The liberation of oppressed people across the world depends on the liberation of black people in this country."

Is Black Power a Marxist movement? No. At least not yet. In fact, the danger of the leaders being sucked into a Marxist establishment is just as great as that of their being absorbed by the American establishment. In either case Black Power will become a white movement again—dominated by white ideologies, plugged in to a white tradition. In which case it will be neutralized in a different way.

Black Power thus claims to be relevant not only to American black people but to people of all colors, everywhere, who are held down in tutelage and subservience by the big white powers—whether American, European or Russian. It claims to be relevant also to the dissatisfied and disengaged within U.S. society (the hippies). *It is part of a world movement of refusal and rejection of the value system we call western culture.* It is therefore at least implicitly critical of Christianity as a white man's religion and accepts Christianity only as somewhat radically revised: "Christ was (literally and historically) a black man!" (Actually, there is a certain typological point to this, but I cannot discuss it here.)

What is to be said about Black Power? What does it mean to a serious—therefore radical—Christian? I for one do not believe a radical Christian has a moral obligation to manufacture molotov cocktails in the cellar and smuggle them into the ghetto. Nor do I believe he has a moral obligation to convert the Black Power movement back to non-violence (which is unlikely anyhow).

I do believe that the Christian is obligated, by his commitment to Christ, to seek out effective and authentic ways of

128

peace in the midst of violence. But merely to demand support and obedience to an established disorder which is essentially violent through and through will not qualify as "peace-making."

There are no easy and simple solutions to this problem, but in the long run the evil root that has to be dealt with is the root of violence, hatred, poison, cruelty and greed which is part of the system itself. The job of the white Christian is then partly a job of diagnosis and criticism, a prophetic task of finding and identifying the injustice which is the cause of *all* the violence, both white and black, which is also the root of war, and of the greed which keeps war going in order that some might make money out of it.

The delicacy and difficulty of the task are due of course to the fact that, in spite of all good intentions, Christians themselves have at times come to identify this evil of greed and power with "Christian order." They have confused it with peace, with right, with justice and with freedom, not distinguishing what really contributes to the good of man and what simply panders to his appetite for wealth and power.

We do not have to go and burn down the slums: but perhaps we might profitably consider whether some of our own venerable religious institutions are not, without our realizing it, supporting themselves in part by the exploitation of slum real estate, or capitalizing in some other way on a disastrous and explosive situation.

In any case, we have to make a clear decision. Black Power or no Black Power, I for one remain *for* the Negro. I trust him, I recognize the overwhelming justice of his complaint, I confess I have no right whatever to get in his way, and that as a Christian I owe him support, not in his ranks but in my own, among the whites who refuse to trust him or hear him, and who want to destroy him.

129

Religion and Race in the United States

THE IDEA OF *kairos*—THE TIME OF URGENT AND PROVIDENTIAL decision—is something characteristic of Christianity, a religion of decisions in time and in history. Can Christians recognize their *kairos*? Is it possible that when the majority of Christians become aware that "the time has come" for a decisive and urgent commitment, the time has, in fact, already run out?

There can be no question now that the time for a certain kind of crucial Christian decision in America has come and gone. In 1962, and finally in 1963, there were "moments of truth" which have now passed, and the scene is becoming one of darkness, anarchy and moral collapse. These, of course, still call for a Christian response, a Christian decision. But it might seem that the responses and decisions of Christians will necessarily be less clear and more tragic because it is now apparent that there is little left for Christians as such to do to shape the events—or forestall the tragedies—that are to come. At best they can pray, and patiently suffer the consequences of past indecision, blindness and evasion. They cannot lead and guide the nation through this crisis, but they can still help others, if they choose, to understand and accept the sufferings involved in order to make a creative and constructive use of the situation for the future. Are they really likely to do this? Who can say?

In the Negro Christian non-violent movement, under Martin Luther King, the *kairos*, the "providential time," met with a courageous and enlightened response. The non-violent-Negro civil rights drive has been one of the most posi-

130

tive and successful expressions of Christian social action that has been seen anywhere in the twentieth century. It is certainly the greatest example of Christian faith in action in the social history of the United States. It has come almost entirely from the Negroes, with a few white Christians and liberals in support. There can be no question that the Christian heroism manifested by the Negroes in the Birmingham demonstrations, or the massive tranquility and order of the March on Washington in August of 1963, had a great deal to do with the passage of the Civil Rights bill. It must also be admitted, as Bayard Rustin, a Negro non-violent leader, has pointed out, that without the Christian intervention of white Protestants and Catholics all over America, the bill would not have been passed. The fact that there is now a Civil Rights Law guaranteeing, at least *de jure,* the freedom of all citizens to enjoy the facilities of the country equally is due to what one might call a Christian as well as a humanitarian and liberal conscience in the United States. However the Northern Negro is, generally speaking, disillusioned with the Churches and with the Christian preaching of moderation and non-violence. His feeling is that the Churches are part of the establishment (which in fact they are!). They support the power-structure and therefore (he believes) keep the Negro deluded and passive, preventing him from fighting for his rights.

The passage of the Civil Rights Bill has only brought the real problem to a head. The struggle for rights now enters a new and more difficult phase.

Hitherto the well-intentioned and the idealistic have assumed that if the needed legislation were passed, the two races would "integrate" more or less naturally, not without a certain amount of difficulty, of course, but nonetheless effectively in the end. They have also assumed as axiomatic that if something is morally right and good, it will come to

131

pass all by itself as soon as obstacles are removed. Everyone seemed to believe with simple faith that law and order, morality, the "American way of life" and Christianity are all very much the same thing. Now it is becoming quite clear that they are not so at all. Many Christians, who have confused "Americanism" with "Christianity" are in fact contributing to the painful contradictions and even injustices of the racial crisis. For the one thing that has been made most evident by the long and bitter struggle of the South, and now of the North, to prevent civil rights legislation from being passed or enforced or made effective, is that the legislators and the police themselves, along with some ministers and indeed all those whom one can call "the establishment," seem to be the first to defy the law or set it aside when their own interests are threatened. In other words we are living in a society that is not exactly moral, a society which misuses Christian cliches to justify its lawlessness and immorality.

And so there are many who think that non-violence has not proved itself a success. It is considered naive and oversimple and it does not get real results. Certainly non-violence postulates a belief in the fundamental goodness of human nature. But this attitude of optimism can come to be confused with shallow confidence in the morality and intrinsic goodness of a society which is proving itself torn by vicious internal contradictions. Non-violence still continues to be used as a tactic, but the days of its real effectiveness are apparently over. It will probably never again convey the message it conveyed in Montgomery, Birmingham and Selma. Those days are over, and it seems that people who believed in all that was implied by non-violence will look back upon those days with a certain nostalgia. For non-violence apparently presupposed a sense of justice, of humaneness, of liberality, of generosity that were not to be found in the white people to whom the Negroes made their

132

stirring appeal. The problem of American racism turned out to be far deeper, far more stubborn, infinitely more complex. It is also part of a much greater problem: one that divides the whole world into what may one day turn into a huge revolutionary interracial war of two camps: the affluent whites and the impoverished non-whites.

One reason why non-violence apparently cannot continue to be a really effective instrument for the vindication of Negro rights is this: it seems that the willingness to take punishment and suffering, which is essential to non-violent resistance, cannot mean the same thing to the Negro minority in the United States as it meant to the Hindus in their vast majority facing English colonialism in India. There, Hindu non-violence bore witness to overwhelming strength. In the Negro ghettoes of America it has turned out to mean, to Negroes and to whites in general, another admission of Negro inferiority and helplessness. The Negro is always the one who lets his head be bashed in. Whether or not this is what non-violence really means, the confused image of it has now become unacceptable to many activists in the struggle for civil rights, while resentful whites, north and south, are not willing to see its true meaning in any case. The Negroes on the other hand, more and more disillusioned not only with white reactionaries but also with ambiguous liberals, have tended to take a more desperate course. On one hand there has been an increasing trend toward unsystematic and spontaneous violence, and on the other there has been the systematic campaign for "Black Power" which, not properly understood and not always clearly explained, has managed to frighten white people not a little. We will discuss this further on.

In any case there is more and more violent action on both sides, as it becomes increasingly clear that the Civil Rights Law has not really solved the racial problem and that in

actual fact the ghetto existence of the Negro has only become better and more inexorably defined by his inability to
take advantage of the rights that have been granted him
only on paper and too late.

The Negro is integrated by law into a society in which
there really is no place for him—not that a place could not
be made for him, if the white majority were capable of
wanting him as a brother and a fellow-citizen. But even
those who have been theoretically in favor of civil rights are
turning out to be concretely reluctant to have the Negro as
next-door neighbor. The so-called "white backlash" manifests a change from tolerant indifference to bitter hatred on
the part of some Northern whites. It is virulent and passionate and one hears the word "nigger" spat out with a venom
which one had thought belonged to the past. And there are
reasons, for violence and gratuitous attacks on white people
by Negroes are common everywhere in the North. The
Negro's clear awareness that he is still despised and rejected,
after years of bitter struggle and deception, has destroyed
his confidence in legal and peaceful methods. Perhaps he is
beginning to want something besides "rights" that are purely
Platonic—an opportunity to unburden himself of his bitterness by violent protest, that will disrupt a social "order"
that seems to him to have proved itself meaningless and
fraudulent.

The problem is much more complex, much more tragic,
than people have imagined. To begin with, it is something
that extends beyond America. It affects the whole world.
The race problem of America has been analyzed (by such
writers as William Faulkner, for example) as a problem of
deep guilt for the sin of slavery. The guilt of white America toward the Negro is simply another version of the guilt
of the European colonizer toward all the other races of the
world, whether in Asia, Africa, America or Polynesia. The

racial crisis in the United States has rightly been diagnosed as a "colonial crisis" within the country itself rather than on a distant continent. But it is nevertheless closely related to the United States' problems in South East Asia and in Latin America, particularly with Cuba.

The fact that non-violent resistance did not fully succeed and the fact that its partial failure clearly disclosed the refusal of white America to really integrate the Negro into its social framework has radically altered the Negro's evaluation of himself and of his struggle. Whereas before he might have been willing to believe it possible for him to find a place in white society, he has now largely ceased to find real integration either credible or desirable. True, there are probably countless middle-class Negroes who are able to find life tolerable and who seek only to avoid further trouble and violence. But there are far more numerous Negroes for whom the present situation spells nothing but despair and total rejection from a society which to them has no real meaning. To these Negroes, if any political self-awareness makes sense at all, it is one in which they begin dimly to recognize themselves as identified with the colored races in all parts of the world which are struggling to assert themselves and find their proper place in it. The slogan "Black Power" implies not only the intent to use political means in order to gain what is granted the Negro by law and refused him in fact. It implies a consciousness of revolutionary solidarity with the colored in other parts of the world. This has been brought sharply to attention by the fact, for example, of Negro protest against fighting against "other colored people" in Vietnam, and fighting them for the interests of the white United States. Thus the Vietnam war, ostensibly being fought for "freedom" and "against communist oppression" is seen to be fraught with its own very unpleasant ambiguities. And this in turn brings into focus

135

all the doubts which radicals, white and Negro alike, are raising about the sincerity of our claim to be the most democratic society on earth.

The civil rights struggle has therefore, in largely abandoning its reliance on non-violence, made a very significant shift in its position. It has changed its basic assumptions. It no longer takes for granted that American society is just, freedom loving and democratic and that the ways to satisfy the just claims of the Negro are built into our system. On the contrary, it takes for granted that our society is basically racist, that it is inclined toward fascism and violence, and that the rights of Negroes cannot be guaranteed without real political power.

When a nation is torn by contradictions, the problem can be apparently "simplified" and "clarified" if unpleasant choices are excluded and if one falls back on primitive positions—on crude and satisfying myths—for instance the myth that "it was all started by the commies." If the whites insist on attributing to Communism the responsibility for every protest which releases the frustrated energies of the Negro, the Negroes in the end will begin to respect and trust Communism. Up to the present they have been supremely indifferent towards it. Their new international consciousness will dispose them more and more to look with respect toward Red China which claims to lead the colored people of the world in revolution.

In one of the big riots of 1964, the one in Harlem in mid-July, when the streets were filled with people in confusion, running from the police; when bricks and bottles were pelting down from the rooftops and the police were firing into the air (not without killing one man and wounding many others), the police captain tried to disperse the rioters by shouting through a megaphone; "Go home! Go home!"

A voice from the crowd answered: "We are home, baby!"

136

The irony of this statement, and its humor, sum up the American problem. There is no "where" for the Negro to go. He is where he is. White America has put him where he is. The tendency has been to act as if he were not there, or as if he might possibly go somewhere else, and to beat him over the head if he makes his collective presence too manifest. The American Negro himself has tried to return to Africa, but the plan was farcical. The Black Nationalists are even now agitating for a part of the country to be turned over to the Negroes—so they can live by themselves. One of the purposes of the violence which those Negro racists actively foment, is to make white society willing and happy to get rid of them. The fact remains that the Negro is now in the home the white man has given him: the three square miles of broken-down tenements which form the ghetto of Harlem, the biggest Negro city in the world, type of all the Negro ghettoes in America, full of crime, misery, squalor, dope addiction, prostitution, gang warfare, hatred and despair. And yet, though Harlem is a problem, it will not become less of a problem if we consider only the negative side. For those who think only of the prostitutes and criminals, Harlem becomes part of the general obsessive national myth of the "bad Negro." The majority of the people in Harlem are good, peaceable, gentle, long-suffering men and women, socially insecure but more sinned against than sinning.

What is to be wondered at is not the occasional mass demonstrations and rioting, not the juvenile delinquency and not the more and more deliberate excursions of small violent groups into other areas of the city to beat up white people and rob them. What is to be wondered at is the persistence of courage, irony, humor, patience, and hope in Harlem!

In a spiritual crisis of the individual, the truth and au-

137

thenticity of the person's spiritual identity are called into question. He is placed in confrontation with reality and judged by his ability to bring himself into a valid and living relationship with the demands of his new situation. In the spiritual, social, historic crises of civilizations—and of religious institutions—the same principle applies. Growth, survival and even salvation may depend on the ability to sacrifice what is fictitious and unauthentic in the construction of one's moral, religious or national identity. One must then enter upon a different creative task of reconstruction and renewal. This task can be carried out only in the climate of faith, of hope and of love: these three must be present in some form, even if they amount only to a natural belief in the validity and significance of human choice, a decision to invest human life with some shadow of meaning, a willingness to treat other men as other selves.

Gandhi long ago pointed out that western democracy was on trial. There is no need for me here to show in how many ways the American concepts of democracy and Christianity are here being weighed in the balance.

The problem of American Christianity is the same as the problem of Christianity everywhere else: Christianity is suffering a crisis of identity and authenticity, and is being judged by the ability of Christians themselves to abandon unauthentic, anachronistic images and securities, in order to find a new place in the world by a new evaluation of the world and a new commitment in it.

In the American crisis the Christian faces a typical choice. The choice is not interior and secret, but public, political and social. He is perhaps not used to regarding his crucial choices in the light of politics. He can now either find security and order by falling back on antique and basically feudal (or perhaps fascist) conceptions, or go forward into the unknown future, identifying himself with the forces that

138

will inevitably create a new society. The choice is between "safety," based on negation of the new and the reaffirmation of the familiar, or the creative risk of love and grace in new and untried solutions, which justice nevertheless demands.

Those who are anxious to discover whether Christianity has had any positive effect on the civil rights struggle seldom ask an equally important question: has the struggle had an effect on Christianity? It has certainly had an effect on the Catholic Church. The case of Father William Du Bay, a young assistant in a Los Angeles Negro parish, is a direct outcome of the racial crisis. His protest was an admitted attempt not only to defend the rights of his Negro parishioners, but also to assert his own right to break through the absolutely ironbound restrictions of clerical submission to canonical authority, not as an act of willful disobedience but as a protest that the priest owes a higher obedience—to the demands of charity and justice—which cannot be shrugged off by simply leaving all responsibility to rest upon superiors. Whatever may have been the rights and wrongs of the case, which was a rude shock to Catholic authority, Father Du Bay was clearly trying to say that he did not believe that the inaction of his bishop entitled him to be passive himself, and that there is such a thing as public opinion in the Church. Not all Catholics have agreed, but all have taken note of this assertion!

The mystique of American Christian rightism, a mystique of violence, of apocalyptic threats, of hatred, and of judgment is perhaps only a more exaggerated and more irrational manifestation of a rather universal attitude common to Christians in many countries. The conviction that the great evil in the world today can be identified with Communism, and that to be a Christian is simply to be an anti-Communist. Communism is the antichrist. Communism is the source of all other problems, all conflicts. All the evils

139

in the world can be traced to the machinations of Communists. The apocalyptic fear of Communism which plays so great a part in the Christianity of some Americans—and some Europeans—resolves itself into a fear of revolution and indeed a fear of any form of social change that would disturb the status quo.

This mentality which we have summarized as "Christian violence" becomes more and more irrational in proportion as it implies both an absolute conviction of one's own rightness and a capacity to approve the use of any means, however violent, however extreme, in order to defend what one feels, subjectively, to be right. This is an axiom. This totalism admits no distinctions, no shades of meaning. "Our side" is totally right, everyone else is diabolically wicked.

Naturally, this synthetic and sweeping "rightness" is compounded of many unconscious doubts and repressed fears. Nor are all the fears repressed. But they take a more or less symbolic form. There is no question that the white racists of the South willingly admit a certain fear of the Negro. The fear is part of their mystique and indeed accounts for a great deal of its emotional power. It is the quasi-mystical obsession with the black demon waiting in the bushes to rape the virginal white daughters of the old South.

The literal truth outdoes all caricature, and it gives us a clue to the mentality and mystique of the "Christian violence" which is coming into being here and there all over the United States, not only among fanatical sects and not only in the South. The intensity of emotion, the sacred and obsessional fear, rising from subliminal levels and reaching consciousness in a panic conviction of spiritual danger, judges all that seems menacing and calls it diabolical. But everything seems menacing and therefore the most innocent of oppositions, the slightest dissenting opinions, calls for the most extreme, the most violent and the most ruthless

140

repressions. At the present time, the Southern pseudo-mystique of sexual and racist obsessions (and of course there have been rapes, and seductions, of whites by Negroes, as well infinitely more rapes and seductions of Negroes by whites) now joins with the deeper and more universal fear of revolution. This combination results in a peculiarly potent climate of aggressive intolerance, suspiciousness, hatred and fear. When we consider that this self-righteous, pseudo-religious faith has its finger terribly close to the button that launches inter-continental ballistic missiles, it gives us food for thought.

The American Negro is well aware of all these obsessions in his regard. He realizes better than the benevolent white liberal to what extent these subliminal fears exist in all white Americans. The tensions created by this dangerous situation are going to increase as the Negro, consciously or otherwise, renounces his hopeful and friendly expectations and begins to test his capacity to shake the foundations of white society by threats of violence.

Well then: what of the *kairos*? Shall we say that it has passed and left the Christian Churches only half awake? It depends upon the sense the Christian gives to his *kairos*. It is certainly possible for us to recognize that we have missed a chance for significant social action. We can edify the world with those subtle and contrite self-examinations which we often substitute for purposeful activity. Or we can do worse, and involve ourselves in the righteous and apocalyptic fury of those whose "Christianity" has emptied itself of serious meaning in order to become a fanatical negation, a refusal of reality, and a ritual hunting of Communist witches.

For those whose Christianity is still a religion of truth and love, not of hate and fear, I think the first thing to do is to admit that our *kairos* is perhaps not always likely to be what

141

we expect. Are we, for example, justified in assuming so complacently that *kairos,* in race crisis, means an opportunity for us as Christians to step in and settle everything with a few wise answers and the adoption of the right attitudes? Are we not called upon to re-evaluate our own notions and see that "right attitudes" are not enough and that it is not sufficient merely to have goodwill, or even to go to jail gloriously for an honest cause? We need a little more depth and a keener sense of the tragedy (or perhaps the comedy) of our situation: we are living in a world which is in many ways "post-Christian" and acting as if we were still running things, still in a position to solve all the world's problems and tell everybody what to do next. It might help if we realized that in fact most people have lost interest in our official pronouncements, and while the fanatical type of Christian still thrives on the belief that he is hated, the rest of us are beginning to realize that the wicked world can no longer take the trouble to do even that. It is simply not interested.

This, as a matter of fact, is no disaster. It is really a liberation. We no longer have to take ourselves so abominably seriously as "Christians" with a public and capital "C." We can give a little more thought to the reality of our vocation and bother less with the image which we show to the world.

If there is a *kairos,* and perhaps there still is, it is not a "time" in which once again we will convince the world that we are right, but perhaps rather a time in which the crisis of man will teach us to see a few sobering truths about our own Christian calling and our place in the world—a place no longer exalted and mighty, or perhaps even influential.

In fact we are learning that we are as other men are, that we are not a special kind of privileged being, that our faith does not exempt us from facing the mysterious realities of the world with the same limitations as everybody else, and with the same capacity for human failure. Our Christian calling does not make us superior to other men, does not entitle us to judge everyone and decide everything for everybody. We do not have answers to every social problem, and all conflicts have not been decided beforehand in favor of our side. Our job is to struggle along with everybody else and collaborate with them in the difficult, frustrating task of seeking a solution to common problems, which are entirely new and strange to us all.

The American racial crisis which grows more serious every day offers the American Christian a chance to face reality about himself and recover his fidelity to Christian truth, not merely in institutional loyalties and doctrinal orthodoxies (in which no one has taken the trouble to accuse him of failing) but in recanting a more basic heresy: the loss of that Christian sense which sees every other man as Christ and treats him as Christ. For, as St. John said: "We know what love is by this: that he laid down his life for us so that we ought to lay down our lives for the brotherhood. But whoever possesses this world's goods and notices his brother in need and shuts his heart against him, how can the love of God remain in him? Dear children, let us put our love not into words or into talk but into deeds, and make it real." (I John 3: 16–18)

We do indeed have a message for the world, and the Word of God is still as alive and penetrating today "as any two-edged sword." But we have perhaps taken the edge off the sword by our short-sightedness and our complacency. The Christian failure in American racial justice has been all too real, but it is not the fault of the few dedicated and non-violent followers of Christ. It is due much more to the fact that so few Christians have been able to face the fact that non-violence comes very close to the heart of the Gospel ethic, and is perhaps essential to it.

But non-violence is not simply a matter of marching with

143

signs and placards under the eyes of unfriendly policemen. The partial failure of liberal non-violence has brought out the stark reality that our society itself is radically violent and that violence is built into its very structure. We live in a society which, while appealing to Christian ethical ideals, violently negates its Christian pretensions and in so doing drives a radical minority to desperation and violence. The white Christian cannot in such a situation be content merely to march with his black brother at the risk of getting his head broken or of being shot. The problem is to eradicate this basic violence and unjustice from white society. Can it be done? How?

Events and Pseudo-Events:

Letter to a Southern Churchman

I HAVE PUBLICLY STATED THAT I WOULD NO LONGER COMMENT on current events. People ask why. There are many reasons, and I might as well say at once that they are reasons which may possibly be valid for me only, not for others. In any case I did not make this decision for anyone but myself. Nor would I have made it unless I had previously made my position clear in the areas of greatest urgency—race and peace.

First of all, I mistrust an obsession with declarations and pronouncements. While silence can constitute guilt and complicity, once one has taken a stand he is not necessarily obliged to come out with a new answer and a new solution to insoluble problems every third day.

After all, was it not Bonhoeffer himself who said it was an "Anglo-Saxon failing" to imagine that the Church was supposed to have a ready answer for every social problem?

When one has too many answers, and when one joins a chorus of others chanting the same slogans, there is, it seems to me, a danger that one is trying to evade the loneliness of a conscience that realizes itself to be in an inescapably evil situation. We are all under judgment. None of us is free from contamination. Our choice is not that of being pure and whole at the mere cost of formulating a just and honest opinion. Mere commitment to a decent program of action does not lift the curse. Our real choice is between being like Job, who *knew* he was stricken, and Job's friends who did not know that they were stricken too—though less obviously than he. (So they had answers!)

If we *know* that we are all under judgment, we will cease to make the obvious wickedness of "the others" a fulcrum for our own supposed righteousness to exert itself upon the world. On the contrary, we will be willing to admit that we are "right-wised" not by condemning others according to our law or ethical ideal, but by seeing that the real sinner whom we find abominable and frightening (because he threatens our very life) still has in himself the ground for God's love, the same ground that is in our own sinful and deluded hearts.

To justify ourselves is to justify our sin and to call God a liar.

Second, there is the nature of my own vocation to the monastic, solitary, contemplative life—the vocation of Job! Of course this monastic life does not necessarily imply a total refusal to have anything to do with the world. Such a refusal would, in any case, be illusory. It would deceive no one but the monk himself. It is not possible for anyone, however isolated from the world, to say "I will no longer concern myself with the affairs of the world." We cannot help being implicated. We can be guilty even by default. But the monastic and contemplative life does certainly imply a very special perspective, a viewpoint which others do not share, the viewpoint of one who is not directly engaged in the struggles and controversies of the world. Now it seems to me that if a monk is permitted to be detached from these struggles over particular interests, it is only in order that he may give more thought to the interests of all, to the whole question of the reconciliation of all men with one another in Christ. One is permitted, it seems to me, to stand back from parochial and partisan concerns, if one can thereby hope to get a better view of the whole problem and mystery of man.

146

A contemplative will, then, concern himself with the same problems as other people, but he will try to get to the spiritual and metaphysical roots of these problems—not by analysis but by simplicity. This of course is no easy task, and I cannot claim that I have discovered anything worth saying. Yet since I have been asked to say something, I will at least hazard a few conjectures. Take them for what they may be worth: they are subjective, they are provisional, they are mere intuitions, they will certainly need to be completed by the thinking of others. If they suggest a few useful perspectives to others, then I am satisfied.

I am more and more impressed by the fact that it is largely futile to get up and make statements about current problems. At the same time, I know that silent acquiescence in evil is also out of the question. I know too that there are times when protest is inescapable, even when it seems as useless as beating your head up against a brick wall. At the same time, when protest simply becomes an act of desperation, it loses its power to communicate anything to anyone who does not share the same feelings of despair.

There is of course no need to comment on the uselessness of false optimism, or to waste any attentions on the sunlit absurdities of those who consistently refuse to face reality. One cannot be a Christian today without having a deeply afflicted conscience. I say it again: we are all under judgment. And it seems to me that our gestures of repentance, though they may be individually sincere, are collectively hollow and even meaningless. Why?

This is the question that plagues me.

The reason seems to be, to some extent, a deep failure of communication.

* * *

There is a great deal of talk today about the Church and the world, about secular Christianity, religionless religion

147

and so on. It seems to me that religionless religion is certainly a result of this failure of communication. (Here I am distinguishing Bonhoeffer's disciples from Bonhoeffer himself.) Seeing that traditional and biblical language simply does not ring any bells in the minds of modern men, the apostles of religionless religion have discarded that language and decided thereby to avoid the problem of communication altogether. Having done so, however, they seem to have also gotten rid of any recognizable Christian message. To reconcile man with man and not with God is to reconcile no one at all. It is the old problem of the social Gospel over again. When the life expectancy of the average secular ideology today is about five years (barring a few notable exceptions that have become orthodoxies, like Marxism and Freudianism) it seems rather irresponsible to identify the Gospel with one or the other of them.

Assuming then that the Church has something to communicate to the world that the world does not already know, what does this imply? First of all, we must try to clarify the relation of the Church to the world. It seems to me false simply to say that the Church and the world should be considered as perfectly identified, as indistinguishable, and leave it at that. After all, there is still I John 2: 15–16 to be considered.

This judgment of the world as by definition *closed in upon itself* and therefore *closed to any revelation that demands to break through its defensive shell* is surely one of the key ideas of the New Testament. By the Incarnation and Cross Christ does in fact *break through* the defensive shell not only of sin and passionate attachment, but of all ethical and religious systems that strive to make man self-sufficient in his own worldly realm.

The Church and the world are related in a dialectic of identity and non-identity, yes and no, nearness and dis-

148

tance. The Church is Christ present in the world to reconcile the world to Himself. The world is therefore not
purely and simply Christ. There is a question of acceptance
or refusal. If we are dealing with the self-revelation of a
cosmic Christ who is gradually becoming visible in man,
simply as *man,* the decision for this Christ becomes a kind
of poetic commitment to pantheistic vitalism or something of
the sort, not an acceptance of the Gospel in the obedience
of faith. In other words "Christ" is then only a symbol for
the world as a closed-system. Such a symbol may seem
inspiring; but it is idolatrous. Further, if Christ is simply
manifesting himself in man's history, whether we do anything about it or not, then there is no need either of dialogue or of dialectic between the Church and the world. By
this dialectic of challenge, faith and love, word and response,
we break out of the closed system. If we forsake this forward movement toward eschatological fulfillment, then we
plunge into the interminable circling of the world upon
itself. No amount of religious cliches can make this encapsu-
lation a true "freedom."

It seems to me that one of the great obligations of the
Christian is to keep the eyes of his faith clear of such confusions. And the monk above all has to keep free from this
circling-in-desperation, this closed system, which is essentially pagan and which implies a hidden servitude to the
elements and the powers of the air in St. Paul's sense (Gala-
tians 4: 3,9). (I readily admit, with Luther, that in practice
the monk who makes monasticism a "law" automatically
fails in his primal obligation.)

Though there are certainly more ways than one of preserving the freedom of the sons of God, the way to which I was
called and which I have chosen is that of the monastic life.

Paul's view of the "elements" and the "powers of the air"
was couched in the language of the cosmology of his day.

Translated into the language of our own time, I would say these mysterious realities are to be sought where we least expect them, not in what is most remote and mysterious, but in what is most familiar, what is near at hand, what is at our elbow all day long—what speaks or sings in our ear, and practically does our thinking for us. The "powers" and "elements" are precisely what stand between the world and Christ. It is they who stand in the way of reconciliation. It is they who, by influencing all our thinking and behavior in so many unsuspected ways, dispose us to decide *for* the world *as against* Christ, thus making reconciliation impossible.

Clearly, the "powers" and "elements" which in Paul's day dominated men's minds through pagan religion or through religious legalism, today dominate us in the confusion and the ambiguity of the Babel of tongues that we call mass-society. Certainly I do not condemn everything in the mass-media. But how does one stop to separate the truth from the half-truth, the event from the pseudo-event, reality from the manufactured image? It is in this confusion of images and myths, superstitions and ideologies that the "powers of the air" govern our thinking—even our thinking about religion! Where there is no critical perspective, no detached observation, no time to ask the pertinent questions, how can one avoid being deluded and confused?

Someone has to try to keep his head clear of static and preserve the interior solitude and silence that are essential for independent thought.

A monk loses his reason for existing if he simply submits to all the routines that govern the thinking of everybody else. He loses his reason for existing if he simply substitutes other routines of his own! He is obliged by his vocation to have his *own mind* if not to speak it. He has got to be a free man.

What did the radio say this evening? I don't know.

150

What was on TV? I have watched TV twice in my life. I am frankly not terribly interested in TV anyway. Certainly I do not pretend that by simply refusing to keep up with the latest news I am therefore unaffected by what goes on, or *free* of it all. Certainly events happen and they affect me as they do other people. It is important for me to know about them too: but I refrain from trying to know them in their fresh condition as "news." When they reach me they have become slightly stale. I eat the same tragedies as others, but in the form of tasteless crusts. The news reaches me in the long run through books and magazines, and no longer as a stimulant. Living without news is like living without cigarettes (another peculiarity of the monastic life). The need for this habitual indulgence quickly disappears. So, when you hear news without the "need" to hear it, it treats you differently. And you treat it differently too.

In this perspective you are perhaps able to distinguish the real happening from the pseudo-event. Nine tenths of the news, as printed in the papers, is pseudo-news, manufactured events. Some days ten tenths. The ritual morning trance, in which one scans columns of newsprint, creates a peculiar form of generalized pseudo-attention to a pseudo-reality. This experience is taken seriously. It is one's daily immersion in "reality." One's orientation to the rest of the world. One's way of reassuring himself that he has not fallen behind. That he is still there. That he still counts!

My own experience has been that renunciation of this self-hypnosis, of this participation in the unquiet universal trance, is no sacrifice of reality at all. To "fall behind" in this sense is to get out of the big cloud of dust that everybody is kicking up, to breathe and to see a little more clearly.

When you get a clearer picture you can understand why so many want to stand in the dust cloud, where there is comfort in confusion.

The things that actually happen are sometimes incredibly horrible.

The fog of semi-rational verbiage with which the events are surrounded is also terrible, but in a different way.

And then, beside the few real horrors, there are the countless pseudo-events, the come-on's, the releases, the statements, the surmises, the slanders, the quarrels, the insults and the interminable self-advertising of the image-makers.

We believe that the "news" has a strange metaphysical status outside us: it "happens" by itself. Actually, it is something we fabricate. Those who are poor artisans make only pseudo-events. These are the tired politicians and businessmen, the educators, writers, intellectuals and tiredest of all, the Churchmen.

Others are better at it: they know how to make real bad news!

*　　*　　*

Reading the Vulgate I run across the Latin word *simulacrum* which has implications of a mask-like deceptiveness, of intellectual cheating, of an ideological shell-game. The word *simulacrum*, it seems to me, presents itself as a very suggestive one to describe an advertisement, or an over-inflated political presence, or that face on the TV screen. The word shimmers, grins, cajoles. It is a fine word for something monumentally phony. It occurs for instance in the last line of the First Epistle of John. But there it is usually translated as "idols" . . . "Little Children, watch out for the simulacra!" —watch out for the national, the regional, the institutional images!

Does it not occur to us that if, in fact, we live in a society which is par excellence that of the *simulacrum*, we are the champion idolaters of all history? No, it does not occur to us, because for us an idol is nothing more than a harmless

Greek statue, complete with a figleaf, in the corner of the museum. We have given up worrying about idols—as well as devils. And we are living in the age of science. How could we, the most emancipated of men, be guilty of superstition? Could science itself be our number one superstition?

You see where my rambling has brought me. To this: we are under judgment. And what for? For the primal sin. We are idolaters. We make *simulacra* and we hypnotize ourselves with our skill in creating these mental movies that do not appear to be idols because they are so alive! Because we are idolaters, because we have "exchanged the glory of the immortal God for the semblance of the likeness of mortal man, of birds, of quadrupeds, of reptiles . . ." we fulfill all the other requirements of those who are under God's wrath, as catalogued by Paul in Romans 1: 24–32.

Our idols are by no means dumb and powerless. The sardonic diatribes of the prophets against images of wood and stone do not apply to our images that live, and speak, and smile, and dance, and allure us and lead us off to kill. Not only are we idolaters, but we are likely to carry out point by point the harlotries of the Apocalypse. And if we do, we will do so innocently, decently, with clean hands, for the blood is always shed somewhere else! The smoke of the victims is always justified by some clean sociological explanation, and of course it is not supersitition because we are by definition the most enlightened people that ever happened.

The things that we do, the things that make our news, the things that are contemporary, are abominations of superstition, of idolatry, proceeding from minds that are full of myths, distortions, half-truths, prejudices, evasions, illusions, lies: in a word—*simulacra*. Ideas and conceptions that look good but aren't. Ideals that claim to be humane and prove themselves, in their effects, to be callous, cruel, cynical, sometimes even criminal.

153

We have no trouble at all detecting all this in the ideologies of *other* nations, other social groups. That is at least something! But it is not enough. We cannot begin to face our real problems until we admit that these evils are universal. We see them in others because they are in ourselves. Until we admit that we are subject to the same risks and the same follies, the same evils and the same fanaticisms, only in different forms, under different appearances (*simulacra*) we will continue to propose solutions that make our problems insoluble. We will continue to be deadlocked with adversaries who happen to be our own mirror image.

❃　　❃　　❃

My thesis is now clear: in my opinion the root of our trouble is that our habits of thought and the drives that proceed from them are basically idolatrous and mythical. We are all the more inclined to idolatry because we imagine that we are of all generations the most enlightened, the most objective, the most scientific, the most progressive and the most humane. This, in fact, is an "image" of ourselves—an image which is false and is also the object of a cult. We worship ourselves in this image. The nature of our acts is determined in large measure by the demands of our worship. Because we have an image (*simulacrum*) of ourselves as fair, objective, practical and humane, we actually make it more difficult for ourselves to be what we think we are. Since our "objectivity" for instance is in fact an image of ourselves as "objective," we soon take our objectivity for granted, and instead of checking the facts, we simply manipulate the facts to fit our pious conviction. In other words, instead of taking care to examine the realities of our political or social problems, we simply bring out the idols in solemn procession. "We are the ones who are right, *they* are the ones who are wrong. We are the good guys, *they* are the bad guys. We

154

are honest, *they* are crooks." In this confrontation of images, "objectivity" ceases to be a consistent attention to fact and becomes a devout and blind fidelity to myth. If the adversary is by definition wicked, then objectivity consists simply in refusing to believe that he can possibly be honest in any circumstances whatever. If facts seem to conflict with images, then we feel that we are being tempted by the devil, and we determine that we will be all the more blindly loyal to our images. To debate with the devil would be to yield! Thus in support of realism and objectivity we simply determine beforehand that we will be swayed by no fact whatever that does not accord perfectly with our own preconceived judgment. Objectivity becomes simple dogmatism.

As I say, we can see this mechanism at work in the Communists. We cannot see it in ourselves. True, of course, our dogmatism is not as blatant, as rigid, as bureaucratically dense, as monolithic. It is nonetheless real. That is to say, it is based on *refusals* that are just as categorical and just as absolute.

These refusals are made necessary by a primary commitment to a false image which is the object of superstitious worship. The fact that the image is not made of stone or metal, but of ideas, slogans and pseudo-events only makes it all the more dangerous.

❂ ❂ ❂

A more complex syndrome in our mythical thinking. I shall call it "justification by snake-handling."

Let me say at once that I am not trying to ridicule the good, simple people in the Tennessee mountains or in North Carolina who every once in a while gather in their little Churches, work themselves up into a state of exaltation and then pass around a live rattlesnake from hand to hand. There is a kind of rugged starkness about this primitive

155

fundamentalism that calls for a certain respect, and I am reminded that in the novels of Flannery O'Connor due honor was not denied to primitives. The people Flannery O'Connor depised were those whose mental snake-handling was more polite and less risky, more sophisticated and adroit, more complacent and much less honest, based on the invocation not of Mark 16:18, but of something at once more sinister, more modern and more obscure.

I take the mountain people as my starting point simply because in them the cycle is stark and clinically clear. And they are aware of what they are doing.

The rest of us do it without recognizing the analogy.

I do not say we do it every day. Snake-handling is reserved for moments of crisis, when we feel ourselves and our myths called into question. It is our reaction to deep stirring of guilt about ourselves and our images. We handle snakes in order to restore the image to a place of perfect security.

In Christian terms, the mental snake-handling is an attempt to evade judgment when our conscience obscurely tells us that we are under judgment. It represents recourse to a daring and ritual act, a magic gesture that is visible and recognized by others, which proves to us that we are right, that the image is right, that our rightness cannot be contested, and whoever contests it is a minion of the devil.

Here is the scenario.

First, a drab, uninteresting or over-organized, bored existence. Or at least an obscure feeling that your life is not quite as meaningful as it ought to be. That there is not only something lacking, but probably *everything* lacking. The more obscure and diffuse the feeling, the better. If you are hardly aware of it at all, fine. Most Americans on any day of the week can, if they reflect a little on it, see that they easily meet these qualifications. Even if one has all he needs in material goods, he can still feel as if he lacked *everything!*

Second, you have to connive with a group of other people who feel the same way, at least implicitly. You may perhaps come to an agreement with them in actual discussion together, or you may simply (more often than not) find that you and a lot of other people have all seen the same thing on TV or somewhere and are all reacting to it in the same way. I will not go into bizarre details about snake-handling in small fanatical groups of adepts and snake-handling on the national level. Let's keep it simple. First, you are bored and dissatisfied. Second, you find yourself in collusion with others who react as you do to some event.

Implicitly or explicitly you agree on some course of action which is at the same time *symbolic, arbitrary and dangerous.* These three characteristics are essential. There may be others. But at least the act has to be symbolic. If the symbolism is unconscious, so much the better. The act or event has to be arbitrary, irrational, and in a sense provocative. It must not only be more or less unreasonable, it should, if possible, even openly *defy* reason. Indeed it may be totally irrelevant. If at the same time it is an act which defies morality, public or private, this may enhance its value. But that is not essential. It must at least be basically irrational. If it is completely useless and irrelevant, so much the better. And it must be dangerous, if not physically then at least socially or morally. The event brings one face to face with destruction or grave harm, if not danger to life and limb, then a danger to reputation, to one's social acceptability, one's future.

However, while the event may implicitly defy ostracism or hatred on the part of an out-group, it strengthens the bonds of the in-group, those who have agreed to engage in the symbolic and arbitrary activity together. At this point, we recognize characteristic adolescent behavior, but teen-agers have no monopoly on it, except in so far as we are in fact a teen-age society—a society that likes to play "chicken" not with fast cars, but with ballistic missiles.

The symbolic, irrational and perilous event must prove something, at least to those who perform it. The thing it attempts to prove must be some basic value in themselves: that they are *alive*, that they are *real*, that they *count*, or (as in the case of the authentic snake-handlers) that they are *the Chosen*. In fact, it is a *substitute for divine judgment*. Instead of waiting around in uncertainty, one forces the issue. One does something drastic and "conclusive."

Naturally, not all who enact such events are necessarily believers. One does not have to believe in God—one merely needs to have an "image"! This mental ritual is a component in our contemporary idolatries.

Finally, and this is the point, those who have come together, who have agreed, who have performed the irrational, quasi-initiatory act, who have "proved themselves" thereby, who have stabilized their common image, *are now in a position to judge others*. By creating this situation of challenge, by constructing this "event," they have proved themselves to be "the ones who are right." They have not done this by thinking or reasoning, nor by discussion, dialogue, investigation: they have done it by a ritual and initiatory action in which they enjoyed the sense of self-transcendence, of escape from the monotony and the affront of a meaningless existence. And note that it is a cycle that is all the more easily set in motion when existence is in fact more really drab, when the mentality of the participants is more genuinely desperate, when the inner contradictions they seek to escape are all the more inexorable.

Though by its nature this event is arbitrary, unnecessary, and in some sense fabricated, if it is sufficiently drastic it can become far more than a pseudo-event. It can become an act of genuine horror. It can lead to incalculably tragic consequences. If, in handing the rattlesnake around, somebody gets bitten, it is no longer a pseudo-event. Yet nevertheless, in its origin, the event was artificial, fabricated and indeed uncalled for.

Some examples: on the international level, a paradigm of snake-handling and pseudo-event was the Berlin crisis, turned on and off periodically, for the sake of effect. It reached its paroxysm in Cuba, and shortly after that Krushchev's snake-handling days were over.

The big fuss about fallout shelters in this country was another episode of the same kind, and it was our reaction to the Berlin crisis. A purely symbolic and irrational exercise.

The philosophy of escalation, with its mystical degrees and esoteric meanings, is a form of intellectual snake-handling. To "think of the unthinkable" is to display one's prowess in handling a cosmic copperhead without dismay. Since the copperhead is only abstract at the time the feat is not uncomfortable. But in this area myths can suddenly and without warning turn into unpleasant realities. In point of fact, our snake-handling in South East Asia is not abstract—but, as I said before, I am not commenting on events.

On another level, we all participate in one way or another in this national or international snake-handling when we get into the act in some more or less dramatic way. A lot of our protests and demonstrations, even when they are perfectly valid and reasonable in themselves, take the form of political snake-handling. This, I submit, robs them of their real value, because it isolates our action and protest in a closed realm of images and idols which mean one thing to us and another to our adversaries. *We no longer communicate. We abandon communication in order to celebrate our own favorite group-myths in a ritual pseudo-event.* "News" is largely made up of this liturgy of pseudo-events and irrelevant witness. Let us realize that "Ideals" and "purity of

159

heart" may easily cover a snake-handling approach to political reality.

Everywhere, from extreme right to extreme left, we find people in our society who become "sanctified," set apart, chosen, sealed off in a ritual game of some sort by reason of events enacted in honor of images. They move step by step, taking the nation with them, into realms of commitment and of absurdity, areas where, by virtue of the fact that one has agreed to face some very select irrationality *one is quarantined from the ordinary world of right and wrong.*

The man who has agreed with his peers in the enactment of a symbolic, dangerous and arbitrary event has thereby put himself and them beyond good and evil. They have all entered together into the realm of the gods, and in that realm they find that their action has had amazing consequences: it changes the whole meaning of truth and falsity; it imposes on life an entirely new logic; one must follow on from one irrationality to the next in a demonic consistency dictated by machines.

But here of course, I am speaking of mental snake-handling only at the highest and most mystical echelons of the technological elite. Down on our pedestrian level there is no such mystical security, no such permanent election. We are not initiated into a whole new kingdom of sacred irresponsibilities. We have to repeat some crude fanatical stunt again and again because it never quite takes. However, we have the privilege of remotely participating in the snake-handling exploits of the high-priests of policy and strategy.

On this liturgy of pseudo-events the survival of the human race—or at least its sanity and dignity—are now made to depend.

Our salvation, on the contrary, cannot be sought in this realm of images and idols, of fabricated events and unclear meanings.

*　　*　　*

After all this rambling and conjecturing, it is time to draw a few conclusions. Should the Church turn to the world of modern man and identify with him completely? In all his legitimate aspirations, in all his authentic human hopes and aspirations, obviously it must. If not it betrays him and betrays the Gospel. "Insofar as you did it to one of the least of these my brothers, you did it unto me." (Matthew 25:40) But the Church betrays herself and modern man if she simply identifies with his superstitions, his image-making, his political snake-handling and his idolatries of nation, party, class and race.

The Church has an obligation *not* to join in the incantation of political slogans and in the concoction of pseudo-events, *but to cut clear through the deviousness and ambiguity of both slogans and events by her simplicity and her love.*

"To be simple," says Bonhoeffer, "is to fix one's eye solely on the simple truth of God at a time when all concepts are being confused, distorted and turned upside-down. It is to be single-hearted and not a man of two souls . . . *Not fettered by principles but bound by love for God.* The simple man has been set free from the problems and conflicts of ethical decision."

It is unfortunately true that the Church has to repent of remaining enclosed in parochial concerns, and turn to the outside world. To turn to the world is to recognize our mission and service to man and man's world. We are not in the world for ourselves, for our own spiritual advantage, but for Christ and for the world. We have a mission to reconcile the world with Christ. How can we do this if we do not "turn to the world"? At the same time, in turning to our fellowman and loving him, we will ourselves be reconciled with Christ. What other point has there ever been in preaching the Gospel? Unfortunately the simple business of "making converts" has sometimes obscured all deep understand-

161

ing of what this turning to the world really means as *event*.

The Church is indeed concerned with news: the Good News. The Church is concerned with real events: saving events, the encounter of man and Christ in the reconciliation of man with man. In a sense, there is no other kind of event that matters and there is no other news that matters. To abandon this news, and become implicated in the manufacturing of pseudo-events in order to create an "image" that will then attract converts . . . This is an affront to the world and to Christ. Can it be entirely avoided? I do not know, but one thing must be said about it now: *it has ceased to have any meaning whatever to modern man.*

If *image* means *idol*—and it does—then the Church too can unfortunately make an idol of itself, or identify itself too closely with other idols: nations, region, race, political theory.

Obviously the Church is present in history and is responsible to man in his historical predicament. But let us not take too superficial and too distorted a view of history. Our over-sensitive awareness of ourselves as responsible for "making history" is a grotesque illusion, and it leads us into the morass of pseudo-events. Those who are obsessed with "making history" are responsible for the banality of the bad news which comes more and more to constitute our "history." The Church that takes all this too literally and too seriously needs to go back and read the New Testament, not omitting the book of *Revelation*.

The genuine saving event, the encounter of man with Christ in his encounter of love and reconciliation with his fellowman, is generally *not newsworthy*. Not because there is an ingrained malice in journalists but because such events are not sufficiently visible. In trying to make them newsworthy, or visible, in trying to put them on TV, we often make them altogether incredible—or else reduce them to

162

the common level of banality at which they can no longer be distinguished from pseudo-events.

Finally, no matter how you doctor it, *the pseudo-event cannot be turned into a saving and reconciling event.* Whether it is a display of political snake-handling, or some other demonstration of man's intent to justify his existence by seeing himself in the morning paper, no matter how noble and how Christian the intention may be, no man is ever going to come to the truth through pseudo-events, or be reconciled with his fellowman as a result of pseudo-events. On the contrary, by its very nature the pseudo-event arouses anxiety, suspicion, fear of deception and a full awareness of the inherent weakness of the position which it is supposed to justify.

The great question then is how *do* we communicate with the modern world? If in fact communication has been reduced to pseudo-communication, to the celebration of pseudo-events and the irate clashing of incompatible myth-systems, how are we to avoid falling into this predicament? How are we to avoid the common obsession with pseudo-events in order to construct what seems to us to be a credible idol?

It is a nasty question, but it needs to be considered, for in it is contained the mystery of the evil of our time.

I do not have an answer to the question, but I suspect the root of it is this: if we love our own ideology and our own opinion instead of loving our brother, we will seek only to glorify our ideas and our institutions and by that fact we will make real communication impossible.

I think Bonhoeffer was absolutely right when he said our real task is to bear in ourselves the fury of the world against Christ in order to reconcile the world with Christ (a statement that does not accord with the superficial worldliness of some of Bonhoeffer's disciples). But let us take care that

163

the fury of the world is not merely directed against our own ethical or political ideals, worse still our image of ourselves incarnated in our particular mode of symbolic protest.

When I began this letter I did not promise an answer, I only promised a question. Our own lifetime will not suffice to bring us close to the answer. But the root of the answer is the love of Christ and the ground is the sinful heart of sinful man as he really is—as we really are, you, and I, and our disconcerting neighbor.

The Hot Summer
of Sixty-Seven

THE FOLLOWING PAGES ARE PRESENTED WITHOUT APOLOGY
for their inadequacy. Who can pretend to give a satisfactory
explanation of the events in Newark, Detroit, and so many
other northern and Eastern cities in this summer of nineteen
sixty-seven? These are my own hasty and personal reactions.
They were not originally intended for publication at all. I
simply wanted to share a few ideas with my friends, and
particularly with readers of an essay I had previously written—"Letters to a White Liberal"—during the "Birmingham Summer" of 1963. This essay was published in the book
Seeds of Destruction. Many readers thought that my views
were too pessimistic. Recently, however, I was gratified by
the way in which one of my reviewers—Martin Marty, who
condemned the book—took back his judgment and admitted
that the events of this summer put things in a different light
(*National Catholic Reporter,* Aug. 30, 1967).

In the "Letters to a White Liberal" I was interpreting the
efforts of Dr. Martin Luther King to solve the race problem
by Christian non-violence. I said at that time that this was
the *last chance* to really do something by a peaceful revolution and that it was perhaps already too late. I maintained
then, as I do now, that the only possible solution was for
Negroes and whites to pool their resources and work together for a radical and creative change in our social structures. The only hope of peace and order would be, I think,
the creation of a truly new and truly "Great Society" in
which the two races could share the same advantages not
only on paper but in fact. I held (and still hold) that only

a deep Christian renewal of conscience and consciousness on the part of black and white could make this possible. In other words political change, however momentous, would be useless without reconciliation. I felt that in 1963 there was still a chance of this taking place, but that time was just about running out. I added that if this failed, the only prospect was violence. In fact, the murder of the three civil rights workers in Mississippi the following year, the Liuzzo and Daniels murders, then Watts were all steps in the direction of hopelessness.

It also seems to me that the gradual, irreversible escalation in Vietnam has had a lot to do with the violence at home. There is such a thing as mental contamination. Bad ideas can be very contagious. In Vietnam the U.S. has officially adopted the policy that the best way to get across an idea is by fire and dynamite. Is it surprising that the Negro has caught on, and decided that he will try a little bit of the same? Note also that Vietnam seems to teach another perilous lesson: we know how to escalate, but we apparently don't know how to reverse the process and de-escalate. There is only one way: up. Make it hotter. Make it worse. This does not make the prospects for the future in our cities very pleasant. The Negroes are very likely to escalate too, without knowing how to put the thing in reverse. In my opinion, this is practically certain. And obviously white society is not going to stand around idly and let it happen without a reply in kind, indeed without anticipating it perhaps with "preventive first strikes." We'll see.

The Black Power movement has now, in any case, replaced Christian non-violence. Dr. King no longer retains his position of preeminent moral authority as the greatest Negro leader. But though the Black Power movement is trying to channel the exploding energies of the Negro ghettoes in a political direction, we can see that the violence of today

166

is, and the violence to come will probably be, more and more aimless, nihilistic, arbitrary, destructive and non-amenable to reasonable control.

Already it is evident that those whites who reviled Dr. King as a "Communist" and rabble rouser will have reason to regret that the guidance of the Negro struggle for rights has slipped from his hands into the hands of those who hold rifles.

Indeed, this is no longer a Negro struggle for legal rights but a more elemental, nihilistic revolution which these notes will attempt to consider.

I would like to emphasize two points: 1. The situation is now really serious. Violence will *certainly* continue. 2. This demands great realism and foresight on the part of everyone. We must learn to deal with this and all our other critical problems with as few delusions as possible, whether they be optimistic or fatalistic and destructive. The point is this: we are on the edge of revolution, perhaps even a limited civil war. Certainly a kind of civil cold war. But can we keep this violence from becoming purely catastrophic? The problem of racial conflict is part and parcel of the whole problem of human violence anyway, all the way up from the suppressed inarticulate hate feelings of interpersonal family and job conflicts to the question of the H-bomb and mass extermination. The problem is in ourselves. It is everybody's problem. The racial conflict is only *one* symptom.

In order to understand the racial violence that confronts us we need first of all to interpret what it is trying to say. When we see pictures of Detroit looking like a city that has just undergone an air raid we realize that this is no longer a political struggle to obtain rights guaranteed by law in the existing order of things. What we have, on the contrary, is a massive attack on the order itself. What is being attacked is not just regional prejudice, not just "police brutality," but

167

the system we live in. This is not a campaign for civil rights, it is in effect a kind of declaration of war. The Negroes are saying, on various different levels, that white American society is so unjust, so corrupt, so hopeless, so tied up in its own inner contradictions that it deserves to be attacked and even, if possible, destroyed. The end justifies the means. No means are to be considered foul. Every form of trickery and violence has been used against them and they intend to return the compliment.

Why are the Negroes, themselves American citizens, saying such a drastic thing? (And of course here we have to qualify: to what extent is this what they are "all" saying? To what extent is this still only the contention of a rabid minority? To what extent can we still avoid driving all the moderate Negroes to this same extreme position? I am concerned here only with spelling out the message of the current riots.)

There is one snap answer: Communists. This is a knee-jerk reaction that is so tired, so automatic, so futile that it is fatal. It cannot give a true understanding of what we are contending with. It makes us hunt imaginary enemies instead of trying to confront the complexities of a human problem that is terribly near. It puts the root of the evil thousands of miles away, it exonerates our own system from all defect and all guilt, and makes us forget to look for the solution where we have to find it: in our own backyard. In fact, in our own heart.

It is true that the Negro revolution in our country is in fact part of a world revolution. And the Communists are trying to exploit that world revolution for their own ends. But this is something much deeper and more elemental than a political revolution, and if it is not understood in depth it can lead to fatal mistakes. The Negroes of America have become conscious of the worldwide nature of the violent conflict which they interpret in terms of color. Whether this interpretation is naive, false, stupid and so on is beside the

168

point. It is an interpretation which, for better or for worse, is gradually coming to have an ever greater influence everywhere. I fully admit that it may be absurd to look at things that way, it may even be suicidal: but nevertheless we live in a world which for practical purposes is now a racist world. God knows it should not be!

The Negroes of America have—at least the most militant elements have—adopted a fundamentally racist position. They wish now not to become integrated but to assert their own identity in the most forceful possible manner and, if possible, even to separate from the whites. Obviously, apart from the dreams of fanatics, such a separation is completely impossible. Racism which attempts to evade the problem simply intensifies it. Meanwhile the Negroes interpret the war in Asia as a color-war, in which they are asked to support white power in an attempt to subjugate Asian colored people. Once again, this is a sweeping over-simplification: but it is what people are thinking, and it is a basis for their decisions. Drastic decisions to bomb and burn at home.

Now this same pattern is reproducing itself all over the world. Everywhere, in Africa, Asia, Melanesia, you find movements that are something more than political. They are messianic, quasi-political, eschatological movements which all have certain factors in common: they are violently hostile to white European-American civilization, and they are anti-Christian because they identify Christ as a "white God." Yet at the same time they tend to incorporate a kind of Christian eschatology with elements of pagan religion. The result: dedicated, sometimes fanatical, sometimes crazy messianic movements which all believe themselves called to resist, reject and if possible destroy white civilization and to put in its place a new culture which takes on the aspect of a religious messianic Kingdom and a new creation, a totally new kind of existence.

Whatever may be the value of these cultic movements,

169

they are not only very influential but they are symptoms that have the highest significance. They represent an entirely new consciousness, an awakening of an awareness and of an intent that white people can barely grasp, let alone understand dispassionately. Yet it is of the greatest importance for us to *understand* this new consciousness if we can. The place where this new consciousness comes closest to us is in the Negro ghettoes of our own country. The new highly destructive riots are manifestations of this new mythical interpretation of present-day reality: a sense that white society has been judged and found wanting, that it has been consistently cruel, hypocritical, unjust, inhuman. That the day of retribution has come. It is the time of judgment and of blood. All these movements start with a violent repudiation of white culture and of everything that it stands for: i.e., everything that implies its superiority, everything that justifies the subjection of non-white peoples and cultures.

So there is first of all a spasm of rejection. This rejection is most effectively preached by some prophetic figure who is primarily a liberator, also mythologized as a prophet-messiah, and usually (by courtesy of an obliging opposition) elevated in due course to the rank of martyr. Lumumba is a case in point. And in America we have also had Malcolm X, an uncompromising black separatist, who was "martyred" and has now become a symbol of the black man who found his identity by a kind of moral liberation: he was imprisoned in the underworld by the corrupt society of whitey. He fought his way free, became a fearless and lucid black man who realized that no white man could be trusted, et cetera. This is becoming a standard pattern all over the world.

The colored peoples form the vast majority of the world's population, and also are the have-nots in a world where sixty percent of the wealth is in the hands of a tiny minority of

170

Americans. These colored people have, they think, a mission first of all to liberate themselves from the whites, and second, perhaps even to destroy white civilization if this becomes necessary.

Obviously, white civilization is not about to let itself be passively destroyed.

Note that I am simply spelling out the message: I am not saying whether the message is nuts, or whether it may have something to it: I am saying that it has to be taken seriously insofar as it is an expression of impassioned convictions which will gradually take clearer shape in the minds of millions of people in the next ten years or so.

That being the case, we have to readjust our own thinking at least on a few points like the following.

1. Our own well-meant efforts to help solve economic and political problems, at home or abroad, whether by peaceful aid (Alliance for Progress, Peace Corps) or by business or by military support and intervention, are going to be interpreted, rightly or wrongly, as strategy to gain or to maintain control over others. This also goes for the desperate and belated efforts to improve life in the ghettoes at home: playgrounds, schools, and so on. No one is about to accept these as valid solutions of anything.

2. The American ideology of freedom and democracy is now largely discredited everywhere, even among a significant proportion of Americans. The fervent celebration of American ideals by Congressmen and publicists is useful mainly for bolstering up their own morale. In others, even in those who want to agree, this incantation raises more and more serious doubts. Can we possibly be sincere about these grandiose concepts? Do we believe that they are likely to be used in really constructive ways to solve our problems? Or are they going to become fanatical shibboleths to justify an armed and violent reaction on the part of white society

171

against the attacks leveled against it? In other words, is "freedom" simply going to become the copyrighted trademark of the States Rights types, the KKK, the CIA or the Pentagon? In other words will "freedom" simply mean armed repression? What I am saying is this: our American ideals and principles can retain their credibility only insofar as they are capable of *radical adaptation* to this crisis, and *creative response* to a turbulent time that is heavy with unimagined possibilities both for growth and for pathological decay. Slogans are not enough. And slogans backed up with machine guns and napalm are not inspiring much real belief! They only consolidate hatred and determined opposition. "Freedom" cannot retain its meaning if it continues to be only freedom for some based on the violent repression of others.

3. Instead of merely reacting emotionally to the threat of violence and destruction, we need to understand the spiritual and psychological implications of the present crisis, first of all in the Negro in America and then in the colored races everywhere. The non-violent movement in America worked (and doubtless continues to work) only for a few dedicated and trained specialists who really understood it and practiced it rightly. For the majority both of Negroes and of whites, its message has never been really clear. For the American Negro, in an intense identity crisis, feeling himself a morally mutilated non-person reduced to playing a role determined entirely for him by someone else, non-violence was not yet practicable. Only for exceptionally mature and spiritually gifted people (of whom there are perhaps still many) was it really meaningful. For the penniless and hopeless Negro who stood aside and viewed it from afar, non-violence simply reinforced the feelings of hopeless passivity and despair which were his. On the other hand, an appeal to violence, an assurance that he could burn houses and loot

172

stores with relative impunity, proved an outlet to explosive suppressed hate—more satisfying to him than just being beaten over the head for the ten thousandth time by a Southern cop, without recourse to anyone on this earth.

It is pointless to say that the laws guarantee the Negro all the same rights as white people. We know that the laws are not enforced and the Negro is often denied his obvious rights; but also economically speaking the Negro remains in the same position as he was before, perhaps worse. He is convinced that there is no real place for him in our established society except the very secondary place which we will give him. It is a psychological impossibility for most white Americans really to accept a Negro as an equal, in every respect, and the violent struggle against open housing has proved it. This incidentally is one of the reasons why Negroes have finally resorted to a war on white property which may eventually attain very serious proportions (sabotage of central power plants or of water supply). In short: the Negro considers that it is impossible for him really to acquire a place as an equal in this society of ours. Such being the case he will do the best he can to louse things up and make them unpleasant for whitey. It is perhaps not a rational or virtuous decision in terms of our own very nice ethic, but he is no longer interested in our own very nice ethic. We must not be too surprised if he fails to respond to our exhortations in this regard—especially when they emanate from the Chief of Police.

4. The real problem as I see it is this: the limited and distorted view which almost inevitably dictates a white reaction of violence. Now that the Negro in America has clearly and articulately declared war on white property and white power—if not already on the white man as such—the reaction of the whites is easily predictable. I already pointed to it four years ago. A violent clamp-down, ruthless retaliation,

173

both organized and non-organized, official and unofficial. An all-out indiscriminate effort to put down the Negro at any cost. Let us be quite clear about it: the Negro himself seems to be provoking this kind of reaction. He seems to *want* this kind of reaction. The seriousness of this possibility of violence arises not from a logical sequence of political and economic causes, but from pathological involvement in violence on both sides, white and Negro.

The problem as I see it is no longer merely political or economic or legal or what have you (it was never merely that). It is a spiritual and psychological problem of a society which has developed too fast and too far for the psychic capacities of its members, who can no longer cope with their inner hostilities and destructiveness. They can no longer really manage their lives in a fully reasonable and human way—only by resort to extreme and possibly destructive maneuvers. A nuclear arms race. A race to get on the moon. A stupid war in Asia that cannot be won by either side. An affluent economy depending on built-in obsolescence and the ever increasing consumption of more goodies than anyone can comfortably consume. A bored, ambivalent over-stimulation of violence and sex. We are living in a society which for all its unquestionable advantages and all its fantastic ingenuity just does not seem to be able to provide people with lives that are fully human and fully real.

There are wonderful people in it, and it is a marvel we are not ten times crazier than we already are, but we have to face the fact that we live in a pretty sick culture. Now if in this sick society, where there are a lot of very scared, very upset, very unrealistic people who feel themselves more and more violently threatened, everyone starts buying guns and preparing to shoot each other up (remember the fuss about the gun in the fallout shelter in 1962), we are going to have an unparalleled mess. The result may eventually be that people will decide that the only way to maintain some semblance of order will be the creation of a semifacist state with storm troopers and, yes, concentration camps. And many will be quite ready to accept it if the Negroes continue to make them ready.

To sum it up: the problem as I see it is this. The Negro has in some sense abandoned the struggle for Civil Rights. He has given up Christian non-violence as futile idealism. He has decided that whitey only understands one kind of language: violence. The Negro has concluded that if whitey wants to terrorize Vietnamese with napalm and other cozy instruments of war, he should have a little taste of what fire and terror feel like at home. So in effect the Negro is declaring guerilla war on white society. "The Negro" I say, meaning those who have decided to take upon themselves the mandate to represent all black men by acting in their name. Obviously, the majority of Negroes would still prefer to go on as best they can and at least have relatively peaceful, relatively livable lives. These moderate Negroes will perhaps have the worst time of all, caught in between two violent groups of extremists and becoming the victims of everybody. They will be tempted to become extremists themselves. Their choice is limited. They cannot join the KKK!

Now the Negro knows, or should know, that he cannot really win this kind of civil war. But he can become so provocative as to dislocate this highly organized technological system of ours. If President Johnson continues trying to pull the country together by getting it more and more involved in fighting an outside enemy (Asians) and if the country gets mixed up in a war with China, and if the Negro then decides it is a good time to shake the foundations here at home . . . I need not elaborate on the picture. It could be catastrophic. But in any event, there is nothing in sight

175

but the violence of desperation *unless* it turns out that the SNCC people are smart enough to really gain some kind of political power for the Negro and get him really implicated in the affairs of the nation. Maybe! I would not gamble on it myself. The forces involved are too unpredictable, and far too explosive.

A victorious Negro revolution is out of the question unless the country is crippled by some disaster (such as nuclear war or catastrophic collapse of economy). The most likely thing is that extreme provocation by irrational violence may create such disorder and such panic in the country that a new order based on force (a police state) may have to be established. In that event, the possibility of extremists on the white side taking over and ruling by irrational and arbitrary violence is very likely. Even "prison camps" for Negroes and then for other unacceptables are not beyond the bounds of possibility. At times one feels that the Negroes are unconsciously willing to provoke this.

Much as we may all sympathize with the frustrations of the Negro, and much as we may tolerantly understand his drive for a new sense of identity by means of aggressive and separatist assertion, we cannot get around the fact that this is simply another form of the same racist delusion that keeps cropping up everywhere in different forms. The trouble with delusionary thinking is that, starting perhaps from a basis of reality (or even from no real basis whatever!), it proceeds to exempt emotion and violence from all reasonable control. It creates a sense of transcendent justification, of absolute validity, a seemingly plausible claim to be beyond good and evil, in an area where anything goes. The result is an explosion of emotion, an orgiastic climax of hate which carries everything before it until its power is spent. We have seen this at work in Nazism—its extreme manifesttation, backed by all the instruments of political and military power. We have seen it in Russian anti-semitism, in French hatred of Algerians, in Arab hatred of Jews, in conflict between Hindu and Moslem, between Sudanese Moslems and Black Africans. We see it in South African apartheid and in American segregationism.

The new segregationism now preached by the Black Power movement is unfortunately no improvement. It is little more than desperation, which substitutes the emotional orgy for a hopeless and frustrated effort to achieve anything by ordinary political means. The only thing that can be said for it at the moment is that it is probably not yet as general as it seems. It is taken with full seriousness by a minority of Negro extremists. It is still taken, I think, with a grain of salt by the majority of American Negroes who know it won't work but who are perhaps secretly hopeful that it will stir things up enough to influence the whites more forcefully than anything that has so far happened. In my opinion, the real aim of the Black Power people is still probably to use the noise about separation as a threat rather than as a serious political policy. On the other hand, we are in a climate of dangerous mental contagion in which there is no guarantee that anyone will continue to act reasonably once an emotional chain reaction gets going. In a situation like this, the delusions on both sides reinforce and aggravate each other, and there is enough emotional violence packed into America today to blow the whole place sky high, no matter how reasonable some of us may still hope to be.

One of our own tasks (and perhaps now it is too late to tackle it effectively) is the serious examination of the delusions behind our own thinking. For instance: what about the contradiction implied in our willingness to preserve the Union by a resort to violence that will inevitably destroy it? Or, alternately: what about the internal contradiction in our apparent willingness to preserve "freedom" by institut-

177

ing a police state? This simply ties in with so many other contradictions: our determination to "liberate" South East Asians from Communism by burning them, if necessary, to death. Of course we'd much rather do it by giving them candy bars but, when the chips are down. . . . The big question to which all these others add up is: have our formulas about democracy finally become just that, empty formulas, and masks for delusionary thinking? If that is the case, then we had better get to grips with reality. The Negroes are trying to point to a redefinition of reality: they are saying that they find themselves in a society in which theoretically everything is fine for them and where in fact they have no hope of being fully accepted in every way as human beings on an equal basis with others. The affirmation of this has now become so strident and so harsh that, whether you agree or not, you are bound to listen. This does not make all the conclusions automatically right. On the contrary, the stridency and hate may simply be attempts to *enforce* impossible conclusions.

On the other hand, we have to recognize that a climate of irrationality and panic is just what the extremists of both sides thrive on. If everyone is kept in a state of fear and uncertainty, if tensions are maintained at a high pitch, then explosions and reprisals can be managed by those who think they will profit by them. The policy of the Black Power movement is twofold: to use this threat of revolutionary terror in order to give the Negro himself more confidence, and in order to get some kind of leverage with which to work on whitey. In other words, it is an attempt to consolidate all American Negroes into a bloc with unequivocal bargaining power. But this bid for power rests on the exploitation of free-floating and radically uncontrollable violence which may at any time get out of hand. If and when the violence becomes so widespread as to disrupt American society, there may be a real civil war, and the Black Power program takes this as a realistic, acceptable option.

Much as I hate to see such a situation arise, I still feel it is one to which the Negroes have been driven by us. I believe we still have to take this into account in our attempts to respond. I do not think any form of white extremism will be an adequate answer. And I do hope that we will keep our heads enough to prevent a complete polarization, a split which makes all reasonable communication between the races impossible. We must continue to treat our Negro friends as persons and as friends, not as members of a hostile and incomprehensible species, and it is to be hoped that they will do us the same honor. Above all, the Negro has a right to self-respect in his identity as a person of his race and we must continue to do all that we can to help him in this—as well as doing all we can to see that his human and civil rights are guaranteed him, even when he may seem to be acting in such a way as to forfeit them in the eyes of a truculent and critical white society.

As Christians, we must remember that in Christ there is no meaning to racial divisions. There is no white and black in Christ: but if Christianity is being discredited in the eyes of Negroes, that does not dispense us from our duty to be authentic Christians toward the Negro whether he likes us or not. It is not our job to convince him that Christianity is "true" or "genuine," but to live up to what we ourselves profess to believe, so that we may not be judged by God for a mere lip-service that has (as we now begin to realize too late) reached the proportions of worldwide scandal.

Appendix: The Question of Guilt

A number of readers of "Letters to a White Liberal" object to the idea that the racial conflict and its consequences are largely the "fault" of the white race, and that it is necessary to admit "guilt" in a certain sense, in order to deal with the problem. Of course the word "guilt" may be ambiguous here. At the same time, it is possible that these readers have an exclusively individualistic notion of responsibility. They do not feel they are "at fault" or responsible for a wrong except when they have made a deliberate personal choice of something they know to be out of line, and feel shame for having done so. They do not believe that they have made any such choice in regard to Negroes, and do not see how any responsibility attaches to them. They think they are not "unjust" to the Negro and that they owe him nothing. They are in fact free to sit back and condemn everything he does. The Negro is the one who is "wrong."

There is, however, such a thing as collective responsibility, and collective guilt. This is not quite the same as personal responsibility and personal guilt, because it does not usually follow from a direct fully conscious act of choice. Few of us have actively and consciously *chosen* to oppress and mistreat the Negro. But nevertheless we have all more or less acquiesced in and consented to a state of affairs in which the Negro is treated unjustly, and in which his unjust treatment is directly or indirectly to the advantage of people like ourselves, people with whom we agree and collaborate, people with whom we are in fact identified. So that even if in theory the white man may believe himself to be well disposed toward the Negro—and never gets into a bind in which he proves himself to be otherwise—we all collectively contribute to a situation in which the Negro has to live and act as our inferior. I am personally convinced that most white people who think themselves very "fair" to the Negro show, by the way they imagine themselves "fair," that they consider the Negro an inferior type of human being, a sort of "minor," and their "fairness" consists in giving him certain benefits provided he "keeps in his place," the place they have allocated to him as an inferior. I would like to say that this state of mind is itself an act of inhumanity and injustice against the Negro and is in fact at the root of the trouble with the Negro, so that anyone who holds such opinions, even in the best of faith, is contributing actively to the violence of the present situation whether he realizes it or not. One of the reasons why the Negro has finally in desperation become so hostile and truculent toward Whitey is that he wants to bring this fact out into the open. He wants to push things to the point where no one can any longer pretend that by treating the Negro as a minor and a semi-savage he is being "just" and "fair." On the contrary, this kind of treatment is part of a whole subtle system of moral and psychological oppression which is essentially *violent*. Anyone who has such an attitude is then partly responsible for what is going on, and in that sense "guilty."

In the case of collective guilt like this, as also in other such cases (favoring an unjust war, participating in the economic oppression of colonials, and so forth), it is necessary for a man who wants to be in good faith to cease identifying himself with actions that are causing the evil in question, and to disclaim any intention of further participating in these acts, while also doing whatever he can to restore the balance of justice and of violated rights. The problem is of course that in deep and complex problems of this nature, the responsibility goes far into the area of the unconscious attitudes and prejudices we all have, and in that area we cannot control all our reactions at will. That is what makes the whole thing so terribly hard. But we must at least desire to have a lucid, honest and non-mythical view of the hard realities, in order to try to deal with them.

181

The Meaning of Malcolm X

THE *Autobiography of Malcolm X* IS A BOOK OF DECISIVE importance. It is widely read, especially on campuses, and it is certainly helping to crystallize revolutionary thought among students. For one thing, it adds immeasurably to the picture of Malcolm X formed by the mass-media during his life, and gives us some idea of the possibilities that he might have actualized if he had not been brutally eliminated from the political scene. The picture most of us had of him was inadequate, though not altogether untrue. We saw him as a militant, rigid, somewhat fanatical agitator, absolutely committed to a naive racist mystique and to a religious organization which was made to sound like a Negro SS. This was partially true of the Malcolm X who came dramatically into view in the early sixties as the most active organizer of the Black Muslims, the right-hand man of their founder, Elijah Muhammad. Malcolm X was then known to be a former thief and hustler who had become a Black Muslim in prison. He received a grudging and fearful respect as one who sought to rehabilitate others like himself by the discipline of an organized religious and paramilitary existence. He and his cohorts explicitly rejected the values of white society along with the white man's image of himself, of the black, and of the world at large.

Even if there were no more to his life than this, his autobiography would not be without interest. But this book shows that there was much more. To begin with, Malcolm X was undoubtedly more gifted, more intelligent, more flexible than he appeared to be when he was deliberately

182

effacing himself behind the ideas and programs of "The Honorable Mr. Elijah Muhammad." Also, his loyalty to the Muslim leader, which seems to have been both simple and genuine, was perhaps too naive. If the Black Muslims had not turned against him and expelled him, Malcolm would possibly have remained content with limitations that seriously restricted his growth. It may be added that the story of his break with the Black Muslims, and even more the story of his death, remain very mysterious. Was he murdered by his former brethren? There is plenty of evidence that he *expected* them to murder him. But he knew himself to be menaced also by others. The epilogue added to this story by the reporter to whom it was narrated does not help us to penetrate the mystery of his assassination. It is certainly strange that Malcolm X should have been gunned down by three men in the front row of the auditorium where he habitually spoke to his own followers, that the men got away even though a special detail of twenty policemen was supposed to have been posted in the hall. Nothing has ever been made public that offers any satisfactory explanation of the murder.

The story of Malcolm X falls into three distinct parts. The son of a Negro preacher, who was also a Black Nationalist and was murdered by whites, Malcolm moved in his teens from a small town in Michigan to Roxbury, the Negro ghetto of Boston. There and in Harlem he got mixed up in every kind of underworld activity: numbers, dope, pandering, burglary. Operating with a small gang of thieves which included two white girls, he was caught and sentenced. In prison, he began to read voraciously. He was converted to the Black Muslims by letters from one of his brothers. Already in prison he became a propagandist for the teachings of Elijah Muhammad, and as soon as he was out of jail he went to meet the Black Muslim leader. In a short time he proved himself to be an unusually effective organizer, and thanks to his efforts the Muslims began to spread all over the country, attracting a great deal of attention in the mass media by their denunciations of the whites and their absolute segregationism. Like the Black Nationalists of Marcus Garvey, the Muslims declare that they wish to live completely separate from the "white devils," and are looking for separate territory in which to do so.

Can all this be completely dismissed merely as a racism which is by definition a pure myth? Certainly there is a generous element of illusion in the way the idea is elaborated. But is there nevertheless an element of truth in the inexorable refusal to accept *any* profession of sincere friendship, interest, compassion from *any* white man? Malcolm X later recognized that his own earlier refusals were too absolute, that some kind of dialogue between the races had to be possible, some kind of collaboration had to be admitted. Yet he felt that the ordinary white liberal professions of sincerity were not good enough, and he insisted on a tactic of refusal which declared, both implicitly and explicitly, that however honest the white man might feel himself to be subjectively, the Negro could not objectively accept his protestations of concern at their face value. They were bound to prove deceptive because the white man could not change his essentially distorted view of the relationship between the races. Even when the white man indulged in a veritable cult of the Negro, he betrayed his basic conviction that the Negro was somehow more of an animal, a distinct and exotic species of human being. Observation of whites visiting Harlem in search of certain types of recreation made this supposition rather plausible. Meanwhile, even the most decent, most buttoned-up kind of liberalism still consists in an invitation to Negroes to come and join a superior race—together with concrete refusals to tolerate too close an intimacy when the invitation is accepted.

184

On the other hand, the Black Muslims offer a rather sketchy and not always accurate presentation of the teachings of Islam. On the grounds that Islam is "the original black man's religion," the Black Muslims of America preach a predominantly negative doctrine; anti-Christian and anti-white. In spite of the fact that Malcolm protested against being stereotyped as a preacher of race hatred, there is unquestionably a strong racist element in the Black Muslim code. This is, in fact, a ghetto religion, and the story of Malcolm's relations with Elijah Muhammad suggests that without a ghetto basis for his power, Elijah Muhammad would not last long. The Black Muslims are not without their positive qualities (they do after all help hundreds of Negroes to recover their dignity as human beings who feel that life has a meaning). But they apparently believe a rather unusual amount of naive mythology (including an elaborate account of how the white race was produced by "bleaching" out a certain number of Negroes, over a stretch of many generations, on the island of Patmos—or was it Cyprus?). One might also remark in passing that the idea of Islam as a "black man's religion," contrasted with Christianity as a religion of white slave traders, is a bit over-simplified. After all, the Arab Muslims have always been energetic exploiters of the raw slave material which black Africa presented to them, and they have consistently justified themselves with words like these from the *Koran:* "We have raised some people above others by degrees so they might force one another to compulsory labor" (43:32). In short, both Christians and Muslims have known how to make use of their Scriptures to justify racial injustice when occasion demanded.

Meanwhile, in post-colonial Africa, the relations between Black Africans and Arab Muslims are by no means cordial (witness the bloody conflict in and around the Sudan and Senegal). Nor does this apply merely to rivalry between Muslims and Black Christians. Native Africa is as tragically

185

divided by racial authority as any other part of the world.

The whole second part of the life of Malcolm X, the chapters devoted to his life as a Black Muslim, are rather disconcerting. In order to understand them we have to realize that they are made up of material narrated by Malcolm to his ghost-writer during the time when he was still a loyal follower of Elijah Muhammad, and no changes were made in this material afterwards. Hence the middle section of the book, a faithful portrait of the Black Muslim militant who preached that all whites were devils, measures up to what we were all led to expect by the mass-media. It is an incredible mixture of sincerity, mythology, and militant devotion to what Malcolm believed to be the real cause of the Black Man—the only way to solve his problems. He preaches a foreshortened, impassioned, obsessive racist eschatology which, for all its sweeping ruthlessness, has so far not directly promoted any really significant political action, whether violent or non-violent. But it has certainly contributed much to a particular outlook which, exploited and distorted by the mass-media, has increased tensions, tightened polarities, and doubtless had much to do not only with "hot summer" rioting but even with the death of Malcolm X himself.

The most impressive thing about the *Autobiography of Malcolm X* is, however, the way in which Malcolm outgrew this phase of his development. His expulsion from the Black Muslims was evidently due to jealousies and rivalries within the movement. The peculiar religious temperament of Elijah Muhammad, filled with inner contradictions and inconsistencies not uncommon in certain messiah types, undoubtedly had much to do with it. Malcolm was evidently too big and too smart for the movement, and though he honestly tried to remain an obedient subordinate, this was not possible. He had definitely taken over the center of the stage, and so he had to be driven off it. When he was once again on his own

186

he quickly discovered a whole new dimension of things. He began to get a much deeper, more mature, more sophisticated and more nuanced understanding of the revolutionary situation. He also, at the same time, experienced an unusual deepening of his religious experience of Islam.

The final chapters of the autobiography show us a completely new person. In fact, for the first time we see Malcolm X as a whole person rather than as a character of great energy driven by the symbiotic obsessions of his ghetto milieu. The central fact in this transformation was the religious experience of the *Hajj*, or the pilgrimage to Mecca, which is one of the basic obligations of a Muslim. (I am now using the term Muslim in its complete and "catholic" sense, and no longer in reference to the Black Muslim foreshortening of Islamism.) Not only was his Islamic faith clarified, not only were many gross misapprehensions corrected, but above all he experienced an extraordinary sense of *community*, of brotherhood with other Muslim pilgrims from all parts of the world, *including many who were white*. After the *Hajj*, which he performed with exemplary devotion and with all the meticulous assent of the convert, Malcolm was no longer thinking in terms of straight racist polarities. Before returning to America, he visited some of the new African nations (where he was a great success) and acquired a new sense of the global revolution of which the Negro revolution in America is only a small part. He saw that it was not a simple question of black angels and white devils in the cities of the United States, but of the formerly colonial, under-developed world, filled with black, white, yellow, red, brown and mestizo populations (in other words the majority of the human race), against a highly developed affluent technological society which cannot really help the others in their struggle for liberation because it needs them to remain in a state of economic and political tutelage.

When Malcolm X returned from his pilgrimage to Mecca,

he had changed in two very important ways. First he was an authentic Muslim with a real experience of the meaning of Islam. Second he was no longer a creature of the ghetto. He was ready to become a world citizen. He had begun to experience contemporary realities in a way that remains inaccessible to white travelers in quest of the exotic who see the whole Third World as a potential Acapulco.

Malcolm X returned to America as a revolutionary who could some day have used his African experience and contacts in ways we can barely imagine. Perhaps few people really understood precisely what his new potentialities were, but evidently both white and black enemies of the man sensed that he was, in their terms, highly dangerous.

The meaning of this autobiography comes clear in the final chapters: Malcolm X first outgrew the ghetto underworld of prostitution, dope and crime. He then outgrew the religious underworld, the spiritual power structure that thrives on a ghetto mystique. He was finally attaining to the freedom and fullness of understanding that gives some (still rare) American Negroes the sense of belonging to a world movement that makes them independent, to some extent, of purely American limitations and pressures. Malcolm grew too fast. He was too articulate. He was made to pay for it. The impact of his message to others that may follow him has only been made stronger and more emphatic by his death.

Malcolm X realized that he would not live to read his life-story in print. This he prophesied correctly. He also several times announced that after his death he would be despised and discredited as a stereotype of racist-hatred. In this his intuition was less accurate. His autobiography reveals a person whose struggles are understandable, whose errors we can condone. He was a fighter whose sincerity and courage we cannot help admiring, and who might have become a genuine revolutionary leader—with portentious effect in American society!

188

Part Four

Violence and the Death of God: or God as Unknown Soldier

SINCE THE ESSAYS IN THIS SECTION SPELL OUT SOME OF THE things I have against the "Death-of-God" theology, it is only fair that I begin by saying what I think can be said *for* it.

First of all, the radical Death-of-God theologians are not only to be taken very seriously as Christians, but they are characteristic products of a real theological revival. The present time, for all its confusions and ambiguities, is certainly one of theological ferment: it is one of the most active periods in the history of theological thought. This fruitfulness and creativity have been due largely to men like Karl Barth, Paul Tillich, Karl Rahner, Jacques Maritain, Rudolf Bultmann and the other well-known names of the first half of the century. There are many others appearing on all sides after the Council. The Honest-to-God set in England is perhaps overly naive, and it is their popular theology that I have tended to question most. In America, there is no coherent still less unanimous Death-of-God movement. There is quite a lot of variety in the thinking of Altizer (often hard to follow), Hamilton (apostle to Playboy) and Vahanian, a serious iconoclast with whom I tend most consistently to agree. In what follows, I am considering the "Death of God" chiefly from the viewpoint of Vahanian.

The basic premise of the Death-of-God theology is not, of course, the old and out-worn scientific atheism of the nineteenth century. For this radical theology, the whole question of God's objective existence is completely irrelevant. The approach is altogether different: man's capacity

191

to experience and to apprehend religious thought and concepts of God. Traditional theology has tended to assume that man experienced in himself a need for ultimate certitude which could only be satisfied by God's manifestation of himself in revealed truth. The Death of God starts by taking it as axiomatic that no modern man in good faith can really have an authentic religious experience that is not an experience of God's *absence*. Traditional theology posits God's hidden presence and works to make that presence manifest. In the light of God's presence and of his love, everything else becomes clear. God is the key to everything. The Death-of-God theology begins with a claim that this whole approach has utterly failed: to argue that man feels in himself a need for God, to go on to speak of the presence of God, and to explain everything else in this light is, it believes, simply to substitute ideas about God for gratuitously assumed "presence" of God and thus to make him all the more inexorably absent. In other words, it is not only that traditional theology proves nothing, but it antagonizes and alienates modern man and makes it all the more difficult for him to find any meaning whatever in the concept of God.

Now this is no new or revolutionary discovery. The approach to God "as unknown" has always had a recognized place in Catholic theology, and Protestantism also asserted from the beginning that a too sophisticated intellectual and rational structure in theology might neutralize the living and personal encounter with the inscrutable God of revelation in faith. Traditional theology itself has always recognized the insufficiency of propositions *about* God and *about* redemption which tend to objectify God and set him off at arms length so that he can be "used" and "manipulated." Such a god becomes completely unreal—a mere convenience, serving man's purposes, a social commodity, a cosmic tranquillizer to be packaged and marketed along with any other product. The Death of God is a necessary iconoclastic protest against every form of popular religion which has blasphemed God by trying to sell him on the same terms as next year's Chevrolet.

Furthermore, the accusation runs (and I run right with it), this conceptualizing of God has tended more and more to identify the God of the Bible and of the Church with the Angel of the West—the Power or principality which is the "Guiding Spirit" of European-American civilization. The hidden God "whom no man shall see and live" and whose only manifestation is "in Christ" has been claimed as visible and present in the spirit, the ethos, the inner drive and the whole cultural outlook of the Western world. Thus the ways and attitudes of the post-Roman, mediaeval, then renaissance, then enlightenment, then technological West, have come to be seen as the vesture and even as the Face of God. Europe and America became the only true locus of His epiphany. Western man became in fact the manifestation of God in and as Christ. Hence the whole problem of the salvation of the world could be reduced to the task of turning everybody else into a more or less plausible replica of Western man. More grossly, to make Africa Christian, one needed only to make it Belgian, German, English, French. More grossly still, to save the soul of the African one needed only to baptize him and enslave him, thus killing two birds with one stone: gaining black souls for heaven and making a fortune out of Alabama cotton.

In other words, the saving knowledge of God in Christ was simply a matter of incorporation, however rudimentary, in some limb of western "Christian" culture. Obviously the Church was not conscious of doing this, and the tension between Church and culture, Church and state, Church and world, was always maintained at least in theory. But how

193

real was that tension? In actual fact, while "the world" was habitually and consistently denigrated, at least in words, the tension between it and the Church was more and more relaxed. In proportion as the world proved itself able to get along without the Church, the Church became less and less demanding, Christianity issued less and less of a challenge, until finally the Church would allow you practically anything as long as you continued to obey and to conform. A few difficult and symbolic issues like birth control, clerical celibacy, one permanent marriage, remained longer than any other, but are now being corroded away too. More and more the demands of the Church resolved themselves into demands for formal and exterior gestures of pious allegiance to God alone with rather more firm commitments to the claims of Caesar.

The clearest example of this has been in war. The French revolution put the Church in a new position vis-à-vis the state. The state now became hostile and demanding. The position of the Church was increasingly defensive—a matter of difficult concordats which guaranteed at least the integrity of the Church *as institution*. In order to protect these guarantees, the faithful had to be ready to meet the demands of the state in other areas. The State was now in need of larger armies. Conscription was becoming more and more universal. Even clerics, even religious, exempt by their very vocation to follow the counsels of perfection, were required to waive that exemption when necessary to protect the interests of the Church institution in an anticlerical nation (such as France). In other words, one of the ways in which the Church protected her institutional structures in potentially hostile countries was to support the nation in its wars.

One of the few real demands for heroic sacrifice still made by the Church was that the faithful put aside their scruples

194

and fears and obey the nation without question when it summoned them to go to war, even against other supposedly "Christian" nations. Theirs not to reason why. The government knew best. They did not have to inquire too minutely into the causes of the war or into the ways by which it was being waged. Suffice it that the bishops, by their approval, implied that the war and everything about it was "just." And the bishops, in their turn, as good patriots, left all these technicalities to the Ministry of War.

Thus it happened that the Christian gave heroic witness to his God and his faith by a meek, unquestioning obedience even unto death in submission to a Church authority that ordered him to submit to a civil authority that was not necessarily Christian—perhaps even anti-Christian.

Thus in fact God was drafted into all the armies and invited to get out there and kill Himself.

As far as Europe was concerned, these rites were already thoroughly solemnized in World War I, but the Second World War guaranteed their full and complete efficacy. The nihilism and black despair of French literary and atheistic existentialism after World War II gave conclusive evidence that God had been a casualty of the war. He had died in it as one—or all—of its soldiers, both known and unknown. For the United States—which underwent a brief spasm of popular religion after World War II—the immolation has proceeded in Korea and most especially in Vietnam.

The effect of this more or less complete identification of God with "western civilization" and with "western society" regarded as still implicitly Christian has been of course that the crisis of western civilization has also been necessarily a crisis of Christianity and of Christian faith. In this crisis, the Christian position has been one of more and more intolerable ambiguity, since in fact the last remaining elements of Christianity in western culture have all but bled away.

195

The reaction of Christians has been somewhat frantic—where there has been any real reaction at all. One tended to lash out wildly against "materialism" and "secularism" and other scapegoat ideas, and to adopt a rather rigid posture of belief in order to maintain some coherent sense of Christian identity. But now that theologians and churchmen themselves are celebrating the praises of matter and of the secular city, this identity has been further undermined.

The true believers in this state of insecurity and frustration, have only manifested more clearly and more pitifully the contradiction of their inner state. They have come out vociferously for the most bizarre, the most fanatical, the most aberrant causes in politics and culture. You can now find the most ardent Christians lined up in the most ridiculous, regressive, irrational parades. If they were concerned only with flying saucers and conversations with the departed it would not be so bad: but they are also deeply involved in racism, in quasi-fascist nationalism, in every shade of fanatical hate-cult, and in every semi-lunatic pressure group that is all the more self-congratulatory in that it is supported by the affluent as well as by the clergy. Such Christianity is of course a mere monstrosity and tends to make us believe that our Christian institutions are, in Vahanian's words only "the lips with which we praise God while our hearts are far from him." He says:

> The survival of the Christian tradition is handicapped rather than helped by the existence of structures that are Christian in name only. It was doubtless easier to make the conversion from pre-Christian to Christian than it is from post-Christian to Christian. . . . Ultimately, organized religion, with its variegated paraphernalia by trying to show how pertinent faith is, blunts it and mummifies it, [this leads to] the cultural annexation of God or a deliquescence of faith into religiosity. . . .*

* *Wait Without Idols* (New York: George Braziller, 1964)

196

In such a situation, who needs atheists? The unbelief of believers is amply sufficient to make God repugnant and incredible.

Here we have to take account of the positive Christian affirmation made by the death-of-God theologians. It is this: the deformation of God, due to the manipulative exploitation of Him in the official concepts, is self-destroying. "God is man's failure." The intentness with which official Christianity seeks to make God relevant to man makes Him so irrelevant that there remains but one alternative: to declare Him dead. Then the true God, the God who is "absent," comes to life again.

When the god invented by man "dies" (he never really lived) then the true God is once again mysteriously present precisely because "God is absent." For Vahanian, Biblical religion shows us once for all that man's basic obligation to God is iconoclasm. That sounds wild, but it is only a reformulation of the first two commandments.

The chief problem of the Death-of-God theology as I see it is not that its language is calculatingly and consistently insulting to the Church, nor that it deliberately makes use of near-blasphemy in its contention that the official concept of God has now become blasphemous. All this can be understood when it is seen in the atmosphere of creativity and prophetism which surely is a sign of theology in our time. The real problem is that the Death-of-God theology too easily falls short of the prophetism to which it lays claim. It is often mere sophomoric anti-religion and anti-clericalism, and seems to end by subjecting man more completely and more arbitrarily to the massive domination of post-Christian secularism. My feeling is that the Death-of-God theology simply issues in acquiescence to political totalism, the police state—whether capitalist or communist makes little difference. Either way, by conventional Christianity or by the

197

Death of God, we seem to end up rendering everything to Caesar.

Nevertheless, the challenge issued by the Death-of-God theology is not to be evaded. In order to disentangle Christian faith from the crisis and collapse of western culture, and open it to entirely new world perspectives, we have to be able to renounce the mighty spirit that has let himself be set up in the place of God: the Angel of the West.

The Unbelief of Believers

THERE EXISTS AMONG BELIEVERS A VAGUE PRESENTIMENT OF rampant godlessness in America. This fear is perhaps not without foundation but, like so many other vague fears clothed in conveniently dreadful mythology, it sees monstrous evils in the wrong places and ignores the humdrum pathology of everyday life. America is not being undermined by a godless underground any more than it is honey combed with secret communist cells. There is of course a systematic militant atheism which has a rather brave and aggressive ring of nineteenth-century crusading liberalism about it. An atheism of this type is of course a kind of religion and it has its own devout believers, its own rituals, its own conviction of persecution and martyrdom, its own private canonizations. We have no quarrel with this determined sincerity.

More serious is the phenomenon of a general pervasive indifference and complacency which are spread out among believers and non believers alike. This is what Martin E. Marty sets out to study in his book *Varieties of Unbelief* (New York: Holt, Rinehart & Winston, 1964). He is quite rightly concerned by the real unbelief of apparent believers. He examines the religious vacuum in which a variety of obscure superstitions and neuroses amalgamate with the cliches of technology and nationalism to produce a curious half-formulated creed, claiming the support of official and churchly institutions, making occasional and expedient appeals to Christ, the Gospel and Christian ethics, and calling down wrath upon those who rock this "reli-

199

gious" boat. His chief purpose is to meditate upon the way "unbelief is institutionalized and presents as a more or less permanent cultural phenomenon" in American religion. He meditates, he does not denounce. His meditation is nourished above all by considerations on the originality of modern unbelief. In order to do this he has to stand back and view his subject (as he does in his early chapter) in the context of European unbelief which is something more radical than ours. America has yet to produce a prophet of godlessness as articulately disillusioned as Sartre. After all, there can be no serious comparison between the vaudeville platitudes of Ingersoll and the savagely well-aimed intuitions of Nietzsche.

The unbelief of modern man is not the refusal to listen to a God who speaks. It is a subjectively sincere and total lack of interest in the very ideas of a God who speaks, together with a conviction that such a concept can only be a pretext for "bad faith." Modern unbelief is an earnest desire for a complete and integral secularity, a forthright worldliness, but without the solid comforts of middle class spirituality. Indeed, it demands a frank refusal of all spiritual security in any religious system, or in any personal surrender to the Absolute. It is a cool and often bored acceptance of the awful autonomy by which man can indeed make or destroy himself, but in which he is not summoned by anyone to do anything special. His chief problem is in guessing how life is to be given a meaning.

We recognize here the voice of Sartre and the existentialists, who are certainly atheists all the way, and know it, and proclaim it. These are not the unbelievers Dr. Marty finds in our American Churches. Far from it. Statistically, the vast majority of Americans claim some religious belief, or at least refuse to identify themselves openly as unbelievers. And they are doubtless sincere. They have faith and in fact they

200

may be "true believers" with all that this expression, since Hoffer's book on the subject, has come to imply. They persist in invoking the God who is the guarantee of the security they seek, or seem to enjoy. They do not invoke a God who speaks or makes demands, but a God who simply accounts for the rightness and perpetuity of certain material benefits. Their "god" is simply an explanation of and purification for the comfort and confusion of affluent society.

What in fact do they believe in? In success, prosperity, know-how, effort, having fun. Do they have a religious ideology? Yes, it centers around concepts of romantic individualism, nationalism, progress, and a hope that claims to be Christian, sanctioned by certain supposedly Christian ethical norms and cult patterns. Even though "heaven" may provide a comfortable background of myth, this "Christianity" is built on vaguely pragmatic securities, on flimsy and sentimental images, and on the tepid reassurances provided by conformity and togetherness in this world. Here, in the midst of our earnest and comfortable orthodoxy, Dr. Marty detects the "nearness of unbelief" and sees that it is quite different from the "weak faith" that we may sometimes be inclined to call it.

In a word, Dr. Marty suggests that what passes for Christian faith among many Americans is perhaps less respectable, intellectually and spiritually, than the concerned atheism of those whose unbelief implies the courageous assumption of loneliness, dread and risk. Certainly a Christianity that claims to obey God when in fact it is obeying only the imperatives of a marketing and affluent society, must certainly be written off in the end as "bad faith."

The phenomenology of this particular kind of unbelief is exposed in such detail, and its varieties are spread out in so many neatly identified categories, secular and religious, that the reader tends to lose his sense of direction, and when he

201

puts the book down he is not altogether clear what conclusion he has reached. Perhaps this muting and tempering
of conclusions is deliberate. Such a study could easily be
harsh, indeed furious. But the author has elected to avoid
prophetism and stick to the more acceptable tone of objective sociology, content with the hope that the reader or the
reviewer will not remain insensitive to the book's prophetic
undertones.

One might be tempted to ask if this is an age in which
prophecy can afford to be spoken only in undertones: but
one is brought up short by the deafening clamor of so many
who claim to be prophets that in the end one must accept
the wisdom with which Dr. Marty prefers to keep his doors
open to civilized dialogue.

It must be admitted that the book quietly and devastatingly makes a few really dreadful points about American
religion—but Dr. Marty never departs from that tolerance
and openness which, though they may seem to permit a certain religious and moral inauthenticity among us, remain
nevertheless a genuine source of hope for the rational
dialogue which alone can help us find our way as Christians
in the world of the future.

It is certain that much in our supposed Christianity is in
fact a deplorable cult of idols. But the itch for crusading
which makes itself felt precisely in those areas where Christianity is most inflamed with fundamentalism and integral-
ism offers no real hope of a corrective. On the contrary, Dr.
Marty perceives very wisely that the more vociferous ecsta-
sies of some of our Christians, both Protestant and Catholic,
may proceed from the fact that their lives have been informed by nationalism more than by faith.

Carleton Hayes has assured us that the "syncretism of
nationalism and Christianity is strikingly noticeable in the

202

United States," and Dr. Marty adds: "Nationalism can produce an ecstasy which few other idolatries can." Christianity today, when it is not suppressed outright by the state, tends to assume an "adjectival" relation to the state. A "Christian nationalist" is one whose Christianity takes second place, and serves to justify a patriotism in whose eyes the nation can do no wrong. In such a case, it becomes "Christian faith" and "Christian heroism" to renounce even one's Christian protest and to obey the dictates of the (unchristian) Nation without question. Instead of that Christian independence which realizes that the Nation itself may come under the higher judgment of God, there arises the notion of a "Christian" obedience in which the faithful are urged to accept the national purpose on the justification of any and every means. They renounce all judgment and choice in order to follow secular authority blindly since "the Government knows best."

Thus when Christianity becomes subordinated to a practical cult of one's nation, one's society or one's secular way of life, and when religion becomes indissolubly wedded in fact to a totalist social structure (even one that still aspires to be called democratic) it happens that the secular society itself assumes the functions of a Church mediating between God and man, to such a point that the pastors themselves tend to look to the state as a font of divine decisions in the practical order. All dissent in the civil sphere thereby automatically becomes a religious betrayal and a spiritual apostasy.

The great question then is one of clarification. We can no longer afford to equate faith with the acceptance of myths about our nation, our society, or our technology; to equate hope with a naive confidence in our image of ourselves as the good guys against whom all the villains in the world are leagued in conspiracy; to equate love with a mindlessly

203

compliant togetherness, a dimly lived and semi-radiant compulsiveness in work and play, invested by commercial artists with an aura of spurious joy.

What matters, however, is not simply to set conformity over against dissent, to call the one evil and the other good, and be satisfied with that. The perspectives of Dr. Marty's book are wider. He sees that the job of the dissenter is not merely to accuse, to upbraid and to condemn, but, after showing the need for spiritual awakening and constructive analysis, to break open the way to dialogue and keep it open.

Apologies to an Unbeliever

THIS IS NOT GOING TO BE AN EASY TUNE TO SING. TO BEGIN
with, it is not one of the currently popular numbers. Still less
one of the older and more time-worn routines. But I see you
are already suspicious. I do not dispute your perfect right
to be so. You *should* be suspicious. That is the first thing I
have to say. Not that you need me to say it. But perhaps I
need myself to say it.

However, if you distrust the word "apologies" and if you
think that I am trying to afflict you with apologetics, please
set your mind at rest. By "apologies" I mean simply what
the word says. I recognize that I have been standing on your
foot, and I am now at last getting off it, with these few
mumbled sentences.

"But who," you say, "is behind that pronoun: who do you
mean when you say 'I'? Do you mean 'the Believer'? Do you
mean your Church? Do you mean the clergy? Do you mean
your monastic Order? Or do you just mean yourself?"

Well, in the first place, I am not entitled to speak in any-
body's name but my own. I am quite sure that what I want
to say will not be endorsed by many of the clergy, and it
certainly is not the official teaching of the Catholic Church.
On the other hand, I take my own faith seriously and am
not a priest for nothing. I am a Believer, though not the
aggressive kind. I would not say these things if I thought
they were not in the deepest sense true to what I believe. At
the same time I am conscious of the futility of being a mere
respectable and secure "Believer" with a capital "B."

So I am apologizing to you for the inadequacy and imper-

205

tinence of so much that has been inflicted on you in the name of religion, not only because it has embarrassed me, and others like me, but because it seems to me to be a falsification of religious truth. In fact, I am secretly grateful to you for refusing to accept so much of the arrogant dictation that they have tried to foist on you. And here you notice that I have a tendency to slip out of my rank among the capital *B*-Believers, and even to edge over a little toward your side, not because I don't believe, but just because things sometimes seem to me a little quieter and more thoughtful where you are.

But in any case, I am definitely speaking from the Christian side of the fence, at once identifying myself with the other Believers—Catholic and Protestant—and reserving the right to disagree with them and even to scandalize them a little. In these terms I speak to you, an unbeliever—or at any rate, one who cannot find it in himself to stomach what I seem to have swallowed without difficulty.

Though it is true that day by day you care less and less what I may have swallowed, and though I am in fact apologizing for the fact that there is still such an exaggerated obsession with the difference between us, I think the time has come (at least for me) to take a new attitude toward our relationship.

At this point, let us get clear about *your* identity. You are, they say, an Unbeliever. On the other hand you are not a professional and militant Unbeliever. The militant Unbeliever is, in fact, a Believer—though perhaps a Believer-in-reverse. I will take care not to patronize you by seeming to doubt your unbelief—though technically it would be more accurate to say that you are a *Non*-Believer rather than an *Un*-believer. You are one who neither rejects belief nor accepts it. In fact you have given up thinking about it because the message of faith does not reach you, does not interest you and seems to have nothing to do with you at all. Or if it does reach you and does seem somehow relevant to you, yet you do not understand how one can know there is such a thing as a divine revelation. The concept of "revelation" is, to you, meaningless.

It is to you that I now say, with all the honesty at my command, that you are a sorely affronted person. Believers have for centuries made a habit out of reviling and disparaging you. Have they perhaps done this in order to fortify themselves against their own secret doubts? Do all these Believers believe in God, or are they more intent upon believing that they themselves are Believers? Are you—the Unbeliever—more useful to them in this devout exercise than God himself?

They not only claim to know all about you, they take it upon themselves to expose the hidden sins which (according to them) explain your unbelief. They exert themselves to make you insecure, to tell you how unhappy you are—as if you needed them to tell you, and as if they were any happier themselves! They weave a thousand myths about you, and having covered you with shame and discredit, they wonder why you do not run to them for comfort. Seeing their failure they try a different approach. Currrently they are playing a game called "God is Dead." But do not take this too seriously. This is only another card in an ideological card game, and what they want, in the end, is the same thing as before: to get you into their Churches. I confess I myself fail to see how the claim that "God is dead" constitutes an argument for going to church.

At this point I am making a public renunciation, in my own name at least, of all tactical, clerical, apologetic designs upon the sincerity of your non-belief. I am not trying to tamper with your conscience. I am not insinuating that you have "spiritual problems" that I can detect and you cannot.

On the contrary, I am writing this for one purpose only: to apologize for the fact that this kind of affront has been, and still is, daily and hourly perpetrated on you by a variety of Believers, some fanatical, some reasonable; some clerical, some lay; some religious and some irreligious; some futuristic and some antique.

I think this apology is demanded by the respect I have for my own faith. If I, as a Christian, believe that my first duty is to love and respect my fellowman in his personal frailty and perplexity, in his unique hazard and his need for trust, then I think that the refusal to let him alone, the inability to entrust him to God and to his own conscience, and the insistence on rejecting him as a person until he agrees with me, is simply a sign that my own faith is inadequate. I do not (in such a case) believe in the love of God for man, I simply itch to impose my own ideas on others. Claiming to love truth and my fellow man I am really only loving my own spiritual security, and using the Gospel as a gimmick for self-justification.

Let me be quite frank about it; the current fuss and shouting about whether or not God is dead, whether or not the Church (or Churches) can make the grade in twentieth-century society, whether or not the Church can regain the attention of modern man (either by guitar playing or liturgical gamesmanship), all seems to me to be rather trivial and beside the point. Where authentic religious concern degenerates into salesmanship it becomes an affront to the honest perplexities of the vast majority of men. I think, frankly, that you are entitled to be left unbothered by the sheer triviality of so much religious vaudeville.

This of course requires much more explanation than I can give it here. For instance, I do not intend to call into question all attempts at religious renewal. If I doubted for a moment that Christianity was alive and developing I would not bother my head with it at all. Yet at the same time I think a great deal of the fuss, argument and publicity in which the renewal seeks to express itself is very ambiguous. Are the Believers trying to convince themselves of their singular importance by selling a new image of themselves? I certainly do not feel that the question of religious renewal is as relevant to you as Church news releases imply. I appreciate your sometimes sympathetic curiosity, your cautious gestures of approval. Yet I think too many churchmen are still toying with the vain hope that their various institutions are going to continue to play dominant roles in society. I very much doubt it! I think the existence of the Christian in the modern world is going to be more and more marginal. We are going to be "Diaspora" Christians in a frankly secular and non-believing society. This is not necessarily as tragic as it may sound, if I can judge by the quality of the Christians from Czechoslovakia, for instance, that I have met!

As you see, I am apologizing because *you* have to suffer from our illusions.

This does not make life very comfortable for you, particularly when, as may happen, you are yourself serious enough about "beliefs" to think twice about adopting one. You hesitate to believe without motives that seem to you to be really worthy of such a perilous commitment. Others are less scrupulous about it. They can have the luxury of peaceful consciences, at very low cost, and they can look down on you into the bargain. (What makes them so sure that they are God's good friends and you are not? Some theologians I know are beginning to speak differently. They are saying that you others may be closer to God and potentially more "Believing" than many of us. This is not new either. Paul had something of the sort to say to the Athenians!)

There was a time when we pursued you everywhere with

209

foolproof arguments for religion in which, as it turned out, you were not interested. We assumed this convicted you of bad faith. More recently, the sharp insights of a Sartre have reminded us that knowing all the answers in advance can itself be evidence of bad faith. Some of us have begun to find routine argumentation rather hollow. Obviously, clear insight is a matter of intelligence and reasonable judgment, not emotion. Yet such insights are not the fruit of argument and cannot be pounded into another by debate. Perhaps if we had debated less, you would have been better disposed to receive these insights in the silence of your own conscience. Faith comes by hearing, says St. Paul: but by hearing *what?* The cries of snake-handlers? The soothing platitudes of the religious operator? One must first be able to listen to the inscrutable ground of his own being, and who am I to say that your reservations about religious commitment do not protect, in you, this kind of listening?

The "absence of God" and the "silence of God" in the modern world are not only evident, but they are facts of profound *religious* significance.

What do these metaphorical expressions mean? They refer obviously to another metaphorical concept, that of "communication" between man and God. To say that "God is absent" and "God is silent" is to say that the familiar concept of "communication" between man and God has broken down. And if you are an Unbeliever it is often enough because such communication is, to you, incredible. We, on the other hand, have insisted more and more that communication with God was credible and was in fact taking place: when *we* spoke, *God* spoke. Unfortunately, the terms in which we have continued to say this did little to make the idea acceptable, or even conceivable, to you. We keep insisting that we and God deal with each other morning, noon and night over closed-circuit TV. These pious metaphors are

210

permissible with certain reservations, but to try to force
them on you can border on blasphemous idiocy. Thus our
very language itself (to many of us still adequate) has
tended to become an important element in the absence and
the silence of God. Does it occur to us that instead of reveal-
ing him we are hiding him? As a matter of fact, the Second
Vatican Council formally admitted this. In the Constitution
on the Church in the World we read that "Believers can
have more than a little to do with the birth of atheism"
when by their deficiencies "they must be said to conceal
rather than reveal the authentic face of God and religion."
(n. 19)

Whatever one may choose to make of this absence and
this silence of God they have to be accepted as primary religious facts of our time. There is no use trying to ignore
them, to act as if they could not possibly have happened, or
to blame them all on somebody else. Much as I might wish
that all men shared my faith—and I wish they did—there
is no point in my sitting and dreaming about it, when in fact
I live in a world in which God is silent, from which he is
apparently absent, in which the conventional routines
designed to celebrate his presence only make the spiritual
void all the more embarrassing. Some Christians still cling
desperately to the idea that if one *admits* all this, one loses
everything!

To admit that this is a world to which God seems not to
be speaking is not a renunciation of faith: it is a simple
acceptance of an existential religious fact. It should not dis-
concert anyone who knows, from the Bible and from the
mystics, that the silences of God are also messages with a
definite import of their own. And this import is not necessarily reassuring. One thing it may imply, for instance, is a
judgment on the self-righteousness of those who trust in
themselves because they are fully respectable and "estab-

211

lished." It may imply a judgment of their affirmations, and suggest that a great deal is being said by God in language that we have not yet learned to decode. Not that there are new dogmas being revealed: but perhaps things that we badly need to know are being told us in new and disconcerting ways. Perhaps they are staring us in the face, and we cannot see them. It is in such situations that the language of prophetism speaks of the "silence of God."

To turn to such a world, in which every other voice but the voice of God is heard and merely to add one more voice to the general din—one's own—is to neglect the ominous reality of a crisis that has perhaps become apocalyptic. In "turning to" this kind of world, I think the Catholic Church intends to respect the gravity of its predicament, and to do a little listening. There is certainly an enormous difference between the solemn anathemas of Vatican I and the more temperate and sympathetic appeals of Vatican II for dialogue.

My apology can be summed up in this admission: we self-styled believers have assumed that we are always right, you were always wrong; we knew, you did not know; we had everything to tell you, but you would not listen. In actual fact while I certainly believe that the message of the Gospel is something that we are called upon to preach, I think we will communicate it more intelligently in dialogue. Half of talking is listening. And listening implies that the other speaker also has something to say.

I know, you do not trust this admission as it stands. There are still plenty of Christians who see the dialogue between the Believer and Unbeliever more or less as that between the old-fashioned psychiatric counselor and his client. The Unbeliever is a madman who must be listened to tolerantly until he is softened up (his "confidence is won"). Then he can be tactfully led to discover the right answers.

212

Without prejudice to the truth of the Gospel and to the Church's authority to teach and interpret the message of Christ, that message still demands to be understood in an authentic human situation. In this situation, men meet one another as men, that is to say as equals, as "fellow servants." Equals listen to one another because they have a compassionate respect for one another in their common predicament.

My own peculiar task in my Church and in my world has been that of the solitary explorer who, instead of jumping on all the latest bandwagons at once, is bound to search the existential depths of faith in its silences, its ambiguities, and in those certainties which lie deeper than the bottom of anxiety. In these depths there are no easy answers, no pat solutions to anything. It is a kind of submarine life in which faith sometimes mysteriously takes on the aspect of doubt when, in fact, one has to doubt and reject conventional and superstitious surrogates that have taken the place of faith. On this level, the division between Believer and Unbeliever ceases to be so crystal clear. It is not that some are all right and others are all wrong: *all* are bound to seek in honest perplexity. Everybody is an Unbeliever more or less! Only when this fact is fully experienced, accepted and lived with, does one become fit to hear the simple message of the Gospel—or of any other religious teaching.

The religious problem of the twentieth century is not understandable if we regard it only as a problem of Unbelievers and of atheists. It is also and perhaps chiefly a problem of Believers. The faith that has grown cold is not only the faith that the Unbeliever has lost but the faith that the Believer has kept. This faith has too often become rigid, or complex, sentimental, foolish, or impertinent. It has lost itself in imaginings and unrealities, dispersed itself in pon-

213

tifical and organizational routines, or evaporated in activism and loose talk.

The most hopeful sign of religious renewal is the authentic sincerity and openness with which some Believers are beginning to recognize this. At the very moment when it would seem that they had to gather for a fanatical last-ditch stand, these Believers are dropping their defensiveness, their defiance and their mistrust. They are realizing that a faith that is afraid of other people is no faith at all. A faith that supports itself by condemning others is itself condemned by the Gospel.

The Contemplative Life
in the Modern World

CAN CONTEMPLATION STILL FIND A PLACE IN THE WORLD OF technology and conflict which is ours? Does it belong only to the past? The answer to this is that, since the direct and pure experience of reality in its ultimate root is man's deepest need, contemplation must be possible if man is to remain human. If contemplation is no longer possible, then man's life has lost the spiritual orientation upon which everything else—order, peace, happiness, sanity—must depend. But true contemplation is an austere and exacting vocation. Those who seek it are few and those who find it fewer still. Nevertheless, their presence witnesses to the fact that contemplation remains both necessary and possible.

Man has an instinctive need for harmony and peace, for tranquillity, order and meaning. None of these seem to be the most salient characteristics of modern society. Life in a monastery, where the traditions and rites of a more contemplative age are still alive and still practiced, cannot help but remind men that there once existed a more leisurely and more spiritual way of life—and that this was the way of their ancestors. Thus even into the confused activism of Western life is woven a certain memory of contemplation. It is a memory so vague and so remote that it is hardly understood, and yet it can awaken the hope of recovering inner vision. In this hope, modern man can perhaps entertain, for a brief time, the dream of a contemplative life and of a higher spiritual state of quiet, of rest, of untroubled joy. But a sense of self-deception and guilt immediately awakens in Western man a reaction of despair, disgust, rejection of the dream

215

and commitment to total activism. We must face the fact that the mere thought of contemplation is one which deeply troubles the modern person who takes it seriously. It is so contrary to the modern way of life, so apparently alien, so seemingly impossible, that the modern man who even considers it finds, at first, that his whole being rebels against it. If the ideal of inner peace remains attractive the demands of the way to peace seem to be so exacting and so extreme that they can no longer be met. We would like to be quiet, but our restlessness will not allow it. Hence we believe that for us there can be no peace except in a life filled up with movement and activity, with speech, news, communication, recreation, distraction. We seek the meaning of our life in activity for its own sake, activity without objective, efficacy without fruit, scientism, the cult of unlimited power, the service of the machine as an end in itself. And in all these a certain dynamism is imagined. The life of frantic activity is invested with the noblest of qualities, as if it were the whole end and happiness of man: or rather as if the life of man had no inherent meaning whatever and had to be given a meaning from some external source, from a society engaged in a gigantic communal effort to raise man above himself. Man is indeed called to transcend himself. But do his own efforts suffice for this?

At this point it would be tempting to analyze the complex new situation that has arisen due to the popularity of hallucinogenic drugs. It is not possible for me to attempt such an analysis. Yet the fact that these drugs exist and are so widely used does require at least a passing mention. The most obvious thing about them is that they are short cuts to "inner vision." They promise contemplative experience without any need to practice the disciplines of the contemplative life. In other words they offer just the sort of thing modern man most wants, the opportunity to eat his cake and have it, to have the best of both worlds, to become a "mystic" without making any sacrifices. Unfortunately, this situation is not one that can be casually blamed on beatniks and irresponsible juveniles. It seems to me that it is only another aspect of that affluence to which official religion has contributed its own measure of confusion and bad faith. It has after all been the claim of official religion—more or less in all the Churches—that religion would act as a happiness pill, would help people to solve their problems, would make life easier and more jolly, and so on. If religion is enthusiastically advertised as a happiness pill, and then a real happiness pill comes along, then I see no justification for religious people complaining that the public likes the competitor's product better. After all, it is cheaper and more effective.

What needs to be made clear, however, is that contemplation is not a deepening of experience only, but a radical change in one's way of being and living, and the essence of this change is precisely a liberation from *dependence on external means to external ends*. Of course one may say that an opening of the "doors of perception" is not entirely "external" and yet it is a satisfaction for which one may develop a habitual need and on which one may become dependent. True contemplation delivers one from all such forms of dependence. In that sense it seems to me that a contemplative life that depends on the use of drugs is essentially different from one which implies complete liberation from all dependence on anything but freedom and divine grace. I realize that these few remarks do not answer the real question but they express a doubt in my own mind.

In any event I believe the reason for the inner confusion of Western man is that our technological society has no longer any place in it for wisdom that seeks truth for its own sake, that seeks the fulness of being, that seeks to rest in an intuition of the very ground of all being. Without wisdom, the apparent opposition of action and contemplation, of work and rest, of involvement and detachment, can never be resolved. Ancient and traditional societies, whether of Asia or of the West, always specifically recognized "the way" of the wise, the way of spiritual discipline in which there was at once wisdom and method, and by which, whether in art, in philosophy, in religion, or in the monastic life, some men would attain to the inner meaning of being, they would experience this meaning for all their brothers, they would so to speak bring together in themselves the divisions or complications that confused the life of their fellows. By healing the divisions in themselves they would help heal the divisions of the whole world. They would realize in themselves that unity which is at the same time the highest action and the purest rest, true knowledge and selfless love, a knowledge beyond knowledge in emptiness and unknowing; a willing beyond will in apparent non-activity. They would attain to the highest striving in the absence of striving and of contention.

This way of wisdom is no dream, no temptation and no evasion, for it is on the contrary a return to reality in its very root. It is not an escape from contradiction and confusion for it finds unity and clarity only by plunging into the very midst of contradiction, by the acceptance of emptiness and suffering, by the renunciation of the passions and obsessions with which the whole world is "on fire." It does not withdraw from the fire. It is in the very heart of the fire, yet remains cool, because it has the gentleness and humility that come from self-abandonment, and hence does not seek to assert the illusion of the exterior self.

Once a man has set his foot on this way, there is no excuse for abandoning it, for to be actually on the way is to recognize without doubt or hesitation that only the way is fully real and that everything else is deception, except insofar as

218

it may in some secret and hidden manner be connected with "the way."

Thus, far from wishing to abandon this way, the contemplative seeks only to travel further and further along it. This journey without maps leads him into rugged mountainous country where there are often mists and storms and where he is more and more alone. Yet at the same time, ascending the slopes in darkness, feeling more and more keenly his own emptiness, and with the winter wind blowing cruelly through his now tattered garments, he meets at times other travelers on the way, poor pilgrims as he is, and as solitary as he, belonging perhaps to other lands and other traditions. There are of course great differences between them, and yet they have much in common. Indeed, the Western contemplative can say that he feels himself much closer to the Zen monks of ancient Japan than to the busy and impatient men of the West, of his own country, who think in terms of money, power, publicity, machines, business, political advantage, military strategy—who seek, in a word, the triumphant affirmation of their own will, their own power, considered as the end for which they exist. Is not this perhaps the most foolish of all dreams, the most tenacious and damaging of illusions?

In any event, it is certain that the way of wisdom is not an evasion. Simply to evade modern life would be a futile attempt to abdicate from its responsibilities and a renunciation of advantages—and illusions. The contemplative way requires first of all and above all renunciation of this obsession with the triumph of the individual or collective will to power. For this aggressive and self-assertive drive to possess and to exert power implies a totally different view of reality than that which is seen when one travels the contemplative way. The aggressive and dominative view of reality places at the center the individual self with its bodily

219

form, its feelings and emotions, its appetites and needs, its loves and hates, its actions and reactions. All these are seen as forming together a basic and indubitable reality to which everything else must be referred, so that all other things are also estimated in their individuality, their actions and reactions, and all the ways in which they impinge upon the interests of the individual self. The world is then seen as a multiplicity of conflicting and limited beings, all enclosed in the prisons of their own individuality, all therefore complete in a permanent and vulnerable incompleteness, all seeking to find a certain completeness by asserting themselves at the expense of others, dominating and using others. This world becomes, then, an immense conflict in which the only peace is that which is accorded to the victory of the strong, and in order to taste the joy of this peace, the weak must submit to the strong and join him in his adventures so that they may share in his power. Thus there arises a spurious, inconclusive unity: the unity of the massive aggregate, the unity of those thrown together without love and without understanding by the accidents of the power struggle. Seen from the point of view of "the way" this unity is nothing but a collective monstrosity because it has no real reason for existing and is not a unity at all. However insistently it may claim for itself the dignities of a truly communal and human existence, it does not elevate man by a truly communal and interpersonal cooperation. It only drives him with mad and irresistible demands, exploiting him, alienating him from reality and demanding from him a blind irrational and total subjection. The life of the collective mass is such that it destroys in man the inmost need and capacity for contemplation. It dries up the living springs of compassion and understanding. It perverts the creative genius and destroys the innocent vision that is proper to man in communion with nature. Finally the collective mass becomes a vast aggregate of

220

organized hatred, a huge and organized death-wish, threatening its own existence and that of the entire human race.

The mission of the contemplative in this world of massive conflict and collective unreason is to seek the true way of unity and peace, without succumbing to the illusion of withdrawal into a realm of abstraction from which unpleasant realities are simply excluded by the force of will. In facing the world with a totally different viewpoint, he maintains alive in the world the presence of a spiritual and intelligent consciousness which is the root of true peace and true unity among men. This consciousness certainly accepts the fact of our empirical and individual existence, but refuses to take this as the basic reality. The basic reality is neither the individual, empirical self nor an abstract and ideal entity which can exist only in reason. The basic reality is being itself, which is one in all concrete existents, which shares itself among them and manifests itself through them. The goal of the contemplative is, on its lowest level, the recognition of this splendor of being and unity—a splendor in which he is one with all that is. But on a higher level still, it is the transcendent ground and source of being, the not-being and the emptiness that is so called because it is absolutely beyond all definition and limitation. This ground and source is not simply an inert and passive emptiness, but for the Christian it is pure act, pure freedom, pure light. The emptiness which is "pure being" is the light of God which, as St. John's Gospel says, "gives light to every man who comes into the world." Specifically, the Gospel sees all being coming forth from the Father, God, in His Word, who is the light of the world. "In Him (the Word) was life, and this life was Light for all men, and the Light shone in darkness and the darkness could not understand it." (John 1:4–5)

Now very often the ordinary active and ethical preoccupations of Christians make them forget this deeper and

221

more contemplative dimension of the Christian way. So active, in fact, has been the face presented by Christianity to the Asian world that the hidden contemplative element of Christianity is often not even suspected at all by Asians. But without the deep root of wisdom and contemplation, Christian action would have no meaning and no purpose.

The Christian is then not simply a man of goodwill, who commits himself to a certain set of beliefs, who has a definite dogmatic conception of the universe, of man, and of man's reason for existing. He is not simply one who follows a moral code of brotherhood and benevolence with strong emphasis on certain rewards and punishments dealt out to the individual. Underlying Christianity is not simply a set of doctrines about God considered as dwelling remotely in heaven, and man struggling on earth, far from heaven, trying to appease a distant God by means of virtuous acts. On the contrary Christians themselves too often fail to realize that the infinite God is dwelling within them, so that He is in them and they are in Him. They remain unaware of the presence of the infinite source of being right in the midst of the world and of men. True Christian wisdom is therefore oriented to the experience of the divine Light which is present in the world, the Light in whom all things are, and which is nevertheless unknown to the world because no mind can see or grasp its infinity. "He was in the world and the world was made by Him and the world did not know Him. He came into His own and His own did not receive Him." (John 1: 10-11)

Contemplative wisdom is then not simply an aesthetic extrapolation of certain intellectual or dogmatic principles, but a living contact with the Infinite Source of all being, a contact not only of minds and hearts, not only of "I and Thou," but a transcendent union of consciousness in which man and God become, according to the expression of St. Paul, "one spirit."

222

Though this contemplative union is an extreme intensification of conscious awareness, a kind of total awareness, it is not properly contained or signified in any particular vision, but rather in non-vision, which attains the totality of meaning beyond all limited conceptions, by the surrender of love. God Himself is not only pure being but also pure love, and to know Him is to become one with Him in love. In this dimension of Christian experience, the Cross of Christ means more than the juridical redemption of man from the guilt of evil-doing. It means the passage from death to life and from nothingness to fullness, or to fullness in nothingness. Thus the contemplative way of ancient Christian monastic tradition is not simply a way of good works and of loving devotion, fine as these are, but also a way of emptiness and transcendence in union with the crucified Christ. The Cross signified that the sacrificial death which is the end of all lust for earthly power and all indulgence of passion is in fact the liberation of those who have renounced their exterior self in order to dedicate their lives to love and to truth. Christ is not simply an object of love and contemplation whom the Christian considers with devout attention: He is also "the way, the truth and the life" so that for the Christian to be "on the way" is to be "in Christ" and to seek truth is to walk in the light of Christ. "For me to live," says St. Paul, "is Christ. I live, now not I, but Christ lives in me."

This is a summary outline of the meaning of Christian contemplation, a meaning which calls for much greater development particularly in all that concerns the sacramental and liturgical life of the Church. Such is the way of contemplation.

One need not be a monk to turn this way. It is sufficient to be a child of God, a human person. It is enough that one has in oneself the instinct for truth, the desire of that freedom from limitation and from servitude to external things which St. Paul calls the "servitude of corruption" and which, in fact, holds the whole world of man in bondage by passion, greed, the lust for sensation and for individual survival, as though one could become rich enough, powerful enough and clever enough to cheat death.

Unfortunately, this passion for unreality and for the impossible fills the world today with violence, hatred and indeed with a kind of insane and cunning fury which threatens our very existence.

Science and technology are indeed admirable in many respects and if they fulfill their promises they can do much for man. But they can never solve his deepest problems. On the contrary, without wisdom, without the intuition and freedom that enable man to return to the root of his being, science can only precipitate him still further into the centrifugal flight that flings him, in all his compact and uncomprehending isolation, into the darkness of outer space without purpose and without objective.

Honest to God

Letter to a Radical Anglican

YOU PROBABLY REMEMBER THE MINISTER IN ONE OF EVELYN Waugh's novels: I think it is *Decline and Fall*. After a life of humdrum and secure devotion, he suddenly wakes up one morning with the awful thought that perhaps he does not really know "what it is all for." He rouses his wife and makes this doubt known to her. She brightly replies "Well, if you have such doubts, the only thing to do is resign." This he immediately does.

I know it is unkind to think of this in connection with the much discussed book* of the Anglican Bishop of Wool-wich, but really *Honest to God* in its agonized sincerity and its profoundly concerned confusions makes me think of Waugh's picture of the naive minister, deliberately intended by its author to be typological.

So now your Bishop has discovered that God is not a God "out there," not seated on a throne in the empyrean heaven, not overseeing an earth-centered universe. I should have thought it was about time. And the Bishop is now faced with the task of "thinking what to put in the place (of this mythical image)." With Bultmann he will demythologize, and for this I am not so sure that he deserves to be "trampled to death by geese" (Kierkegaard). I for one am perfectly at home with the idea that mythical and poetic state-

---

* *Honest to God*, by J. A. T. Robinson (Philadelphia: Westminster Press, 1963).

ments about God are not adequate representations of Him, but I am also used to thinking that no conceptual knowledge of God is perfectly adequate, and therefore when I see the Bishop busy with "framing new concepts" I would be inclined to say he still had not grasped the extent of the problem. His anguish should perhaps be greater and more existential than it actually is. He quotes Tillich and Bonhoeffer, but does he measure up to them? He protests with them against "conditioning the unconditional," and yet I cannot help feeling that his book is, more than anything else, a job of "reconditioning." With profound conviction and unquestionable truth, Dr. Robinson declares that the Christian image has become inadequate in the modern world. He even goes so far as to say that we ought to be able to get along without any image at all, and this is a form of iconoclasm which I would be quite willing to take seriously, at least with certain theological clarifications. Yet the whole purpose of the book seems in the end to be the presentation of a new and more acceptable "image" of the Christian: the fully modern, concerned, committed "secular" Christian, in the world and of it, emancipated from religious myth, and able to travel along with existentialism and practice the new morality without guilt feelings. But is it so important to create this image? Is it not an idol like any other?

Since the book is chiefly preoccupied with the frustrated condition of a ministry unable to communicate its message, I wonder if after all this is not another, more sophisticated, better documented, manual of Christian salesmanship. Is it a declaration of Christian insecurity in a world where Christianity is no longer popular or even acceptable? Is it simply a desperate attempt to escape a religious shipwreck and find security in fellowship, any fellowship? The Bishop is aware that such questions are raised by his book, and he defends himself. How convincingly?

These questions concern us all. The coverage and commentary on the Vatican Council have also been very sensitive to the "image" of Catholicity in a godless world. Naturally there has been not much iconoclasm, and the decor of the Council as well as some of its theology is still quite baroque. The Bishop of Woolwich makes it clear that he wants nothing of the sort, and in this he probably voices secret desires and convictions of many Roman Catholics.

Among the geese that have trampled the Bishop to death few have been Roman. I do not want to bring up the rear of the parade with a few Capitoline platitudes and the weak, superior wit of one who lives in another world, safely wrapped in the arms of dogmatic infallibility and curial surveillance. If I write about *Honest to God* at all it is because I belong to the Bishop's world, sympathize with his problems, recognize them as being in some way my own. But that is precisely why I think the book does not say enough, or say the right things. And, in fact, it is saying something other than it seems to say. To begin with, this is not the kind of book that can be judged purely and simply by its theological propositions, and it is not with these propositions that I am concerned (except to say that I find his Christology impossible). The book *appears* to be chiefly concerned with theology, indeed with a complete "restatement" of Anglican theology, a theological revolution. In actual fact it may be an abdication from theology, an evasion of the theologian's hard and unrewarding task. The way to make theology comprehensible to modern man is to get rid of it. Is this the theological message of *Honest to God?* And yet Dr. Robinson is deeply, sincerely, "honestly" concerned with faith in God—a fact which some of his critics have overlooked. He really believes that theology has become an obstacle between man and God rather than a way to God. He wants to liberate faith from a dead language. But is this not a *semantic* problem first of all? Should it not be treated as such?

Bishop Robinson grew up at Canterbury, which I knew at least briefly in my childhood, and he went to the same college as I at Cambridge. I do not think we were both at Clare at the same time. We might have been. It is clear that he was always a churchy type, and at that time I was not. I believe I showed up in chapel at Clare just once (it was a charming Caroline place with deep choir stalls in which we sat in surplices). When I was at Cambridge I was precisely the kind of person who, as his book complains, finds the Church unintelligible. My attitude was a common Cambridge attitude of total indifference to religion, and his Anglicanism is a Cambridge-like response to this kind of problem.

In the collection of reviews and letters called The *"Honest to God" Debate** which must be read in connection with the book itself, a Cambridge man of my time (not identified) has this to say:

> Had such thinking as has led to *Honest to God* been the case in my Cambridge days (some thirty years ago now) I might well have found my way into the Church. . . . But at Cambridge I just couldn't face the dreariness and impracticability of this Church image. . . .

These are not my own feelings. I would agree that I was not impressed by the image of the Anglican Church or of any other. But I am not sure I would have been led to any Church by Bishop Robinson's book.

Yet in all fairness I must admit that I think that I discovered the meaning of Christian faith when I found out that the usual mythological and anthropomorphic picture of

* The *"Honest to God" Debate, Some reactions to the Book* Honest to God, ed. David L. Edwards (London, SCM Press, 1963, 287 pp.).

God was not the true God of Christians. That is to say that, radically, my experience was close to that which I think underlies Dr. Robinson's book: the direct and existential discovery of God beyond concepts and beyond myths, in His inexpressible reality. Whether one speaks of Him as *ens a se* and pure act (which are the notions that gave me a certain amount of light) or whether one accepts Tillich's idea of God as the "pure ground of all being" (as Bishop Robinson does), the important thing is a spiritual awareness of the supreme reality of God. God is in some sense *beyond* all apologetic proof because all argumentation that goes from beings to His Being still leaves one with the impression that He is "*a* being" among other beings, "*an* essence" like other essences (though of course above them all), "a nature" in the midst and at the source of all other natures. This does not do justice to transcendence or rather it gives a completely false idea of transcendence as a separation in physical space, a location "outside" the universe.

I was very struck, on page 29 of *Honest to God*, by the fact that the Bishop of Woolwich is in spirit rather close to St. Anselm, though he might be the first to deny it. Dr. Robinson is saying (and I agree) that if one is too anxious to "prove the existence of God" one is liable not to be "honest to God" but indeed to misrepresent Him grievously and create a false image of Him that will be little more than a scandal and a pretext for unbelief.

Though St. Anselm is ordinarily represented as a man who was eager at all costs to discover an airtight apologetic proof for God's existence, I do not think this is the whole story. Certainly Anselm was a Dialectician and was fully confident that his dialectic had power to convince. But what he was saying in his argument (wrongly called "ontological") was that God was *the one being whose existence required no proof*. He cannot but "be." To question the "existence" of

Him Who *is*, is tantamount to conceiving Him as possibly existing or not existing, as having somehow "come into being." Since He cannot not be, any question of His possible existence is irrelevant. To me the important thing about this is the religious intuition of God's aseity, not the supposed force of the dialectical proof. I hope to say this more fully elsewhere. In any case, it seems to me to be in harmony with the best intuitions in *Honest to God*.

And that is why I disagree with Bishop Robinson in his conviction that his thesis and his problem are utterly new. They are not new, they are perfectly traditional. When *Honest to God* speaks disparagingly of the *via negativa* in traditional theology, the author seems to be under the misapprehension that this was nothing but a rejection of the wicked world. In fact it was a passing beyond positive concepts, a direct flight to God "without concepts" or by negative concepts (He is "not this," not that"). Those who are so intent on de-mythologizing should not forget the real import of the Thomist doctrine of analogy (not so fashionable these days). In any case, Dr. Robinson ought to re-read Pseudo-Dionysius. From the very beginning Christians have been aware that the New Testament revelation of God was entirely revolutionary: the Father of Our Lord Jesus Christ is not "a God" among others, even the Highest God. He is the Father dwelling in light inaccessible, and seen only in the Son. He is seen in Christ precisely as *Son* of Man, and when the Risen Lord "ascends" (this upsets Bishop Robinson), then the invisible God is manifest in the Church through the Spirit of Christ and through the love which makes men one in Christ. I think that in this confession of faith (apart from the supposedly "mythical" character of some expressions) Bishop Robinson and I would substantially agree.

What then is his problem? It is a very real one. Stated in

Bonhoeffer's terms (and the full statement of the problem must be sought in the *Letters from Prison,* written by the Evangelical minister who was one of Hitler's victims) it is the fact that the usual language of religion and of the Bible has apparently ceased to have any meaning whatever for modern man.

It is not so much that the symbolic and "mythical" statements of revealed truth are "false" but that they very often convey the opposite to what they are intended to convey. Hence, says Bishop Robinson, with Bonhoeffer, to try to force outmoded and irrelevant concepts of God on modern man is an affront, an "attack on the adulthood of the world." It means, in effect, a foolish attempt to frighten the modern skeptic into thinking he has problems which he has become incapable of having, and then producing a *Deus ex machina* to rescue him from his supposed plight. Let us be frank: much popular religion in our time, including the writing and preaching of not a few Catholics, has something of this about it. Even where the language and dogma may be impeccably correct, they may mask a puerile and magic psychology of religion and a complete misunderstanding of Christian truth. The great heretics today are perhaps to be sought, as Karl Rahner has suggested, among those who are technically orthodox and at the same time profoundly insensitive to the inner meaning and spiritual implications of Christian revelation.

Though I agree with the Bishop's diagnosis, I fail to see where he has provided any kind of remedy. To go back to Cambridge: I remember one evening in A's rooms, at St. Catherine's. A. had discovered some believers who were very alive and whose ideas, he thought, were new. He invited me around to meet them, and to discuss religion. I do not remember who they were (the strange thought just hit me: what if one were called J. A. T. Robinson? But none was from Clare). It was one of those typical undergraduate discussions. We said nothing very profound. They were good men. They were earnest. They were "honest to God." I explained in detail that I had no interest whatever in religion, in God, in any Church, and that I saw no possible reason for taking an interest in such things. That if I thought I had some motive to be interested, I would doubtless be able to find some meaning in what they said. But as far as I was concerned it simply made no difference. I couldn't care less.

Then one of them, the most articulate, without dismay and in impeccable "honest to God" terms, said: "If that is the way you feel, you are at least not deceiving yourself, and so I think that if you ever *do* get a motive, you will take faith very seriously." If he turned out in the end to be right, then perhaps I owe something to his prayers.

Now these men were giving me the Bishop Robinson treatment. Nothing was said about God not being "out there"—presumably because this was accepted by all as quite obvious. Nothing was said about religious myth. Yet fundamentally the approach was like that of the Bishop of Woolwich: the *honesty* pitch. Shall I sum it up this way? "Yes, I know that the idea of God is silly, religion seems meaningless, and all that. Frankly it is a bit meaningless to me at times. But you can see I am honest, and I admit you are honest. Why don't we go one step further and say that your honesty should be just like mine and then you will find yourself to be a Christian!" Very engaging! But it led nowhere. It was precisely at this point that all communication broke down. But according to Robinson it is at this point that communication is, by magic, supposed to begin.

This discussion represented precisely the kind of difficulty Bishop Robinson has in mind. It is a difficulty of communication in which understanding and progress are blocked by

232

confusion and irrelevancies. Two sets of statements are made and they appear to confront one another, but in fact they rest on entirely different presuppositions and axioms. They seem to be attacking the same problems, and perhaps in fact they do, but on entirely different levels. What is formulated as a problem on one level cannot be conceived to be a problem on the other, and hence what is proposed as a solution on the first level is in fact only a difficulty on the second. Hence the impression that one interlocutor, under the pretense of helping the other, is in fact hindering him and tying him up in ambiguities. The more clear, convincing and compelling the arguments become, the more they are experienced as fatuous, meaningless and even as unconsciously dishonest. But it should be clear that this is a *semantic* difficulty first of all. Surely Cambridge, where I. A. Richards wrote and lectured on *The Meaning of Meaning*, ought to have made that long since clear. It is still not clear in *Honest to God* which has been presented and accepted as theology, and therefore condemned as theology. That is why its point has often been missed.

Bishop Robinson has many exciting quotations from Tillich, Bonhoeffer, Bultmann and others. These are profound thinkers and even when one cannot agree with them, one can accept the urgency of the problems they pose and the depth of the experience from which the problems arise. But when *Honest to God* claims first of all to be stating a brand new problem peculiar to our age, proposing *a radical restatement and re-interpretation of Christianity* and a complete turning away from outmoded "religion" with its "supranatural myths" to "this world," to "man" and to all that is unabashedly "secular," it naturally awakens certain expectations and a definite alarm. Since I am not easily alarmed, I went into the book with lively expectations but found nothing more than a rather woolly hopefulness, and com-

233

plete vagueness about "the world" in which our future is to be sought without compromise and without any backward looking toward a discarded myth of heaven.

It seems to me that the Bishop has really not answered the questions his book has raised. He has so accentuated the division between natural and "supra-natural" (his term), "religious" and "secular" that he is no longer able to rise above his two terms and come out with a dialectical synthesis. He is caught in the division and ends by committing himself to one half of it, to the exclusion of the other. Abandoning an unqualified commitment to the "religious myth" and to God as a *Deus ex machina,* he firmly lays hold on the world because "God is in the world" and nowhere else. So the more secular one is, the more one discards the trappings of religion, the more one is united to God-in-the-world. One must in this way re-interpret the Christian obligation to suffer with God in His world: by resolutely abandoning the consolations of "religion" and plunging into a seemingly godless secularism out of love for God's world and of the people in it.

It is easy to see how shocking this message sounds to conservative Anglicans, and there have been not a few who, like the minister's wife in *Decline and Fall,* suggested that the time had come for the Bishop of Woolwich to resign his see and turn his attention to something more in harmony with his thesis—bartending, for example. But I am still not certain that this courageous, indeed despairing attempt to enter into fellowship with the godless is really calculated to establish communication with them.

If there is to be communication, then there is presumably something to communicate. But as E. I. Mascall has pertinently remarked, in a review of *Honest to God:* "If Dr. Robinson is right in saying that 'God is teaching us that we must live as men who can get on very well without Him,' then the Church has no need to say anything whatever to secularized man, for that is precisely what secularized man already believes." (*The Honest to God Debate*, p. 93)

I should say, as a rough guess, that at least a million people have read this book and doubtless many more are acquainted with the controversy about it through the newspapers, magazines and TV. Who are all these people? Are they the godless seculars who have long since dismissed religion from their mind and who are incapable of "having a religious problem"? Remember, one of the ideas the Bishop takes from Bonhoeffer and makes axiomatic is that Christianity is trying to awaken problems in the mind of the man who no longer has any religious difficulties, in order to make him "need God" in this sense. What it may do, for readers who are troubled about the viability of Christian ideas, is make them more comfortable with a religionless religion, that is nevertheless sincerely "Christian."

To judge by the letters reprinted in the *Honest to God Debate* the people who have been most "helped" (and they have certainly been at least stimulated) by the Bishop's book are those who, having a vaguely Christian background of some sort, or having been "practicing Christians" whether Anglican or Protestant and then fallen into doubt, have drawn comfort from the fact that there was a Bishop who understood their difficulty because he shared it. A large number, perhaps the majority of those who articulated comment on the book, were clergymen or university dons and students, or professional people: all of them very conscious of the lack of rapport between Christianity and secular society. All have agreed that it was both subjectively and objectively dishonest for the Church (of England) to go on pretending to be completely convinced by the language of traditional theology. Presented with a choice of "where to stand" they have elected to stand rather with the secular and godless world (believing that this is really "where God is") than with the religious and theological culture of their Fathers. As Bishop Robinson says very beautifully: "For Christianity the holy is in the depth of the common." Taken as it stands, this statement is pure Gospel gold. But in its context it becomes rather more drossy.

What *is* the worldly, the secular, the common? The Bishop of Woolwich makes no distinctions, no qualifications. But surely, if he remembers the existentialist background of his mentors, he must have some sense of the *verfehltes Dasein*, the forfeited, alienated and unredeemed "giveness" that constitutes "the self-in-the-world" for the Christian existentialist. Surely, a passive and uncritical acceptance of whatever "is there" is no way to find "God in the world." A naive enthusiasm and ill-considered commitment to the latest secular optimism is surely not enough to constitute that "true religion" which "consists in harmonizing oneself with the evolutionary process as it develops ever higher forms of self-consciousness." If it is, then the Bishop of Woolwich, for all the refinement of his thought and sophistication of his reading, is giving us little more than the old amalgam of agnosticism, laissez faire and bourgeois hopefulness which has been the stock in trade of religious liberalism for the last hundred years. This may be some comfort to the religiously confused who have still not made the total break with religion. But I have small difficulty imagining what a convinced Marxist might have to say about it.

This is not a book for the unbeliever, though the Bishop hopes it is. Speaking from my own experience, I would say that thirty years ago I would hardly have read the first ten pages. For the complete unbeliever, the very question of religion and Christianity is irrelevant, and the fact that a Christian Bishop happens to admit that he sees its irrelevance is of no interest whatever. That is the Bishop's business.

236

The strange thing is that today, being by the grace of God a believer, a monk and a priest, I have read the book with very real interest. Its problem, which is of no concern to an unbeliever, is very real to a believer. We all realize that as Christians we have to make up our minds about our position in an unchristian world, a "diaspora." Whether we like it or not, we have to accept the diaspora situation if we want to be honest. In this I agree, as Karl Rahner would, with Bonhoeffer, the Bishop of Woolwich, and so many others, including also Karl Barth. It would be absurd to try to convince ourselves, with the triumphalists, that the Catholicism of the Council of Trent (or the Anglicanism of Cranmer) is about to make a victorious comeback and sweep all godless philosophies from the scene.

I for my part am not disturbed at being one of a minority, and if it ends up with me being a minority of one, then, by God's grace, I will accept the fact with equanimity and hold to my theology which is that of Catholic tradition. This will not prevent me loving those who disagree. If occasion arises, I will certainly try to make that theology comprehensible to those who do not hold it with me. I will do this not because I want to be officially correct, or to be approved by a curia which may (let us suppose) have been blown off the face of the earth by an H-bomb. I will do it not because I think the concepts are fashionable and acceptable to twentieth-century man. I will do it because it is my way of being "honest to God" and loyal to the grace which has, as I believe, brought me to the awareness of the unknowable and unspeakable One who is present to me (I gladly agree here with Tillich and the Bishop) in the pure ground of my being. I will do it in my own terms, which may have something of St. John of the Cross, something of St. Thomas, something of the Greek and Latin Fathers, something also of Tauler and Co., of Christian existentialism, and something

237

even of Zen. I think that if the Bishop of Woolwich were a little more aware of these traditional expressions of honesty to God, his book would be more viable than it is.

As it is, however, I think that *Honest to God* is an expression of sincere but misdirected concern: a concern to find "fellowship" with modern secular man on a level that is still ambiguous and superficial because it still attempts, though with all decency and much tact, to "sell" a reconditioned image of a Christianity that is "worldly," "religionless" and free of myths. This may be all very well, but the unconditional character of the Christian concern, to use the Bishop's own language, demands that at some point one confront "the world" with a refusal. We know, in fact, that Bonhoeffer did just this. He certainly did not pretend to find God in Nazism. He gave his life in protest against such an illusion.

Yet this, in conclusion, leaves us with one sobering reflection. It was Bonhoeffer the "religionless," Bonhoeffer who sought "God in the world," who died protesting against Nazi worldliness when the vast majority of the religious, the orthodox, the officially other-worldly and impeccably Christian, lined up behind Hitler's armies and marched in the godless military parade even when they knew they were supporting a government that was determined to destroy their Churches.

No matter what one may say about *Honest to God*, there is something of this intransigent sincerity in it: something that cannot be belittled or ignored. It is more than mere goodwill. I have seen some privately circulated lectures of the Bishop of Woolwich which are far more important and more exciting than *Honest to God* and theologically much deeper. There is something stirring here and the noise over one book must not make us inattentive to what is to come.

The Death of God and the
End of History

THE PURPOSE OF THESE NOTES IS REFLECTIVE RATHER THAN
polemical. That certain Christian theologians are saying
"God is dead" is a fact of some cultural and perhaps even
religious importance. It is important as a critique of traditional Christian ideas, but it also has a special significance
in so far as it preaches a radical "Christian worldliness."
Since all Christians, both radical and conservative, are
deeply concerned with the question of Christianity's relation to the modern world, and since that world is in fact
undergoing revolutionary changes which we must admit we
do not fully understand, it is appropriate to consider the
God-is-dead theology in some of its practical consequences
for all of us who, whether we like it or not, are involved in
this revolution. And we may ask: is the God-is-dead theology really as radical and as revolutionary as it claims to be?

1

First of all: what is meant by the current solemnization
of the "death of God"? It claims to be an act of fervent
Christian iconoclasm which is vitally necessary both for
Christianity and for the "world" since without it (so the
argument runs) Christianity cannot recover any relevance
at all in the modern world and the world itself cannot discover its own implicit and unrecognized potentialities, as
the area in which God is most active in his seeming absence.
For when we recognize he is "not there" we act freely and
in our freedom he "is there." The idea is deliberately left

239

ambiguous, elusive, deceptive. It is paradoxical, dialectical, and it aims to open up perspectives for further development: hence it refuses to make definitive statements once and for all. The kerygma of the "death of God" is then, in fact, *not* a categorical affirmation that "God does not exist" over against a dogma of his existence. Still less is it a declaration that he "never existed." It is rather a declaration that the question of God's existence has now become irrelevant. An announcement of "good news": God as a problem no longer requires our attention.

To begin with, it is no longer necessary (so they say) to assume that because we exist, God exists. In other words, God has for so long been treated as a necessary hypothesis "to explain our existence" that he is no longer of any importance to us when we cease to need or to desire any such hypothesis. This is a perhaps justifiable reaction against a shallow and basically rationalistic apologetic for Christianity which has surely lost any meaning today, but we may remark in passing that it has nothing to do with any authentic understanding of the God of Christian theology or of Christian mysticism. What is involved, however, is a repudiation of *all* discussion of God, whether speculative or mystical: a repudiation of the very notion of God, even as "unknowable." Any claim whatever to know Him, or to know what one is talking about in discussing Him, is dismissed a priori as infected with mythology. At the same time, it is implicitly admitted that this mythology *was once* relevant, but is so no longer.

The language of theology and of revelation has "died" on us, so the argument runs. The words have lost their meaning. Or the meaning they have kept is purely formal, ritual, incantatory, magic.

Thus the "death of God" means also a repudiation not only of traditional theology but also of metaphysics. Some-

240

times (by Catholics who favor this approach) the "death of God" is presented sympathetically as the death of hellenistic metaphysics and the return to a Biblical concept of God which is presumably "non-metaphysical." The death of God therefore implies resurrection. He is not really dead. This offhand recognition of the Bible would seem to be too facile, and one wonders if those who make it have really been reading the Bible lately. Is Biblical language really what they consider relevant to modern man? For the more radical Protestant "God is dead" theologians, this new theology itself is post-Biblical, the Biblical revelation of God is discarded, and even theology itself is discarded. The new theology is an anti-theology. Along with God, the Bible, theology and revelation have "died" too. This is a more consistent and complete rejection of *all* traditionally acceptable language about God. No talk of God is acceptable any more, whether Hellenistic or Hebraic, metaphysical or Biblical. There is nothing left but complete silence about God, since God Himself is completely silent. What then? A quietistic void? No. The confession of God is replaced by another confession which is explicitly and formally a confession of "the world" and (only if you are very much in the know) an implicit and secret confession of the nameless one that we don't talk about any more but who is hiddenly present just where the Churches say he can least be: in the depth of secularity, worldliness and even sin. (The concept of sin is of course dead.)

2

The affirmation of the death of God is then not to be regarded in any way as a metaphysical or theological statement about the ultimate cause or ground of being. It prescinds entirely from the actual existence or non-existence of

241

God and goes beyond all speculation on this or any other question. It is the expression of a "happening" in the consciousness of man. It is rather a matter of "personal witness," the epiphany of a new state of consciousness, a new mode of being in the world, a new relationship to the secular world. This is a "confession," both public and "Christian." The avowal of the "death of God" is a kind of Augustinianism turned inside out, a *confessio peccati* and a *confessio laudis* in which the secular world, not God is singled out for praise, and the sin which is confessed is the sin not of infidelity but of belief. But this cannot be understood if it is regarded as atheism and apostasy (except in a purely superficial sense) because far beneath the surface the *confessio* remains a paradoxical, extreme and kenotic witness to God. A witness of self-emptying in honor of the God who has so emptied himself as to die on the Cross and *not* rise again to resume his former transcendence. He remains only as immanent, empty and hidden in man and in the world. He is present more especially in those who deny him and repudiate him and refuse to recognize him.

One can detect more than a hint of masochism and guilt in the kenoticism of the God-is-dead consciousness, but perhaps this is blended with a note of genuine humility that is more attractive than the intransigence and aggressivity of some who take the affirmation of God's existence to be the basis for the affirmation that they themselves are always right and justified in everything because they are believers.

The kenotic witness of the God-is-dead Christian takes this form: a confession of having sinned against the world, of having insulted the adulthood of man by having believed in a transcendent God. At this one falls at the feet of the world to beg pardon and, by that token, recognizes that "secular man," the non-believer, who simply experiences God as dead, absent and incredible, and makes no bones

242

about admitting it, is closer to God than the believer who claims, in bad faith, to experience the divine presence. The basic dogma of the God-is-dead theology is that any claim to an experience of the reality of God and of his relevance for life on earth today is bound to be fraudulent or at least illusory. The ground of this theology is not a metaphysical or theological assumption about being or about God, but a psychological and epistemological assumption about human consciousness in the modern age. Whereas traditional theology sets explicit dogmatic limits to what can and cannot be rightly affirmed about God's self-revelation, the God-is-dead theology sets implicit and not clearly defined limits to what modern man is actually capable of experiencing honestly. The basis of traditional theology is a dogmatic and objective divine revelation. The basis of God-is-dead theology is man's present subjective state of consciousness which can be tested as authentically modern if it corresponds to "the world of our time" in its historical, technological, political actuality. But just as the traditional believer may assume that his own experience of a saving God (insofar as it corresponds to the *sensus Ecclesiae*) is a valid starting point for any discussion of God, so the God-is-dead Christian assumes that his experience of the world (vindicated by a certain correspondence with the experience of the nearest available nonbeliever) is a valid starting point for any discussion of the world and of the modern consciousness.

Thus we find something of the same ambiguities that we have always encountered in the past. The fervent proselytizer who wants to make converts share his own experience of being saved is replaced by the Christian who is completely "hip" to the modern world and will not listen for a moment to anyone who he suspects does not experience the modern world exactly as he does. Insofar as he has com-

243

mitted himself to a *confessio laudis* of the modern world, he instinctively regards as suspect any tendency to question or criticize "the world." More precisely he resents any questioning of the pragmatic, technological, sociopolitical understanding of the world as autonomous and self-sufficient.

The "death of God" is thus the proclamation of a self-consciously post-Christian attitude. What is that? A post-Christian attitude is first of all based on an assumption: that the essence of Christianity is the summons to choose between God and the world. Faced with this "either/or," the Christian must choose God and reject the world. The sinner chooses the world and rejects God. (St. Augustine spelled this out with his two loves and two cities.) But the post-Christian choice is the reverse of this: to choose the world and proclaim that God is dead is the authentic (rather than "virtuous") choice. It is the choice of love and openness. To choose God and reject the world becomes the inauthentic, loveless, insincere choice. Why? Because in fact the "Christian" choice has become perverted by centuries of corrupt and insincere manipulation. Hence the post-Christian decision is now necessary. If one is interested in saving any vestige of Christian honesty, he must look to the post-Christian choice. In this regard the judgment of man replaces the judgment of God. He who chooses God is condemned by the world for fraud and evasion. Christianity too saw this, but it believed the judgment of the world was to be despised and withstood. As long as the Christian was an authentic martyr, this was quite true. But when his denial of the world became confused with the defense of a Church institution in league with the world, the denial was ambiguous.

In order to understand this more clearly, we have to realize that the confession of the death of God is a bid for solidarity, for communion, for a discovery of a new and more real "union in Christ" which is outside and beyond the institutional barriers which the Church, in centuries past, erected against "the world." Here we find what is most valid and cogent in the new critique of institutional religion: that "the Churches" have created a separate world within the world, a world claiming to be "sacred," while surreptitiously gaining and retaining for themselves every possible worldly advantage and privilege. This ecclesiastical world identifies itself as "holier" and "better" than any other society by virtue of external rites and signs, and presumes to condemn and to vilify all that is real, valid, alive, creative, forwardlooking in order to maintain its own traditional advantage. That this has been done in the name of God, and that those who do this have claimed, by virtue of their fervor in vilifying the world, that they are the true children of God, has therefore contributed to the "Death of God" in the eyes of the modern world.

We can rather easily understand a reaction against the stereotyped opposition by which traditional religion tended to set up God, the supernatural and the sacred over against the world, the natural and the secular, in a dualism that no longer seems valid or practical today. Unfortunately, it seems that the God-is-dead Christian has simply perpetuated this same dualism by turning it inside out: but of course, since he is thinking dialectically, he can be credited with sincerity in saying that he hopes to go beyond this dualistic position to a new synthesis. The tension he sets up between the two poles "God" and "world" aims to make us experience the futility of such a tension and to discover that God, who is no longer "present" as Absolute transcendent Being, is secretly present in the world, where he seems to be absent because entirely immanent. Yet is this a valid synthesis? Is the dialectic really vital, the tension really operative? Or is it simply, once again, a "four legs good two

245

legs bad" argument, as in Orwell's *Animal Farm*? (It is true of course that *Animal Farm* culminated in its own peculiar synthesis.)

3

Has the God-is-dead theology merely substituted "history" and "politics" for "metaphysics" and "revelation"? And if so, can that theology be called authentically "modern"? Is it not still implicated in naive nineteenth-century assumptions? Is it not simply a belated Christian "confession" of evolutionism now glorified as a pragmatic, historical mystique? Without pausing here to discuss the New Left Catholics in England (who seem to have something impressive and disturbing to say) we can say that the comfortable "secular city" theorists in America seem to be confessing the praise of an affluent world that does not need, in any significant way, to be changed. There are aspects of the God-is-dead Christianity in America which make its professed radicalism seem a matter of journalistic cliche and little more. Nothing could be less revolutionary in fact than a kind of quietism which simply celebrates and glorifies the muzak-supermarket complex and which ultimately points to the conclusion that Los Angeles is almost the New Jerusalem.

Here it may be well to mention that critics of the modern technological world, whether Christian or not, are the worst of heretics for the God-is-dead theology. D. H. Lawrence, T. S. Eliot, James Joyce, Kafka and others are singled out for special blame. They all look with suspicion upon the modern world, and some of them seek to fulfill their hopes outside the framework of that world. Some of them even hold to the idea that religion is necessary, and that man cannot find any meaning in life without God. On the con-

246

trary, says one of these new theologians, the first principle of the new theology is that man has no need of God and as long as he imagines he needs God he is alienated from reality—the reality of his own world. Salvation is to be found in a worldliness which is "post-modern, pro-bourgeois, urban and political." This worldliness, incidentally, takes nothing terribly seriously. Or so we are told. It is a fun-worldliness in which "Life is a masked ball, a Halloween party" and the place where the party is held is "the city." Especially the American city, for America is farthest along in the new development: "We are the most profane, the most banal, the most worldly of places." The banality of our urban world is not, however, deplored by this theologian: it is acknowledged, accepted and rejoiced in precisely because it is a sign of authentic faithlessness. And we must "not only acknowledge but will this faithlessness." And in so doing, we must realize that the seemingly innocent banality of the surface hides a deeper ugliness, which is also to be hailed with gladness: "(the God-is-dead theologian) knows that his rebellion and unbelief is both deeper and uglier than his bland worldly mask suggests. . . ." Of course this is more subtle than it seems here: it implies a marriage of quietism and revolt which is a little hard to understand. It *accepts* everything "with passivity" yet waits for some inexplicable breakthrough, some ultimate coming that will happen in the midst of the urban (or suburban?) bourgeois world. Already the American God-is-Dead movement seems to be an entirely post-Marxian and new-bourgeois movement.

Hence it seems at times to be considerably less than revolutionary. The enthusiasm for the secular city coincides with fervent praise of American affluence, which is in fact rooted in the enormous military-industrial complex and therefore in the Vietnam war. Though the God-is-dead movement repudiates transcendence, mysticism, inward-

247

ness, divine law and so forth, turning to immanence, out-going love and creative innovation in interpersonal relationships, its substitution of "history" and "politics" for metaphysics and religion may run the risk of ending in conformism, acquiescence, and passive approval of the American managerial society, affluent economy and war-making power politics. Without entering into moral or political polemics on this point, the question I would like to raise is this. It is a question which flows quite naturally from the rather cogent arguments that accuse established religion of having made God incredible and, in fact, of having "murdered" Him. Is the nineteenth century phenomenon of the Death of God, which led to the so-called "post-Christian era, now inexorably followed by a twentieth-century "death of history" and the "post-historic" and "post-political" era? If that is the case, then in abandoning metaphysics in favor of history and politics the God-is-dead people are jumping onto a dead horse and their hope of riding somewhere is vain.

Of course here we must be careful. Slogans about fidelity to history and eschatologies which seek fulfillment by political revolution tend to reflect a Marxist type of radicalism. Those post-Christians who are inclined to Marxism are also confirmed believers in an historical responsibility. But the God-is-dead theology in America already tends, as we have seen, to a more passive and quietistic, a more frankly "post-historic" attitude. We may recall here the dilemma which was faced by Camus: reviled for being "anti-historical" (by Marxist critics) he distinguished two extreme positions which he found equally unacceptable: one which, for the sake of power, uses men as material with which to "make history"—it sacrifices human beings to an absolute a prioristic logic of "history" which is in fact a fabrication. The other position, basing itself on eternal and spiritual values, accepts

248

non-violence and self-sacrifice, but is in fact inefficacious. Camus concluded that both are myths, and that one must be "neither a victim nor an executioner" (neither a yogi nor a commissar) but work out a dialectic of "revolt" (as opposed to "revolution") which consistently refuses to make violence and murder the basis of its system. In his harrowing story of "The Renegade" he caricatured the Christian who foresook his Christianity to join forces with a historicist and political absolutism. Historicism is of course not "history." The question now is: has this mythical reverence for a completely fabricated idea of history so concealed the reality of our development that it becomes a justification for murderous illusions rather than a guide to reasonable action? If so, the Christian who rightly recognizes his historical responsibilities must take care not to be too naive in his reverence for all that is proposed to him in the name of history.

4

A recent article of Hannah Arendt on "Truth and Politics" investigates the well known hostility of power politicians not only toward historical opinions which they regard as inopportune, but above all toward *historic fact*. Hannah Arendt investigates the irrelevance of philosophical truth for political action and brings forth other disconcerting ironies, including the fact that "the blurring of the dividing line between factual truth and opinion belongs among the many forms that lying can assume, all of which are forms of (political) action." She concludes that the plain impracticality of truth tends to make lying much more interesting for men of action since lying is a form of political action, while telling the truth is not. More and more frequently we observe that the distortion of truth in favor of policy is regarded as political "realism." In other words fact becomes ancillary to political *will*. Nor, in this ironic analysis, is rationality at all necessary to politics. Irrationality may prove much more realistic and effective in manipulating opinion and getting things done. There is a political affinity between the desire to change the world and the ability to say, convincingly, that the sun is shining when really it is raining cats and dogs. Not that all politicians are systematic liars, far from it. But a certain distortion always makes things at once more plausible and more persuasive: more likely to be accepted as obviously true. This has probably always been the case, not only among politicians but among all who make use of rhetoric in order to persuade. (One is sometimes utterly astounded by the pious falsification to which preachers resort in narrating anecdotes that are supposed to edify.) But today, with the enormous amplification of news and of opinion, we are suffering from more than acceptable distortions of perspective. Our supposed historical consciousness, over-informed and over-stimulated, is threatened with death by bloating, and we are overcome with a political elephantiasis which sometimes seems to make all actual forward motion useless if not impossible. But in addition to the sheer volume of information there is the even more portentous fact of falsification and misinformation by which those in power are often completely intent not only on misleading others but even on convincing themselves that their own lies are "historical truth." Remember Simone Weil's remark that "official history is a matter of believing murderers on their own word." One of the deeper lessons of Camus's novel *The Plague* is that what is most central, most urgent, and most deadly becomes present to us in life in a way that cannot be accounted for either as news or as history. And we stand alone and helpless, facing what we cannot know, deafened by the "lie-making machine."

Is this elephantiasis of the historic and political consciousness in fact leading to the "death of history"? Not that history will cease to "happen" but we may altogether cease to
know what is happening let alone understand it. It will happen indeed, but only to be transformed, definitively, into
something that it never was. Politics, instead of being a
means by which man can change his world, will have become simply the means of converting political manipulation
into bogus "historical record."

A really valid concern with history and with politics
would seem to assume that one actually knows what is going
on and that one is able to make efficacious decisions on the
basis of that knowledge. But what if in fact the historical
consciousness is merely a consciousness of what is *thought
to be happening*, and the political consciousness leads
merely to a decision to believe that what was said to have
happened actually happened—in order to approve or dis-
approve it in accordance with an accepted line of thought?
Surely in such a case "history is dead," just as "God is dead,"
for the idea of history then becomes fiction which keeps one
from being aware of what is going on and from making
decisions that are really capable of influencing man's destiny
in a free and constructive manner. The historical and political consciousness are then just as much involved in myth—
no more and no less—than the consciousness of the primitive who seeks to help nature along by celebrating fertility
rites in the planting season. If to this fallacious and uncritical "awareness of history" we also add a mystique of man
attaining "full maturity" we may indeed be groping for a
way to appreciate our radically new situation in a world of
rapid technological development, but should we not be a
little careful about elevating this mystique to the status of
unquestioned dogma? And of doing so, moreover, on the
grounds that God is dead? Does not this sometimes end in
a circular argument that God has to be dead because man

is now an adult and man now has to be an adult because
God is dead?

These are not merely captious questions if, in fact, the
God-is-dead theology results in nothing more than a quasi-
Christian mystique of technological man as the summit of
the evolutionary process. There is more involved, today,
than merely acquiring a new self-understanding that will
aesthetically round out man's modern experience and give
it a kind of post-Christian coherence. Man is evidently faced
with decisions of great importance for his own survival, and
he is perfectly aware of this. But he should also be more
aware of the deviousness of his own heart and of his own
propensity to justify destructive tendencies with moral,
religious, philosophical or even scientific rationalizations.
The God-is-dead mystique is as likely as any other to lead
to mystification, and more likely when it naively accepts
certain political or economic mystifications which are
already fully active. The validity of the God-is-dead theology's claim to iconoclasm will have to be proved not only
by the readiness with which he confesses the shallowness
of certain Christian myths, but also by its ability to see
through secular myths as well. Does the new theology simply "liberate" the Christian from traditional Christianity in
order to subject him to a ready-made political or a-political
ideology of questionable worth? Or does it turn him loose
in a world without values, to occupy himself with the infinite variety of possible metamorphoses in his own consciousness, his own awareness of himself in his self-creating
milieu?

One wonders if history and politics are not already largely
self-discrediting. Certainly the efforts of the young (in a
desperation which is as touching as it is original) to find
entirely new styles of common life and action, suggest that
the conventional ideas of history and politics are already, in

252

their eyes, thoroughly suspect. It is not surprising then that they can afford scarcely more than a yawn for a new theology which comes to them claiming to define for them their own experience with terms in which they recognize only the experience of their fathers.

It would seem that the real objection to the God-is-dead movement is not that it is heretical, unorthodox, too iconoclastic, too radical, "too modern," but on the contrary that it is a tame and belated attempt to transfer Christian insights from the realm of traditional objective theology to that of a modern subjective consciousness which in seeking to be perfectly contemporary is already behind the times. Can such a consciousness appeal to the young who already experience certain hopes and anxieties of another order? What these hopes and anxieties may be I, for one, am in no position to define, but I wonder if they reflect a complacent acceptance of our affluent and highly organized society.

Are we in fact witnessing the death, or perhaps the burial, of "history" in its conventionally accepted sense of something that we "make" and which, as the product of our collective actions and decisions, day by day fills up a record of permanent factual truth set aside for future study and reference? Are we deluding ourselves in fabricating a new Christian myth by which we reassure ourselves that this great political mosaic is in fact a kind of jigsaw puzzle in which we (the initiates) know that what is really being formed is the face of Christ? Are we, without knowing it, under cover of these new myths of ours, drifting into a new world of total, predetermined necessity, a new "system" entirely closed to all liberty and impervious to revolutionary change (except for its own immanent technical revolutionism, determined not by man's will but by technology's own capacity for self-perfection in its own realm, without consideration for man's real needs)? In other words, is the old,

253

sacred, closed, magic and cosmic mystery now being replaced by a new, secular, but equally closed, and equally
determined technological mystery? Are we simply coming
back in a circle to a world that is enclosed in itself: no
longer the world of "nature" and of "religion" but the world
of technique and of formal secular celebrations? In either
case, a world of necessity and not of freedom, a world in
which one has only a certain limited freedom within the
confines of a great all-embracing necessity? In the first case,
freedom being for the Gods, in the second, for the technological process itself to go its own way and to determine the
conditions for everyone's existence? In this event, the God-
is-dead theology would seem to represent not so much an
escape from an ancient cosmic religious determinism, as a
return to a new "sacred" enclosed and fully determined universe of technological immanentism in which the only freedom left is the freedom to accept certain innovations in
one's life style (long hair, guitars) and to protest against
universal sameness by nihilism, dope, riot, crime or something else equally destructive and futile.

5

This survey of some problems raised by the God-is-dead
theology may perhaps throw light on problems which are
common to the rest of us who still "believe." On one hand
a professed radicalism in religion, which is in reality an
attempt to adjust religion to modern developments which
it has hitherto resisted—for instance evolutionism, pragmatism, existentialism, Marxism. On the other a "positive attitude" toward the world and the cultivation of a historical
and political consciousness which resolves itself into uncritical acceptance of and solidarity with established social and
political forms, familiar managerial societies, whether capi-

talist or Marxist. But as was suggested above, there are found, in these various "establishments," certain serious ambiguities which lead one to suspect that we are entering a post-historical era in which the concept of "history" becomes confused and misleading, and a mystique of history ends in mystification pure and simple. Is our "turning to the world" merely a matter of abandoning a mediaeval mystique in order to adopt another which died some time ago—perhaps as a casualty of World War I?

There is in this much-publicized movement a sort of pseudo-creativity which has a certain value. It is iconoclastic up to a point, and it does open up new perspectives. But its iconoclastic thrust is applied where success is cheapest, because resistance is weary, formal and half-hearted. The real idols of our time are not religious, they are secular, and the real challenge to Christianity today is not a matter of mere self-criticism and adaptation to the world, but above all the recovery of a creative and prophetic iconoclasm over against the idols of power, mystification and super-control. These tighten upon man and enclose him in a new world of mystery where the myths are no longer religious and spiritual but historical, political and pseudo-scientific.

The attack upon these idols cannot, however, be a mere reiteration of ancient religious values, of spiritual essences, or a mere recovery of inwardness, or a return to eternal principles. Still less can it be an official and ecclesial operation vested with every kind of pontifical approval. Such an attack will be futile if it confines itself to the realm of ideas. As Camus pointed out with great intelligence, the combat based on absolute positions leads inevitably to quietism or to tyranny. In other words to idolatries that ultimately paralyze all action. Wherever idols, religious or secular, are set up as absolutes, as necessary, as final, the human and valid response is an affirmation of man in his concreteness, his

255

limitation, his openness, his potentiality for development. Far from being a mere speculative declaration about man's essence, or a doctrinaire humanism of some sort, this affirmation takes shape in actual human solidarity and communion. Against the mass brutality of war and police oppression, solidarity with the victims of that oppression. Against the inhumanity of organized affluence, solidarity with those who are excluded from any participation in the benefits of almost unlimited plenty. Where "the world" means in fact "military power," "wealth," "greed," then the Christian remains against it. When the world means those who are concretely victims of these demonic abstractions (and even the rich and mighty are their victims too) then the Christian must be for it and in it and with it.

The problem of course is this: in the name of God a worldly Church in the past became an integral part of the secular establishment which it officially reviled. Is it any better for a worldly Church simply to claim for itself a niche in the new, more frankly secular establishment by announcing that God is dead? This is not even good pragmatism. The death of God is something in which the new thrones and dominations are no longer even interested. The ritual confession of God's death and the formal expiation of the sin of having once believed is at best an acceptable entertainment in which the post-Christian may momentarily congratulate himself that he has been received into a fun-community with the demonic powers he can no longer honestly oppose.

Since this essay was first published, the latest and most important book of Thomas J. J. Altizer has appeared. *The New Apocalypse*, a study of William Blake, throws a different light on the God-is-dead movement. Whatever may be the limitations of some of the other writers of this school, it is certain that for Altizer the "death of God" kenoticism does not imply passive submission to power politics. On the

256

contrary, Blake is seen as a model for the prophetic radical Christianity; he was "unique among all visionaries in that he chose to confront the awesome reality of history as the total epiphany of the sacred." But this implies a rejection of the mystique of a purely profane history.

Eliade has shown that "religion" tends everywhere to dissolve history or to evade it. Only the prophetic tradition of the Old Testament, developed by later Judaic and Christian prophetism, accepts history instead of opposing it. But even traditional eschatology tends to equate the consummation of history with its cataclysmic end and the Parousia of the transcendent Jesus.

It must be remarked, however, that Altizer sees the problem of the secularization of history much as I see it. The prophetic tradition has, he says, "been swallowed up in the contemporary West by a radically profane historicism that in granting ultimate value to historical events has abolished any meaning lying beyond them." It has, in fact, yielded to the Faustian temptation to create a meaning of its own "behind" them—a self-justification by crude lies, woven together in a farcical mystique. Altizer quotes Eliade: "Modern man's boasted freedom to make history is illusory for nearly the whole of the human race. At most man is left free to choose between two positions: (1) to oppose the history that is being made by the very small minority (and in this he is free to choose between suicide and deportation); and (2) to take refuge in a subhuman existence or in flight."

This confronts the modern Christian with a pervasive temptation to a "gnostic retreat from history" or to a regressive eschatology which simply calls the Lord of History to come at once and damn everything. "Only the radical Christian," says Altizer (pointing to Blake), "can meet this temptation with the faith that a totally fallen history is finally the redemptive epiphany of Christ." This is an arresting phrase.

What exactly does it mean? Not the Parousia of the Judge from above and outside history but an immanent dialectical acceptance and reversal of "fallen history."

The following quotation will, I think, make Altizer's meaning clear. "Now the time has come for faith to engage in its deepest confrontation with history. Can faith meet the challenge with a final Yes-saying to history, or must it utter a final No to a history that has lost all its moorings in Christendom? No doubt a traditional faith must say that No, but Blake's vision points the way to a total acceptance, if ultimate reversal, of the full reality of a fallen history."

This is something quite different from mere acquiescence in the manipulation of history by power politicians and a supine acceptance of a secularist mystique *on its own terms.* On the other hand it is not a mere Gnostic repudiation of the power struggle as a pure manifestation of evil without any relevance for salvation history. It is, as Altizer says, at once *acceptance and reversal.* A reading of Blake's Prophetic Books will show clearly enough how radical is the reversal! On the other hand, the reversal is not a rejection of history in favor of something else that is totally outside history. The reversal comes from within history accepted, in its often shattering reality, as the focus of salvation and epiphany. It is not that the world of Auschwitz, Vietnam and the Bomb has to be cursed and repudiated as the devil's own territory. That very world has to be accepted as the terrain of the triumph of love not in the condemnation of evil but in its forgiveness: and this is certainly not an easy truth when we confront the enormity of the evil!

Whatever may be the merits of Altizer's arguments in the realm of theology, it is clear that he is not preaching a quietistic acceptance of evil-as-good. On the other hand, not many Christians are yet capable of fully grasping either the import of Blake's visions or the dialectical sophistication of Altizer's thesis.

"Godless Christianity"?

IT IS NOT EASY TO DISCUSS THE CURRENT PATTERNS OF RADICAL Christian thinking that are woven in and out with the conviction that "God is dead." Certainly the remarks that are presented here do not pretend to be an adequate summing up of the Radical Theology which has replaced the New Orthodoxy of twenty, thirty and forty years ago. At present the new thinking is so fluid and has been so distorted by publicity that one would have a hard time saying exactly what it is all about. But it does certainly have a general character and import that call for objective discussion. And in the first place I shall assume that one's reaction need not necessarily be a reflex of horrified and scandalized rejection. I for one do not insist that all the God-is-dead theologians should be hustled at once to the stake and set alight without further consideration. Though I may not agree with their theology, I am still able to sympathize, at least to some extent, with what they are trying to do.

In the first place of course, they are not "atheists." Or rather they are not the old belligerent pseudo-scientific militant atheists. After all there is a significant difference between the proposition that "God is dead" and the proposition that God never existed anyway. So if they are to be called "atheists" (and apparently they would not object to this), the term would have to be used in a very special sense. The claim that "God is dead" is a claim that in the present state of grave religious crisis the old ways of talking about God and indeed of believing in him no longer have any serious meaning for man. This is a claim that is made very seriously and, one might add, very sweepingly too. It implies that those who do try to cling to the traditional Biblical ideas of God in this time of crisis are either stupid, or "not with it," or more reprehensibly, in "bad faith."

Behind this approach to Christianity today lies the awareness of a *crisis of language*, a crisis in communication. It is not just that certain verbal formulas have become questionable and hard to believe. It is not just a matter of certain "myths." What is questioned is not just the language of the Bible and of the Creeds or the speculations of theology, but the whole issue of revelation itself. One might say that the cornerstone of the whole God-is-dead movement (if there is one) is the formal belief that revelation itself is inconceivable. To say God is dead is to say He is silent, that He cannot be conceived as speaking to man, that whether or not He ever spoke in the past, the whole concept of revelation has now become obsolete because modern man is simply incapable not only of grasping it but even of being interested in it at all.

Now I think that here is precisely where the trouble begins. To say that modern man cannot believe in God because God is unbelievable to modern man and to conclude that any modern man who believes in God is therefore faking: this is not only questionable logic but it seems to me to savor a little of the same bad faith of which it accuses the believer. No matter. I am not trying to set up apologetic arguments against the Radical Theology. One of the reasons why the Radical Theology exists in the first place is that it is a reaction of nausea against the insufficiency of apologetics.

The "God" which Radical Theology claims to be dead is, in many respects, a God that never lived anyway: a God of hypotheses, a God of pious cliches, a God of formalistic ritual, a God invoked to make comfortable people more pleased with themselves, a God called upon to justify every kind of cruelty and evil and hypocrisy. If the Radical Theologians claim that the New Testament preached the death of this false God we can only agree, adding meanwhile that the Old Testament did too: such a God is nothing but an idol. Unfortunately there is more to it than this. In sweeping aside all "transcendence," all "interiority," all "spirituality" and indeed all "religion" the Radical Theology seems at times to be preaching a kind of quietism. This quietism may be very active indeed: it hustles around in all directions. But it passively accepts the imperatives of a non-religious existence in the place of religion. It is radically secular. It is too uncritical of servitudes from which faiths and the spirit are meant to set us free.

The Bonhoeffer-Robinson school holds that the Christian should relinquish the myths of the past which believed in a transcendent Creator, a judging and redeeming god with a message of salvation. He should be an "adult," forget religiousness and inward piety, build the secular city, because in so doing he will be *closer to God.* Instead of listening for God to tell him what to do in a revealed word, man must build a world in which God will be revealed. Can we say that this view seems implicitly to be based on a choice between God and man? Is this school simply saying: "If we are forced to choose between an arid, formalistic faith in God 'out there' and a dynamic, creative love of man here and now, we will forsake the idea of God and choose man"? In so doing, we believe that we will really be closer to God, in His absolute hiddenness, for He has emptied Himself to become man and is manifesting Himself *only* in man." This option is not without its respectable features. It prefers reality and risk to security and abstract formulations. It is exasperated by a religiosity that argues interminably about God in heaven and shows no concern for man on earth. This religiosity, faced by the same implicit choice, seems to say: "If we are forced to choose between sinful man, his unpleasantness, his limitations, and the eternal Father in heaven, we will certainly turn our backs on man's failure to meet our requirements and prostrate ourselves before the Father in whom we are well pleased."

However, both these choices are misled, because there is in fact no such division in Christianity. It is not a matter of *either* God *or* man, but of finding God by loving man, and discovering the true meaning of man in our love for God. Neither is possible without the other.

It is unfortunately true that sometimes religion is turned against man and indifference, or even hatred of one's brother, is justified by an appeal to the holiness of God. St. John long ago made it impossible for anyone to claim seriously that this attitude could be called Christian. "If anyone declares 'I love God' and yet hates his brother, he is a liar; for he who will not love his brother whom he has seen, cannot possibly love the God whom he has never seen." (I John 4:20) The Radical Theologians seem, however, to be saying that this vice has become so ingrained in Christian habits of thought and institutional structures that in order to get back to an honest and direct love of our brother the concept of God, which has become an obstacle, has to be completely removed. They seem to be saying that all talk of God, all formulas of worship, all habits of pious interiority are so infected with sham that anyone who preserves them is bound in spite of himself to be a hypocrite who will always and everywhere seek his own spiritual comfort by rejecting his fellow man in order to affirm an abstract and hypothetical God. Unfortunately, the actual conduct of believers in the past and in the present gives some basis to this dreadful accusation. Yet this does not permit us to take an idyllic view of modern Godlessness. The fact that Christian ideals have undergone corruption does nothing to diminish the horror of the post-Christian "civilization" that is now taking over. When God is indeed "dead" in the lives of men, we see that the void left by His absence is filled with a variety of demons we would prefer not to contemplate. Yet they are there before us at every moment for us to consider: demons of ruthless exploitation, of genocide, cynical and barbarous travesties of justice, perversions of every human and natural instinct. The removal of an inconvenient God has apparently done very little to advance the cause of man.

The Second Vatican Council did not agree that we can appreciate the dignity and adulthood of man only if we decide for him and against God. The dignity and freedom of man, says the Council, remain abortive or deformed without an authentic conscious faith in God. "When a divine substructure and the hope of life eternal are wanting, man's dignity is most grievously lacerated, as current events often attest." (Constitution on the Church and the Modern World, n. 21) Hence the Catholic Church appeals not to dogma alone but to common sense and to the universal experience of our times.

Is it relevant for the Catholic Church to say this? Has any Church the right to claim the attention of modern man? If God is dead, then the Church has nothing more to say—for the Church claims to speak in his name.

This is another dire accusation leveled against traditional belief by the Radical Theologians. The Church has addressed man in his sorrow, in his sin, claiming to bring him not only consolation in his sorrow but redemption from his sin. If only he will listen to her the Church will provide him with a full and final answer. But the answer can only be bought at a certain price: the price of surrender and commitment. In this way, said Bonhoeffer, the Church has exploited man's sorrowful plight in order to gain possession of his freedom. This is the familiar argument of Feuerbach and

263

Marx, who thought the Church simply used man's alienation as an excuse to mystify and manipulate his life for her own advantage.

Atheism alleges that the Church has maliciously exploited the suffering and unhappiness of man in order to force upon him a mythical god who will make everything right and happy in heaven. Here the Radical Theologian joins forces with the atheist. He confronts the Church with the same accusation: that she secretly needs and fosters man's unhappiness in order to keep man under her own tutelage and under servitude to religious myths—that therefore she secretly opposes progress. Her condemnation of the world is then, according to this argument a spiteful attempt to fill man with guilt and fear, to make him hesitant and afraid, and to impede his growth to adulthood.

The argument against the Church and God is stated in its crudest terms by Bonhoeffer (speaking, remember, as a Christian aware of his ambiguous position vis-à-vis the modern world). The Christians, and their "secularized off-shoots . . . the existentialist philosophers and psychotherapists . . . demonstrate to secure, happy mankind that it is really unhappy and desperate . . . in severe straits it knows nothing at all about and from which only they can rescue it. Wherever there is health, strength, security, simplicity they spy luscious fruit to gnaw at or to lay their pernicious eggs in. . . ." Apart from the references to existentialism and psychotherapy, this might almost be quoted word for word from Nietzsche.

To counterattack with familiar apologetic arguments would, in Bonhoeffer's words again, be an affront "to the adulthood of the world—pointless, ignoble and unchristian."

What this argument rests on, however, is the assumption that man is in fact perfectly secure, happy, healthy, simple; that he is not unhappy, not frustrated, not desperate; that where he is in fact "adjusted" he not only does not feel guilt but he behaves kindly, simply, honestly, humanely toward his fellow man . . . and of course above all that he does this easily and habitually without any need for God, for faith, for grace, for sacraments, for revelation. In other words, man is at the point where he is capable of eliminating evil, suffering and unhappiness from his world without recourse to God, by the power of his own science and techniques. His only "insecurity" is then a hangover from his religious excesses in the past!

All that one can say to this is to ask—is this really the case? Is this empirically established? Is man's unhappiness something he is totally unaware of, something invented for him by the Church? Is his only insecurity fomented by religious illusions? Then evil itself is a myth. Auschwitz and Dachau were merely bad dreams. The Stalinist purges were imaginary. Hiroshima was a curious fantasy. The noncombatants burned up by napalm in Vietnam only thought they were burning. Obviously such an argument as this implies a capacity for myth-making hitherto unequalled by any ancient superstition: The atheist cannot possibly go this far, but he does—at least if he is a Marxist—make a few adjustments. Yes, there is evil in this world, certainly. But it is all to be blamed on a certain type of economic system, and on the mystifications of religion. When both are abolished—then all will be well.

Bonhoeffer himself, speculating on the challenge to Christianity, knew well enough there was evil in the world and that it had to be resisted. The lines quoted above were written in a German prison when he had been confined for his activity in the resistance against Hitler, and in a few months, he would pay for his resistance with his life.

As he sat and wrote in his cell, inexorably chosing, one after another, all the "emergency exists" of apologetics, clericalism, ritualism, "inwardness" and "the *salto mortale* (death leap) back to the Middle Ages," he found one way open still. This way can be summed up as an absolute religious *kenoticism,* a Christianity emptied of all, even of God himself. Not that Bonhoeffer does not "believe" in God, in Christ, in the Church, but his theory is that "ultimate honesty" demands that contemporary man live in the world *as though* he had no God. This must be qualified of course: not a life of "godlessness" in the sense of selfishness and immorality, but a life "without God" as a source of comfort, of aid, of support, without God to help our suffering make sense!

"God is teaching us that we must live as men who can get along very well without Him. The God who is with us is the God who forsakes us (Mark 15:34). The God who makes us live in the world without using Him as a working hypothesis is the God before whom we are ever standing."

This passage shows us clearly how far from atheism Bonhoeffer really is. Far from refuting the language of the Bible, Bonhoeffer uses it here. His terms not only echo the poetry of Biblical language but they are deeply impregnated with Biblical ontology. Scholars have pointed out that the Hebrew conception of being in the Bible is profoundly different from that of Greek philosophy—it differs also from that of Western philosophy in general. The Greek mind tends to consider "being" impersonally and objectively in its static aspect: The Hebrew concept is not only dynamic but tends to be personal and to suggest free personal interrelationships and commitments. The "being" of God in the Bible is therefore never merely an abstract conception of an absolute. God is not simply "the Supreme Being" and then, by inference, the "Supreme Manager" of everything. God is not known in His being except to those *for whom He is God.* And He is God *only for those into whose lives He has entered by his saving action.* This encounter, this dynamic, is

266

necessary to any valid Biblical conception of God. It is therefore quite different to speak of the God who is God *for us* and *with us,* and the God who simply "exists." In fact, it is precisely because theologians have talked so much of a god who was in reality not "their God" or "God for them" but only an abstraction and an institutional idol (a projection of their own wishes) that God has ceased to be God "for *anyone*" and hence "is dead." Yet we see at the same time that Bonhoeffer is saying that God's not "being with" us anymore is in fact another more mysterious way of "being for" us, and of being "our God."

Now we see at once that the Radical Theology of Bonhoeffer is not mere atheism. It implies a great purity of faith. One might compare it with St. John of the Cross. But Bonhoeffer is not speaking of or for mystics. He is outlining a program for ordinary Christian life. In so doing he is falling into the same problem as the Quietists. When all Christian life becomes a life of pure love and pure faith without God, without Christ, emptied of everything, then it tends to become in fact a pure void. The human spirit abhors a vacuum. If it is not filled with truth, with God, with love, it will be filled with something else.

This *kenotic* view of God is consistent with Bonhoeffer's view of man's adulthood. It is a kind of extreme faith, so extreme that it turns itself inside out. As the Quietists sought the extreme sacrifice and found it in relinquishing hope of salvation, so Bonhoeffer makes the supreme sacrifice: to live without God in order to be in the company of contemporary man. The dereliction of the mystic becomes the daily bread of the ordinary Christian. But the mystics have extraordinary graces to maintain them, and they retain at least their formal faith, hope and love of God no matter how dark their night. The ordinary man may find it a little difficult to believe in God when he is convinced that "God is dead." If in such a case he abandons all hope in God and places his hope in science, technology, money, comfort, et cetera, what does he have left? Well, he is at least *honest*. He is no longer pretending to be a Christian!

The Anglican Bishop of Woolwich, seizing upon this absolute *kenotic* honesty of Bonhoeffer, demanded to know "Can a truly contemporary person not be an atheist?" The question was not really new, but coming from a Bishop it aroused interest. There was a certain amount of controversy in which of course he admitted that he was not an atheist himself, just as Bonhoeffer has not been an atheist either. But the Bishop's point was that the traditional and Biblical language about God had become (he thought) so completely irrelevant and incredible to modern man that the only way to be "honest" with him was to act as if there simply were no God. Christianity would thus be purified of "religion" and the Christian would henceforth prove his Christianity not by his belief in God but by being a "man for others."

From the point of view of religious psychology there is something to be said for both Bonhoeffer and Robinson. They have clearly diagnosed the modern man's discontentment with the king of religiosity that, for all its sincerity, merely stifles and constrains. Modern man is certainly not at his ease in traditional and ancient religious forms! There is a great and undeniable need for a religious renewal and liberation, since Christianity does indeed promise above all a spirit of freedom and of love, as well as a living and dynamic contact with reality. The Radical Theologians have appealed to modern man's need for a religion he really feels to be authentic and not just a blend of pious imagination and submission to ethical and ritual prescriptions. But in doing so they have concluded that the only religion modern man can accept honestly is no religion at all. Hence they preach a religionless Christianity.

268

Of course their doctrine can easily be caricatured and the rather acrobatic exploit of being "honest to God" by denying Him, and yet still secretly believing in Him anyway, may at times seem a little more complicated than modern man is willing to accept. It is, in fact, far more devious than what sophisticated Christians have always done, accepting the concepts, the images and the symbols of their religion with the realization that these did not adequately convey the full reality of the mysteries which "ear hath not heard and eye hath not seen."

After all, it is no new thing to say that God as he is in Himself is unknown to us and indeed unknowable to any created intelligence. The tradition of apophantic ("non-apparent") theology goes back beyond Pseudo-Dionysius and the Cappadocian Fathers of the fourth century, who long ago taught that if we say "God is," indicating that in Him is the fullness of all that we can conceive of as Being, we must complete it by saying also "God is not" to indicate that the fullness of His Being is far beyond anything that we can conceive of as existing (since all existents we know are limited and circumscribed by their existence). However, we must remember that this tradition of mystical negation always co-exists, in Christianity, with a tradition of symbolic theology in which positive symbols and analogies of theological teaching are accepted for what they are: true but imperfect approximations which lead us gradually toward that which cannot be properly expressed in human language.

Religious formulas and symbols, articles of faith, creeds are not intended to *prove* anything. They are expressions of what has been *revealed*. They are not themselves the whole of revelation. They point to a supernatural truth that is invisible and incomprehensible. If one remains content with the formulas or the symbol and makes it alone the object of one's "faith" then one does not really "believe" in the full

269

sense of the word. One merely subscribes to a religious formula. The object of our faith is not a statement about God but God himself to whom the statement points and who is infinitely beyond anything the statement might lead us to imagine or understand. The purpose of creeds is to define clearly what are the reliable terms in which the revelation of the invisible can be expressed. The terms may even be translated into the language of modern thought, provided one is faithful to their meaning. However, these formulas and symbols *do* tell us the truth about God, and they really enable us to enter into contact with Him, invisibly, in the act of faith. It might be worthwhile to quote a typical passage from St. John of the Cross:

> Remain thou not therefore either partly or wholly in that which thy faculties can comprehend, I mean be thou never willingly satisfied with that which thou understandest of God, but rather with that which thou understandest not of Him; and do thou not rest in loving and having delight in that which thou understandest or feelest concerning God, but do thou love and have delight in that which thou canst not understand or feel concerning Him; for this, as we have said, is to seek Him in faith. Since God is unapproachable and hidden . . . however much it seem to thee that thou findest and feelest and understandest Him, thou must ever hold Him as hidden and serve Him after a hidden manner, as one that is hidden. (*Spiritual Canticle* i, 11, 12)

This is not atheism, it is mysticism, and it is evidently quite different from what Bishop Robinson is talking about.

To know God by "unknowing" is not mere agnosticism. To agree that God is not really to be imagined "out there" is not the same as denying all objective knowledge of his transcendence. To admit, with St. John of the Cross, that we encounter God in the "inmost center" (or "ground") of our own being is not to deny His personality but to affirm it more forcefully than ever, for He is also, precisely, the cause

270

of our own personality and it is in response to His love that our freedom truly develops to personal maturity. A twelfth-century Cistercian, Isaac of Stella, describes this apophantic experience of God as the "falling away of the intelligence not *from* God but *in* God."

Reading Bonhoeffer's statements in his prison letters in the context of his whole work—remembering that he died relatively young, with his thought as yet not completely formed—we can surmise that his "godless" kenoticism was quite probably the result of a deep personal evolution of his genius and his faith. The trouble is that isolated insights like those, taken out of their context, transferred from the realm of subjective experience into that of dogma or theodicy, easily form misleading systems of thought.

In the personal mystical experience of St. John of the Cross, God was known as "unknown," and the All was attained as "Nothingness" (Nada). But St. John did not conclude that therefore the theological language of revelation should be completely revolutionized. He did not proceed to rewrite the Creed "I believe there is *no God.* . . ." On the contrary, precisely because of his mystical and apophantic intuition of God he realized the importance of the solid, simple affirmations of the Creed. The religious experience of the fully mature and experienced Christian is in many ways like that of a child and in other ways totally different from that of a child. Therefore one does not begin by teaching a child these ultimate truths in the paradoxical language of mysticism. Only those with a certain experience of the life of faith are able to apprehend these paradoxical statements without misinterpreting them as "atheism" or "pantheism."

The "absence" of God which is normal at a certain degree of the mystical life should not be made the norm for all contemporary Christianity. It should not be translated from the anguish of personal experience to the abstract formulas of the Creed. The anguish of subjective and personal emptiness must not be objectified and universalized in a flat statement of God's non-existence, when in fact the motive for bearing that anguish is faith in the absolute fullness of His Being and His Love. The whole point of faith is that it enables us to attain to some kind of contact with God who is beyond understanding. One can certainly sacrifice imperfect ideas of God in order to believe more perfectly! But one must believe!

Is it any wonder that if the voice of a theological authority speaks out and confirms the popular suspicion that God is dead and cannot be believed in any longer, this part of the message will be hailed with enthusiasm by those who have no intention of accepting the other part of it: that one must continue to believe even while acting as if God did not exist?

The Catholic Church therefore will continue to teach that "God is" while admitting that for *some* Christians He will be experienced *as if* He were not. She will however carefully distinguish between the godlessness of a world that is either confused or indifferent and has not yet responded to the message of revelation, and the interior darkness of the mystic who has entered deeply into the inexplicable mysteries of the faith which he still firmly believes in its simple and universal and objective formulation. It would be a bit absurd to go about saying glibly that all modern men, atheists, agnostics, communists, nazis, racists, and all the godless in general are really mystics without realizing it!

Yet at the same time—and here I agree with the Radical Theologians—it would seem that there is some mysterious way in which the "God who is dead" nevertheless "lives" and "is present" to those who are incapable of believing in him, perhaps even unable to wish they could believe in him. There is some strange way in which God speaks precisely to those *who do not hear*. And his speech is effective *pre-*

cisely in their not hearing. Indeed, one could go so far as to say that there appears to be a special mercy and love of God for the unbeliever in his sincerity, his honest inability to accept and admit formulas which to him have no meaning. Unfortunately there seems to be no way in which this can be theologically formulated or verified. And yet I believe it to be true. If it is of any comfort to anyone then I am glad. But as I do not know how to develop the idea at present, I will leave it aside.

Notice the symptomatic anxiety of the Radical Theologians about "being contemporary." "Can a truly *contemporary* person not be an atheist?" One gets the feeling that what matters above all is having a recognizable and honored place in the contemporary world. This need is so great that it becomes greater than the need for God. In the first place, I find it hard to see how one can *not* be "contemporary." Surely one has little choice in the matter. This is the kind of thing that is decided quite without us! But then of course there are certain options by which one may be judged on the basis of "contemporariness." We can gladly accept the world of our time, its structure, its organization, its limitations, its risks, its hopes in a "contemporary" way. But what does this mean? The question is important, since the Catholic Church is obviously striving to make precisely this kind of "contemporary" decision about the modern world and its possibilities for good and evil. If the only really contemporary kind of contemporariness is Bishop Robinson's, then the Council should have gone over solidly to atheism, and we must conclude that its failure to do so leaves the Church in the middle ages.

It is obviously absurd to imagine that "contemporaneousness" or "up-to-date-ness" is a value in its own right, as if anything and everything that happens now is the best thing possible merely because it is "contemporary." It is pos-

273

sible to imagine contemporary trends which ought to be denounced, opposed and even fought bitterly. And very often one of the spurious reasons advanced for not resisting such trends is that they are "contemporary" and he who resists proves that he is not of his time. On the contrary it may precisely be his resistance that makes him a true man of his time, if resistance is called for by the real needs of contemporary man.

If we examine this concept of "being contemporary" we find that it is a pure myth and in fact one of the central myths of our society. The myth of contemporariness, like the myth of progress* of which it is a special development, calls for a more profound study than we could possibly attempt here. It is certainly a by-product of our extreme technological virtuosity. The affluent marketing mentality of the capitalist west, in which the individual identity of the consumer is conditioned, to a great extent, by his ability to come up with the latest model in cars, clothes and TV sets just at the right moment, has created the proper atmosphere. If one is not "right" in his outlook, his tastes, his decisions (manifested by the right kind of possessions), one feels that his very existence itself is somehow diminished. One's image

---

* By "myth" I do not mean a lie. A myth is an imaginative synthesis of facts and intuitions about them, forming an interpretative complex of ideas and images. This complex of "values" then becomes central in a meaning-system or world-view, a norm of judgment and of practice. The myth of progress is a synthetic and imaginative evaluation of man and of society which assumes that man is always getting better and better (*qualitatively*) as a result of his *quantitatively* increasing control over matter and nature. This "progress" tends to be regarded as an absolute value in itself. Actually the myths of progress, contemporaneity and so on have become the center of superstitions which are fully as tenacious and absurd as any religious superstitions of the past.

274

has begun to fade. One is on the point of losing reality. Contemporariness is, in fact, status, and status is identity, reality. To be contemporary is to be recognizable as quite up-to-date in a fast moving world where not only tastes but whole world-views in art, science, philosophy, literature and religion are revolutionized every three to five years. To be contemporary is to maintain one's place, to survive in the highly organized and breathless dynamism of the ephemeral. It is a kind of existentialism of fashion, in which there is no solid ontological ground of being, only the constant unpredictable flux of existence. What matters is to be well enough attuned to the slighter signals, indicating the next revolution in ideas, so that one can continue making the right—that is the "contemporary"—options just at the right time. A slight error in timing and one is no longer perfectly "contemporary." One goes under. One drowns in the flux of ephemeral decisions and is superseded by others who have the skill to stay contemporary.

All that is said here about fashions of thought and taste in the capitalist west applies even more to the dogmatic variations of the communist party line. Here one's precise shade of rightness may mean life or death. It pays to be up-to-date and "truly contemporary."

Obviously this brings into being a new variety of "orthodoxy." In place of the more established, traditional kind in which one adhered to a truth that was right once for all, this new secular orthodoxy, which scorns religious tradition, is in fact much more demanding. Here it is no longer enough just to make one right decision and abide by it: one must decide over and over again every day even when today's "right" is yesterday's "wrong." Besides this, whereas the more static type of orthodoxy tended to define rather precisely what one had to accept, here nothing is precise, all

275

must be guessed at and intuited from day to day. Hence the new "believer" has to be much more attentive, much better informed and much quicker on his feet.*

Now since this is the price that must be paid for a hearing in the modern world, and since God is not at all contemporary (He is hidden in the abyss of pure being and outside the flux of temporal existence) then one must apparently abandon God in order to gain a hearing. But the problem arises: once the Christian has gained a hearing, what does he preach if not God, Christ and the Chruch? Well, there are perhaps other things he can do, while waiting for these subjects to become once again fashionable. He can play a guitar. Another aspect of the dialogue with the modern world which the Council unfortunately neglected!

From a Catholic viewpoint, then, the most serious criticism of this admittedly sincere, charitable and concerned "religionless" Christianity is that it does not seem to be Christian. Not that "religion" in the Pauline sense of the "elements" of human ritual and worship is necessary to Christianity but a certain ontological and theological foundation *is* necessary.

In order to gain a hearing in the modern world, in order to "be contemporary" this Christianity dispenses with the Christian revelation of God in Christ and accepts what is in effect a materialistic concept of man. Man is a chance product of biological development. In him matter, inherited from animal ancestors, achieves consciousness. In a primitive state of his growth man was not able to cope with

* It is clear that here we are discussing not Catholic faith but the secular commitment in politics, science, literature and civil life generally: in a word, the problem of "being truly contemporary." Nevertheless in Catholic life there is a certain premium on being "with it" in each new trend—the ability to guess what is really "in" at least today.

276

consciousness without the aid of myths about God, sin, salvation. Now, however, he has reached "adulthood." Man must learn to do without God (since God does not exist—or "is dead"). Man must accept his own existence and make it meaningful by rejecting all the follies and pretenses of "inwardness" and religion and by devoting himself to others in the building of technological society. In fact, mass-society. In other words the "scientific concept of man" has definitively done away with all revelation, and those who still conceive themselves as "believers" must be brave enough and honest enough to admit that if their belief is mere nostalgia that persists, then it becomes irrelevant even to talk about the fact that God is dead. Yet the "religionless religion" still clings to something that constitutes a "message"— it is not a religion, it does not preach God or redemption, yet it does have a kerygma of love. Why? No explanation is given. Love is its own explanation. But then, what is love? How is love itself shown to be no illusion? Is this not merely sentimentality? If we can get along without God, why not get along without love? Why does the logic of kenosis stop precisely where it does? Can we not say that faith in a living God who reveals Himself as love is after all more consistent?

As a matter of fact this ability to get along without God is what, in secular parlance, is accepted as the "adulthood" of man. Thus we see that this "adulthood" is another aspect of the myth of contemporaneity. The adult, modern, contemporaneous man is he who takes it for granted that "God is dead" and gets along without any sense of loss. He can dispense with God. Yet if we look a little closer, we find that this is the result not so much of reasoning as of an act of secular faith. We face the paradox that modern man's self-assurance and unbelief is itself—a belief! And curiously, Christians are using the language of this "belief" in order

277

to make their own faith comprehensible to him. But in so doing, Christians forget that the modern act of belief in unbelief demands a constantly renewed effort to *exclude* and reject God from one's adult world-view. The idea behind Bonhoeffer and Robinson's theology seems to be that if we aid man in his act of unbelief we will bring him closer to God.

Without pursuing this subject further, let us simply say that when one is over-concerned about "being truly contemporary" one may perhaps run wild in one's judgment of what is and what is not "contemporary." Here, I think, we have to admit that it is by no means certain that there exists a contemporary "secular man" for whom the whole idea of God and of Christ is essentially meaningless. It is also exaggerated to say that for the truly contemporary man God is only conceivable as a hypothesis which he no longer needs. Nor is "the scientific concept of man" definitively established as atheistic. After all, there are many of us who have lived through the experience of being "modern" and quite "contemporary" human beings, who have lived fully immersed in a society where God was indeed dismissed as irrelevant, and yet, on receiving the gift of faith, we have realized the truth of the old saying: "believe and you will understand." This is true of intellectuals, artists, technicians, scientists, all kinds of "modern men." It is no doubt quite true that modern man cannot easily grasp the symbols and images, still less the abstract concepts, in which the Church spoke of God one, two or five hundred years ago. But it is not true that modern man is incapable of faith. Faith is not dependent upon this or that psychology, this or that culture, this or that set of symbols. Faith is a divine gift which can break in upon the mind of any man, at any time and in any culture, and in any language, no matter how scientific. But of course if it is to be a fully and articulately Christian

278

faith, it must be a response to Christian preaching of the Gospel message. And here, indeed, we need a contemporary language. There is no doubt whatever that the conventional and well-worn images in which our relations with God and with Christ are expressed, are sometimes irrelevant in the modern world. But yet, where does the trouble really lie? In the "myths" of the Bible? Or rather in our tired, jejune experience of Christian truth? One feels that the trouble is not so much with the Bible or with St. Thomas as with us, with Christians. If we really entered into these truths, really lived them in our "contemporary" lives, they would transmute themselves naturally into terms which would reach our contemporary fellow man. The Council Constitution on the Church and the World frankly admits (n. 19) that much of modern atheism is due in fact to the lamentable example of a pseudo-Christianity in which Christians "must be said to conceal rather than reveal the authentic face of God and of religion." In other words what is required of us is not so much that we discard all the symbols of Biblical revelation and all the traditional terminology of our faith in order to substitute for them a pseudo-scientific religious jargon that would be valid at best for the next ten years. What is required of Christians is that they develop a completely modern and contemporary *consciousness* in which their experience as men of our century is integrated with their experience as children of God redeemed by Christ. The weakness of our Christian language lies not so much in the theology and formulated belief as in the split which has hitherto separated our Christian faith from the rest of our lives. Indeed the job of bridging this abyss has been left to ethics, and the result has not been satisfactory. Our appearance in the world with a few intransigent Catholic positions in ethics has marked us as devout and serious but has not made us more comprehensible to our contemporaries who

279

have no way of knowing *why* we attach such importance to the indissolubility of marriage, for instance. They think it is merely something we have to accept because we are Catholics, and if the truth be told, many of us have no better reasons of our own.

This is certainly one of the things the Council has been saying to us. That if we cultivate a special and eccentric consciousness that sets us apart from the world, if instead of experiencing our faith in a way that is relevant to our time we merely seek refuge from the world in a language of inwardness and of piety that is in fact antiquated and unreal even to ourselves, then we will obviously not be able to communicate any relevant message to our contemporary and unbelieving fellowman. He will observe our piety, he will doubtless give us credit for sincerity, but he will see that we have simply constructed a little mental and spiritual refuge for ourselves, a sanctuary of feeling and nostalgia, something that is inaccessible to the likes of him. And it must remain inaccessible, since he has no motive whatever for wanting such a refuge himself.

The trouble is not all with our unbelieving neighbor. We have hitherto assumed, too easily and too habitually, that his lack of interest in our inner sanctuary was perhaps due to some secret attachment to sin, or some hard core of resistance to grace. But now, with the new attitude of the Church to the World, we are no longer permitted to make such sweeping assumptions. Here we may quote Bonhoeffer again, and this time, though it is one of his boldest and perhaps, to some, most shocking statements, it can be regarded as one of the most penetrating insights of "religionless" Christianity. He says that our acceptance of the "ungodliness" of the world is in some sense preferable to, because more real than, a mere "taking refuge in inwardness." Precisely by virtue of our Christian faith we can become able to see this ungodliness in a new light. *"Now that it has come of age the world is more godless, and perhaps it is for that very reason nearer to God than ever before."**

At this point, if we wanted to be fussy about logic, we might ask what use there is in being "nearer to God" if God is dead? But we must remember that Bonhoeffer's *kenoticism* is the emptying out of all religious thinking, language, "inwardness," habits and attitudes of mind, so that when nothing is left one remains "with God" though there appears to be no God—and one concerns himself henceforth not with ideas of God but with the real needs of other men.

However, to be emptied of theology, religion and inwardness and filled with neo-pagan or pseudo-scientific political ideologies that are even more confusing, does not seem to be much help in bringing men, however surreptitiously, "close to God." For Bonhoeffer himself, no doubt, at the term of a long religious evolution which took him "beyond religion" there was no danger. But what about the confused and troubled "ordinary man" who has lost his bearings

---

* It is interesting that in his latest book the Russian Orthodox theologian Paul Evdokimov makes the same point. "It is possible that the world is nearer now to religious faith than it ever has been. Science no longer presents a difficulty, atheism can no longer advance any serious argument." (*Les Ages de la Vie Spirituelle*, Paris, 1964, p. 40) He adds, however, that the big obstacle is the complacency of the faithful. Here he notably differs from Bishop Robinson and from Bonhoeffer. It is the faithful who claim to believe in God who "act as if He were non-existent." In other words, to act as if God did not exist is not, in Fr. Evdokimov's eyes, grounds for satisfaction. As to the unbelievers, far from finding them totally indifferent, he sees in them a "nostalgie de Dieu" which is "more profound than the self-satisfaction of the believer." This is the view taken by many Catholics also. Fr. Hans Von Balthasar develops an analogous idea: the sinner, for whom God is dead, is close to God's redemptive love, in *Der Wagnis der Nachfolge*, pp. 23–24.

and seeks comfort in a worldly religion of nationalism and racism for example?

We must certainly keep in mind here that Bonhoeffer was absolutely opposed to Nazism, and to all that it stood for. He saw the world of Nazism and tyranny only as an evil to be suffered and opposed in union with Christ. He was not saying that the SS were closer to God than the Christian martyrs and saints. He was not saying that militant atheism should be preferred to the confession of Christ and His Church. But he was saying that the Christian who is true to his faith and true to Christ must now be humble enough and courageous enough to admit that with all his own faith, with all his theology even, he has been an unprofitable servant and the godless world (now not of Nazis but of men of goodwill) in its religious emptiness and foresakeness might well be, by God's inscrutable grace, closer to Him than the believers and the Churches.

Here again, we run into different meanings of the term "the World," even when it is regarded as "godless." Even when, for one like Bonhoeffer, "godlessness" becomes a term of approval, one realizes that the godlessness he approves is not that of the regime that he was determined to overthrow at the risk of his own life. For Bonhoeffer's resistance against Hitlerism and against the peculiar Nazi form of godlessness was dictated by his Christian conscience. Once again we see that in interpreting the statements of this school we must read them entirely in the context of subjective sincerity and personal experience, and in terms of ever changing situations. But unfortunately, when dramatic statements about a holy godlessness are made general and universal they can easily be applied to mean the exact opposite from what they were intended to mean. And how are we to know where godlessness ceases to be "good godlessness" and becomes something to avoid? Does Bishop Robinson go all the way with Sartre, for instance? Is there to be a feast of "Saint Genet" in the calendar of the new Christianity?

The Council Constitution makes quite clear that a systematic atheism which claims for man the freedom "to be an end unto himself" (n. 20) sets itself deliberately and formally in opposition with the Christian revelation that man's source and end are in God and that without God's help he cannot make a right use of his God-given freedom. Atheism asserts on the contrary that man needs to get rid of God precisely because his "illusion" of dependence on God prevents him from attaining adulthood and from making a mature use of his freedom. It is religion, says Marxist atheism, which is keeping man from a full use of his power and knowledge in the construction of a world, a "secular city" in which he will find complete and sufficient happiness.

The Catholic Church will continue, on the other hand, to teach that the love of man is insecure and elusive unless it proceeds from the hidden action of God's love and grace. The love of God is the source of all living and authentic love for other men.

Our long discussion of "religionless Christianity" has been necessary because it is very relevant to what we will discuss later on as the "diaspora situation" of contemporary Christians.

But not all modern thought outside Christianity is "godless." There is also at work an anguished hunger for God which stops short of Christianity since it feels that the ordinary Christian view of God is lifeless and conventional. It seeks to "create" a new symbolic language for the things of God.

Rainer Maria Rilke is in many ways a typical witness of a certain type of modern religious consciousness. He was not "godless." His heritage was profoundly Catholic and yet like so many contemporaries he found much that he could not

283

accept in ordinary Catholic belief and practice. Less Catholic than Péguy, for instance, less Manichaean than Simone Weil, his poetic consciousness adopted a symbolic and spiritual idea of historic cycles in religious vitality. One age finds God in simplicity. The next "builds temples" for Him. The next finds the temples empty and removes the stones of the temples to build houses for men. Then comes another generation which seeks God anew. Rilke thought of himself (at least when he wrote the *Book of Hours*) as a hidden God-seeker in a world when the temples stood empty and half-destroyed. For him, man must anew look *to the future* to find God who would manifest Himself in the history that is to come, not in a new revelation but in a creative effort of man that would make the cosmos once more "transparent." Once again men would be able to see God in His world. This has something in common with the worldliness of Bonhoeffer and of Teilhard de Chardin, and it also appeals to those Christians whose consciousness has been influenced by a Marxist world-view. For Rilke, art itself had a cosmic, religious and prophetic dimension. For the others, science assumes this function. I do not pause to analyze these ideas theologically. I just point to the fact that they are characteristic of the contemporary mind. In fact, Bonhoeffer is very popular today among Christians of the Communist countries. He is probably better read and understood in East than in West Germany. But let us note in passing that Teilhard de Chardin is the one Catholic thinker of our time who is most fully appreciated, even by non-Christians and Marxists, in the Communist countries.

Mention of Teilhard is of course inevitable in any discussion of the Church and the modern world. No matter what may be the ambiguities of his doctrine (which I have no intention of analyzing here) it is incontestable that Teilhard de Chardin has done more than any other Christian to express a deep and living Christian experience in the language of the modern scientific world-view.

In particular he has repeatedly denied that Christians must disparage and reject the world of matter and of science in the name of Christ. On the contrary the heart of his message is that "In the name of our faith we have the right and the duty to become passionate about the things of the earth." Of course even the "scientific world-view" of Teilhard is limited. We must not credit him with scientific omniscience, or with speaking in the name of *every* science. Teilhard was a paleontologist and his insights on evolution are proper to his own study of pre-historic man. They need to be completed by the work of other scientists. But the value of Teilhard is this—he is a Catholic scientist who has given other scientists something to work on—and has opened their eyes to Christian perspectives. If in so doing he has run into criticism both as a scientist and as a theologian, this does not alter the fact that his writings point the way to a new and important horizon in Christian spirituality. Here far more than in the God-is-dead theologians we have a Christian believer, indeed thought by some to be a mystic, who can speak the language of contemporary man without totally compromising his faith in God and in Christ. The respect which he has received in scientific circles, even more among atheists, clearly shows that it is *not* necessary to cry that God is dead before one can get a hearing for the Christian message in the contemporary world.

The name of Teilhard was mentioned more than once in the Council debate on "Schema XIII" and there is no question that the decree itself at times takes on his now familiar tone. We are not surprised that Pope Paul himself is reported to have said (to Cardinal Feltin), "Teilhard is an indispensible man for our times; his expression of the faith is necessary for us."

True, there is still much opposition to the doctrine of Teilhard. But as so often happens, the repressive attempt to silence a voice to which men are eager to respond has only resulted in a more passionate response, and Teilhard has become the symbol of the new Catholic outlook upon the modern world. The very ardor of the devotion to Teilhard and the fervor with which so many have simply identified with him emotionally and spiritually have tended to throw him into a false perspective. But scholars like de Lubac are there to restore the balance, while remaining extremely favorable to Teilhard.

This earnest attempt to express the Christian faith in the language of modern science can surely not be despised, and Teilhard's voice is by now too familiar ever to be silenced. Even those who have never read him—indeed some of his opponents—will be found echoing his language, which has already become common property.

We need more such voices, because we must frankly accept the fact that we live in a culture which, in spite of the Christian elements that still survive in it, is essentially atheistic. The technological humanism of the modern world has built a civilization in which God and religion may at best be tolerated, but in which the prevalent worldview simply excludes God. So true is this that, as we have seen, one cannot seem to be fully contemporary without concurring in this refusal of God (Bonhoeffer attempts to adjust to the refusal without making it himself). But just as the religious refusal of "the world" is ambiguous, so the world's refusal of God and of Christ is even more ambiguous still.

It is a truism to say that the "god" supposedly demolished in atheistic reasoning is no god at all. This straw god is in fact a contingent, limited, fallible, powerless object, a thing among things, at the very best a counterfeit. Such a "god" has no right whatever to exist, but the atheist has very little reason to be proud for seeing it. Yet if he persists in thinking that he has really made a discovery in proving the non-existence of this shadow, it is probably because so many religious people—indeed so many religious books—give the impression that such a shadowy or limited being is indeed the God of religious faith. It is unfortunately true that for many "believers" the God they believe in is not the living God but an apologetic hypothesis.

Index

INDEX